FOR QUEEN AND CURRENCY

FOR QUEEN AND CURRENCY

Audacious fraud, greed and gambling at Buckingham Palace

MICHAEL GILLARD

BLOOMSBURY READER

LONDON · OXFORD · NEW YORK · NEW DELHI · SYDNEY

This edition published in 2015 by Bloomsbury Reader

Bloomsbury Reader is a division of Bloomsbury Publishing Plc, 50

Bedford Square, London WC1B 3DP

First published in Great Britain in 2015 by Bloomsbury Reader

ISBN: 978 1 4482 1550 8
eISBN: 978 1 4482 1549 2

Visit www.bloomsburyreader.com to find out more about our authors and their books.
You will find extracts, author interviews, author events and you can sign up for
newsletters to be the first to hear about our latest releases and special offers.

You can also find us on Twitter @bloomsreader.

For Sparkle and Cool Hand. Shine on.

Contents

Preface

No Old Bill 'ave ever admitted to what we've done … The Queen is going to be mightily pissed off.

This book began with a phone call out of the blue one afternoon in the summer of 2008. The caller was offering an amazing tale that, on the face of it, had everything my news desk at the *Sunday Times* could want: royal indiscretions, high-risk gambling, brown envelopes and greedy, out-of-control Buckingham Palace cops striking gangsta poses on the Throne of England. All of which had seemingly taken place on the watch of Scotland Yard officers paid to protect the Queen and her family during the war on terrorism.

The man at the end of my Nokia identified himself as Paul Page, a 37-year-old recently sacked police officer. It quickly became apparent that the Yard's anti-corruption squad, the Complaints Investigation Bureau (CIB), was investigating Page and he didn't like it. He spoke lucidly but with machine-gun delivery about how, as a Royal Protection officer for ten years, he was now facing charges of threats to kill and fraud. A big fraud, I would soon discover.

Page spat his version of events down the phone: 'I operated a spread betting syndicate from Buckingham Palace. Over 130 officers were involved. CIB stitched me up big time and I can prove it.'

I'd heard it all before, many times: another dirty cop trying to pin his corruption on the undoubtedly venal internal politics of Scotland Yard and the cover-ups that will continue to occur as long as we allow the police to investigate their own.

But Page was different. Through his verbal assault of fact, theory and fuck-peppered anger he made one thing crystal clear. 'You are not a shoulder to cry on,' he said. 'I am not pretending to be innocent.'

It turned out that Page had read a book I co-authored four years earlier about Scotland Yard's phoney attempt at a 'no hiding place' clean-up of corruption in its ranks. That book, *Untouchables*, exposed two decades of double standards and institutional cover-ups by the same anti-corruption squad that was now on Page's case.

As journalists we never know, when we slink, cajole and elbow our way into someone's life, whether we will fathom them. Deadlines, impatience, cynicism and a lack of trust can all work against that aspiration. But I was lucky. When Page found me I found him to be in a confessional state of mind. He had an almost suicidal need to recount and recant for his past actions. And not just what had happened at Buckingham Palace.

Page was ready to blow the whistle on another hidden part of policing: a culture of violence, cover-ups and fit-ups so rarely exposed, let alone publicly justified, by those on the inside. In my experience, when an officer feels scapegoated by his own organisation he loses the will to maintain the siege mentality and conspiracy of silence around modern policing. Page was no exception. He explained:

At the end of the day, they are trying to airbrush out most of what's gone on and say I am guilty on my own. There are loads of people who should be standing in the dock with me. This is their problem: I'm Royal Protection. When these Royal Protection officers are giving evidence you can imagine what it is going to look like. The Queen is going to be mightily pissed off. That's the bottom line. Basically I've threatened them and now I've got it back … I'm happy to go to court. I want to go to court. I'm not trying to say I'm not guilty. I'm guilty of something, I'm sure I am. If it's misconduct in a public office, so are others.

Page had run a gambling syndicate known to its members as the Currency Club. Essentially, it was a hedge fund for cops betting on foreign exchange rates and commodities such as oil and gold in the six boom years leading up to the 2008 crash. Initially, Page operated from the police locker room under the stairs at Buckingham Palace. But later, as civilian investors piled in on promises of returns beyond the dreams of avarice or financial reason, he would drop off cash in brown envelopes from a Range Rover with blacked-out windows that he drove from palace to palace and pub to pub.

'I regret the day I ever expanded it further than just Buckingham Palace. It was the biggest mistake of my life because greed took over everyone,' Page claimed.

The more I looked into the mechanics of the Currency Club, the more it looked like a Ponzi fraud of the kind, but not the size, perpetrated by Wall Street's kingpin, Bernie Madoff, on far more financially savvy and well-heeled punters.

Ponzi schemes, I learned, are quite simple in that early investors are paid from later investors' money. Both Madoff and Page were facing trial at the same time. Their self-delusionary worlds had come a cropper as investor confidence sapped and the world's financial system collapsed.

At his peak, European royals and British lords were among the investors in the illegal hedge fund Madoff had run below the regulator's faint radar. His business grew not just because people liked and trusted Bernie but because he offered investors incredible returns, in return for no questions asked about how he made their money. Healthy commissions were paid to brokers and feeder funds for sending salivating investors his way; and the more they salivated, the more commission the brokers mopped up.

Page operated a similar system of 'lieutenants'. Some were in the police, others were the friends of these uniformed investors. They worked their family and circle of friends for investment in his scheme and received secret commission payments for their enthusiastic advocacy. The whole greedy money-go-round carried on as long as Page regularly paid out the incredible returns he offered well above bank rates.

Before the prosecution could hang, draw and quarter him at the royal courts, I was able to cross-examine Page and his wife Laura about all aspects of their life and the insane way the Currency Club was run. Often this questioning was done amid the family chaos of trying to keep four young boys happy. To his credit, Page never dissembled or feigned memory loss.

I'd like to think my questioning had left him little room to manoeuvre. But the truth is, it was Laura's presence during these sessions and her often withering interjections that stopped any real spin being put on the last eight years of life married to a gambler of other people's money, who'd gone into a free fall of bad decisions and excessive drinking.

Laura had held the family together. She too was facing trial, accused by the Crown Prosecution Service of facilitating the multi-million pound fraud.

Scotland Yard and the Palace never wanted this story to come out, which is why, well before the trial, they made Page an offer it was thought he'd never refuse: resign and save himself, the Queen and Scotland Yard a lot of embarrassment.

His refusal to resign made Page neither madman nor whistle-blower. He was, though, a deeply flawed man, a deluded police officer who thought he was a big swinging dick in the City, where making money appeared as easy as taking sweets from a child.

Rogue cop or scapegoat for a monarchy and police force too big to fail? Good cop gone bad trying to cover up some reckless financial decisions or degenerate gambler who'd set out to rip people off? Either way, I was all in.

By the time their trial started in April 2009, an international cabal of multi-millionaire bankers had inflicted incredible pain on tens of millions of the much less well-off through another type of Ponzi scheme, a global one, involving the trade in toxic mortgage debt. Savings were wiped out, homes and jobs lost and hope gone. Yet this reckless gambling, deception and trickery hasn't resulted in one City suit standing trial.

Whilst I knew by the opening of his trial that Page was guilty, it strongly looked like other Royal Protection officers with dirty hands were being 'looked after', to use a police expression.

As I said, some of the things Page admitted to me were suicidal to his own legal interests. But I believe the public interest would not have been served by his guilty plea in return for a lighter sentence, and no exposition of the management failures that allowed this scandal to develop inside the Royal Protection Squad and at Buckingham Palace.

The intoxicating ability to make money in the commodity, credit and housing booms meant Page's investors didn't carry out simple due diligence. Why would they? He was a police officer, they said. More credibly, Page operated his financial scheme in an era of popular delusion, the delusion being that cheap money and the housing bubble would never end. Free credit allowed Page to binge on gambling and alcohol just as it enabled the British people to embark on a crazy consumer binge.

There was nothing new here. Charles Mackay saw and said it all 160 years ago when capitalism was in its infancy but greed and fraud were not. 'Money has often been a cause of the delusions of multitudes,' he wrote in his seminal work *Memoirs of Extraordinary Popular Delusions and the Madness of Crowds*. 'Sober nations have all at once become desperate gamblers, and risked almost their existence upon the turn of a piece of paper… Men it has been well said think in herds; it will be seen that they go mad in herds, while they only recover their senses slowly, and one by one.'

The decade covered by *For Queen and Currency* was another period of popular delusion and madness of crowds. It started with the death of Princess Diana and ended with the financial meltdown. From 1997 to 2008 was a time of free money; borrow now worry later, buy-to-let mortgages and TV schedules stuffed with property porn for a nation of amateur landlords. The banks were literally throwing money at people on the government-fostered popular delusion that house prices were only going one way: up.

So it was that Page's investors took out cheap loans, gambled their savings or borrowed against their homes to invest in his get-rich-quick-scheme. None engaged professional advice to verify the probity or financial sense of his claims. He offered them returns that were too good to be true, yet they willingly conspired in believing him.

As a business pal of Bernie Madoff once commented on the victims of his multi-billion Ponzi fraud, 'C'mon! They had to know something wasn't right.' Or as a university professor investor who lost his savings bravely admitted to *Time* magazine, 'We knew deep down it was too good to be true … We deluded ourselves into thinking we were all smarter than the others.'

To be fair to Page's victims, where were their role models? It was a period of incredible corruption and greed by politicians and public servants. The MPs and Lords' expenses scandals, many exposed by my newspaper, showed the ease with which politicians felt they could cash in on the housing boom using public funds for mortgages on second homes or improvements to existing ones – moats and duck ponds, anyone?

Without the reckless culture of government-sponsored casino capitalism and irresponsible bank lending, all crowned by light-touch regulation in the City and, as it turned out, at Buckingham Palace and Scotland Yard too, this Royal Protection Squad scandal could never have happened.

Evidence would emerge from the vaults of the Met's anti-corruption squad that Page's dive into financial insanity was spotted well before he hit the water, but shoulders were shrugged and his file gathered dust at Buckingham Palace.

For Queen and Currency is more than a bad-cop story of a big fraud at a great palace. It is also a cautionary tale of the madness of crowds; of how, like Paul Page and his salivating investors, the British people also lost the plot, beguiled as they were by the patter of bankers and politicians who secretly gambled away their future.

Prologue
A crash foretold

21 November 2006.

Paul Page had hardly slept in a week, except when the booze briefly took hold. Awake, he was buzzing with fear and adrenalin.

Days earlier, anti-corruption detectives had come to the house and warned his family they were in danger. Investors in Page's betting syndicate had lost £3 million. One of them had approached a hit man.

Pacing around his living room like a cage fighter, Page's attention was drawn to someone parked oddly across the street. Before he could check it out, the man sped off. Page rushed to his car and gave chase. It ended ten minutes later when he deliberately crashed into his target at a big roundabout.

'Who the fuck are you? Is this a fucking brown envelope job to come sort me out?' Page screamed as he dragged the man out of his wrecked car, a gun pressed to his head.

'Don't kill me!' the man pleaded.

With the sound of police sirens approaching, Page calmly put his weapon down on the grass of the island in the roundabout, raised his hands and watched drivers run for cover.

His eight-year free fall from trusted, Royal Protection officer at Buckingham Palace to half-cut, gun-toting crazy was at last coming to an end.

Part I

Boom (1993–2004)

Chapter 1

Essex princess

July 1993. Police Constable Paul Page was bored. It was a slow summer night shift at Grays police station in Essex.

'Get over to a flat in Lodge Lane,' said the sergeant walking into the office where Page was doodling. 'There's a woman complaining about nuisance calls. Apparently someone's been ringing and putting the phone down. She's only been in the flat a few months. Check it out, will you?'

Page duly drove off, hopeful he was coming to the rescue of a hot girl. But when he arrived at Lodge Lane, an old woman answered the door. The young constable gave an inaudible sigh, introduced himself and quickly established he was at the wrong address.

Minutes later, at about 7.30 pm, the right door was knocked. This time, a dyed blonde in her mid-twenties with a small gap between her front teeth answered. Page was instantly struck. He introduced himself again, this time enthusiastically.

'Hello. I'm PC Page.'

Laura Keenan decided to play with her fresh-faced knight.

Page was well-built and pushing six foot. His ears stuck out because his hair was so short, and his flat nose gave him maturity beyond his years.

'How old are you then?' Laura asked in a deliberately ambiguous tone. Page didn't know whether she was complaining or flirting. Just in case, he added a year to his age. 'Twenty-three,' he replied.

'Ahhh!' she said mockingly. 'Come in.'

Laura's two-year-old son was asleep with the bedroom door open. 'Is the father here?' Page enquired, noticing she wore no wedding ring.

'We split up when my son was born,' Laura explained guardedly, but in a casual tone. 'I've only been here three months. I was living with my mum and dad when Thomas was born.'

Several tea bags later and Page was being hassled by his sergeant wanting to know why the routine inquiry was taking so long.

'Yeah skipper, it's a bit more complicated than I originally thought,' he told his boss, winking at the victim of crime. 'There may be other offences to consider,' he added, for effect.

Page was a natural blagger; one of life's chancers. The self-assured, self-styled cockney wide boy respected the idea of a rule of law and those who enforced it. It appealed to his personality type – what some might call a rescuer, although one with a vigilante edge not afraid to break the rules to dispense his version of street justice.

But he was not a natural policeman of the kind that likes to take orders. He didn't fit easily into a disciplined service of blind obedience. In Page's world, just because a person wearing more elaborate braiding on their arm or a law book under it said something was so, didn't make it so.

That said, to those who knew Page as a boy, it came as little surprise when fifteen months earlier in March 1992 he had announced he was joining Essex Police. At the time he felt he lacked sufficient qualifications for an army officer cadetship and his second choice, the London Fire Brigade, wasn't recruiting. So joining the police seemed a good fall-back.

Around midnight, Laura finally closed the door on PC Page. He had the cheek to claim overtime for his groundwork flirting and the next day was back for more. This time the constable came calling while Laura was in the bath. She thought it was her sister otherwise she never would have come to the communal door in just her towel.

When Laura saw it was Page she blushed. But he persuaded her to let him in on the slim pretext that he had an update on the nuisance caller. Laura was happy to go along with it and, as Page followed her up the stairs, he eyed up her all over salon tan wishing the towel would fall.

A fully clothed Laura shortly emerged and asked PC Page for the latest. 'There's nothing new to report,' he replied with a smirk, before getting down to further gentle flirting.

Two days later, he was on the phone to Laura. 'PC Page here,' he said, still maintaining the veneer of police business. 'Er, I was wondering if you'd like to go out for dinner?'

Laura was twenty-five, unemployed and a single mum on benefits. Her hard-working parents were paying off the clothes catalogue bills she continued to run up. Laura fancied the cocky copper and felt she could have some much-needed fun with him. They arranged to meet at a restaurant bar on a boat in Lakeside, a new, sprawling shopping centre nearby.

That night the conversation flowed easily. Their flirty banter gave way to some discreet intimacy and details about their pasts.

Page explained he was from Leytonstone in east London and had been brought up since he was a baby by his grandparents, because of some family problems that he wasn't ready to go into.

He regularly saw his mum and dad, but talked most warmly about his grandfather. Page then regaled her with the story of how he came to join the Territorial Army when he was just sixteen.

I was the only one of my little gang who got caught trying to steal some kit from their garage on the Lea Bridge Road. Everyone else had it away and this TA officer says to me, 'What are you doing?' I says back, 'I've come to join.' So when I met up with the others, they asked what happened, thinking I'd been nicked, and I told them I'd joined the fucking TA! It was either that or get nicked.

Laura realized her date could talk for England and took her chance to ask if he wanted another lager. It was important that she was seen to pay her own way.

'I can't,' Page replied. 'I'm on late turn.' Laura looked quizzically at him. 'I've got to be on duty later tonight,' he explained.

'Go on,' she urged, reaching down into her shoe.

'What are you doing?' asked Page.

'That's where I keep my money. I didn't want to carry a purse.'

Laura had tapped up her parents for some going-out cash. They were used to it, especially during the weekend. And although generous with his daughter, Laura's father would delight in infuriating her with the same phrase as he handed over the money: 'Don't spend a pound if you've only got a penny.'

Laura was one of five sisters; her dad, Paul Keenan, was a foreman in the local council's housing division and her mother, Marie, worked as a hospital assistant. A natural-born Essex girl, Laura left school at fifteen and worked briefly with her twin in a factory putting labels on tins of mackerel. Before getting pregnant with Thomas, there were spells as an uptown shop assistant and later as an estate agent. But whenever she worked, Laura always lived beyond her means, spending more money on clothes than she could ever earn or wear.

With first-date nerves behind them, over the next few weeks the new lovers spoke regularly on the phone. Some calls went on for hours, especially when Page was working nights.

In August, he took himself off to Los Angeles for a few weeks' holiday. He told Laura it was pre-booked and promised to call her often. In the end he only managed to sneak away twice to dial her digits. The need for discretion was essential as Page was leading a double life.

The young police officer was on holiday with his fiancée of two years. They had met at an east London college when Page was studying computing. But the relationship was on the wane, at least from Page's point of view. Only he couldn't be straight with either of the two women now firmly in his life.

When Page returned from America, Laura let him have it for the too few phone calls. It was his first inkling of her possessiveness and insane jealousy. He liked it, but foolishly tried to pacify her with a travelogue that included the time he saw *Baywatch* being filmed.

Over the following weeks, Page's close police colleagues got to know more about Laura, largely because he was showing her off. In turn, she joked with friends that her new boyfriend was 'stalking' her. 'Whenever I'm up the shops with Thomas in the pram he's there, in his uniform, with his copper mates,' she told them.

In truth, Laura loved his reciprocal jealousy and protective ways, without feeling any sense of suffocation. She felt they had instantly 'gelled'. But on occasions it could be embarrassing. He once clocked her crossing a zebra just before a white-van driver peeped his horn. Page put on the siren and pulled him over.

'Firstly, you're not wearing a seat belt,' he said officiously. 'And secondly, what was you doing to that woman?'

'Come on mate!' implored the driver. 'She was lovely!'

His attempt to find common cause with a fellow geezer fell on deaf ears. 'I know she is,' Page spat back. 'That's my fucking wife!'

The driver wasn't to know the truth and went into a verbal reverse gear apologizing for his inappropriateness.

Page wasn't afraid to put his police colleagues straight either, regardless of their rank. When Laura one day delivered his lunch to the police station, Page walked into the control room to find a number of officers huddled over the CCTV monitor.

'What are you looking at?' he asked.

'You'd give that one, wouldn't you,' replied a sergeant.

'I would, skip, and I am, because that's my missus!'

At this stage of their courtship Laura was the more reserved of the two. She put it down to lingering bad memories of her last relationship with Thomas's father. Page, however, was free-falling in love and often skived off work for some 'victim liaison'. Lying in bed together he would blank calls from the control room asking for assistance.

One day a new skipper at Grays police station wanted to accompany Page on duty. 'I've got a lot of witness statements to take, skip,' said Page, thinking quickly and hoping his boss would back off.

'That's alright, I'll give you a hand,' said the new sergeant. Page persisted and managed to avoid the bonding session. Instead, he sloped off to Laura's to pump her for further information on the still unresolved case of the nuisance caller.

Impressionable colleagues respected Page's strutting confidence. They never grassed him up, preferring to play tricks on the young recruit. One night they sneaked up on the couple's love nest and shone police lights on the bedroom window, as if it was a siege. When Page finally leaned out half naked, there was no one about but he soon noticed that his new J plate Ford Scorpio was plastered with 'POLICE AWARE' stickers on the wind-screen. This was not an occasion for door-to-door inquiries, he thought.

However, the light-headedness of their early relationship took a sour turn when one day Laura called Page at home and his Aunty Pat answered.

'How dare you ring this number,' she said.

'Well, Paul gave it me,' Laura hit back.

'He's engaged!'

'Well, that's not my problem,' she said, after a short pause.

Inside Laura was fuming. She extricated herself from the conversation without appearing floored, but seethed with anger in the hours leading to Page's homecoming. No sooner inside, she tore into him without taking a breath. Page knew it was on top and came clean about the Los Angeles holiday. But he assured Laura that he loved only her and would call off the engagement.

Their relationship survived and spilled into 1994 like a bar brawl. In April, Page enlisted a police friend and requisitioned a riot van to move Laura into a two-bedroom house owned by one of her sisters. Laura made space in the wardrobe for his police uniform. He even persuaded her it was time for the sound of tiny feet – an Alsatian puppy called Max.

But one careless day the tinderbox of their relationship went up following a schoolboy security lapse. Page had left his mobile phone at the home he now shared with Laura. Normally, Laura would have let it ring out but jealousy and mistrust were poison-ing her thoughts.

'Oh hello. Where's Paul?' asked the female voice politely.

'He's not here. Who are you?' snarled Laura.

'I'm his fiancée.'

'Really!' Laura replied sarcastically. 'Then why aren't you with him now? The bitchy banter continued until Laura had had enough and decided to play her top card.

'Oh! And by the way, I'm pregnant with Paul's baby,' she told his fiancée with sweet venom. Just then, Page came home and Laura thrust the phone at him. 'It's your fucking fiancée.'

'I ain't got one,' he blurted out pressing the red button and tossing the handset.

'LIAR!' screamed Laura, and then stormed to the wardrobe to grab his uniform and helmet.

'Please, love!' Page begged as she threw them out of the window.

'Fuck off! And don't ever come back here again.'

The neighbours had started to bang on the wall. 'SHUT UP!' one shouted. This infuriated Laura even more. She leaned out of the window and shouted back, even louder, 'FUCK OFF YOU! We're rowing here.' Turning to Page and pointing at the door, she said: 'And you can fuck off too. And take Max with you.'

Page gathered those belongings that remained in the wardrobe and left without swagger.

The puppy chewed most of Aunty Pat's furniture over the next few weeks. So she was glad to see the back of her nephew when Laura melted and took him back.

This time, Page was telling the truth when he swore to his pregnant girlfriend that he loved only her and would raise Thomas as his own.

The fragile domestic peace didn't stop his colleagues, who now had the measure of Laura, from winding her up. One night they left a highly perfumed police cravat belonging to a flame-haired female officer in Page's sports bag. As predicted, Laura searched it when he was asleep. Her heart beat with rage as she stomped upstairs to confront him. Stuffing the police cravat in his half-asleep face she demanded to know whose it was.

'It was planted by one of the lads,' said Page. 'I didn't do anything.'

Laura covered the cravat with fly spray and threw it at him. 'Take it fucking back,' she shouted.

Many years later, she told me, 'There's not one woman he's worked with that I haven't insulted.'

£ £ £

Page won his black belt in karate at the age of thirteen. In 1988, he was selected to represent England under-17s in the European Championships in Hungary.

As a reward, someone thought the team of largely inner-city boys would enjoy meeting their local MPs at the House of Commons. Page's parliamentarian didn't show, so he was introduced to a young Tory from Henley called Boris Johnson.

The wannabe man-of-the-people clearly wasn't paying attention. He gave Page one of those fake punches to the chest and said, 'Make sure you beat the Japanese.' When he left the room, the karate team looked at each other. 'What a wanker!' they agreed.

Page earned significant career breaks within the police from his talent for karate. Although young, he was mature in a sport that demanded self-restraint. During his interview for Essex Police they'd picked up on his work teaching karate to inner-city Asian and black kids in east and south London. The Leytonstone boy had grown up in a multicultural neighbourhood with many different friends. Through teaching karate to inner-city kids he knew how to gain respect and communicate with young people on the streets.

Like many other forces, Essex was wholly unrepresentative of the ethnic minorities it policed. Yet for Page it was the most natural thing to knock around with black and Asian kids. Casual racism was not a value he shared with the canteen culture of 1990s British policing.

There was, however, another aspect he did embrace wholeheartedly – so-called 'noble cause corruption'. Those on Essex's patch who couldn't be caught red handed but who officers believed were 'at it' would be singled out for beatings and for being fitted up with crimes they hadn't done.

'I accepted and appreciated the hatred of scroats when I joined the police. I didn't need to be sold on the idea. I didn't question the techniques taught us,' Page recalled.

This policing philosophy is in part born of a frustration with the criminal justice system and anger at the lack of respect on the streets. The solution for some police officers is a no legal nonsense approach to physically sorting out criminals and sex offenders who prey on the young, old and vulnerable. In that regard, Page was not by any stretch of the imagination a pc PC.

At Essex, he was given the nickname 'Punchy' because he could be relied on in a fight or when local criminals needed confronting.

'I remember the Battle of Ockenden. We had a thing for these two half-caste brothers. One of them broke the ribs of a dog handler. I got hold of him and strangled him until he cried,' Page recalled. The assault took place in front of a senior officer who didn't say a word, he claimed. 'Back then young cops like me were looking for leadership.'

Other elusive troublemakers would get a beating when they were eventually caught.

A prolific car thief on our patch got caught nicking a car stereo in a car park. He started to fight then hid under one of the cars. It was about 1 am. There was about twenty of us. We dug him out from underneath the car and kicked the shit out of the cunt like a football. [After a while] some [officers] were saying 'Stop! Stop! Stop!' But you know what? He didn't even complain.

Paedophiles were also given a violent lesson when Page was on duty. One was arrested for back chatting and cuffed behind his back so that he couldn't break the fall when thrown into the police van, head first. When he came to in the cells, it was time for another beating.

'The hate' for these people was instilled by old-school Essex officers, said Page. 'There was the thin blue line. And then there was us, the dirty stuff, below it.'

£ £ £

After the British police karate championships, Page drove back to Grays for night duty. His face was black and blue, but he felt good because the Metropolitan Police was head-hunting him.

Sir Brian Hayes, the deputy commissioner of the Metropolitan Police, had apparently encouraged Page to switch forces after seeing him fight for Essex that night.

There were some reservations about transferring to the biggest UK police force. A colleague had warned Page to 'watch his back'. The well-wisher was simply pointing out that in Essex, where you were a name not a number, no one would grass up another officer, unlike the Met where it was impersonal and the politics so venal.

Ironically, Page's transfer to the Met was delayed pending the outcome of an assault complaint he was facing. The incident had taken place on the day Page turned twenty-four. He was called to a children's home on 17 April 1995 to arrest one of the vulnerable boys for criminal damage. Page had the boy in a headlock on the way back to the police station and was forcing him to sing 'Happy Birthday'.

The boy later complained to his social worker. But Page denied it and there was no corroboration, so an internal inquiry dismissed the complaint.

Punchy was going to the Met.[1]

Chapter 2

The 'mobile classroom'

Marylebone is a busy police station covering the north side of London's bustling Oxford Street. Paul Page arrived at his first Metropolitan Police posting in September 1995.

His new patch had a large transient community of shoppers and tourists who attracted all sorts of thieves from street muggers and pickpockets to gangs targeting department and boutique stores.

North of Oxford Street lies the upmarket residential communities of Fitzrovia, Baker Street and St John's Wood, near Lord's cricket ground. As with much of London, here the rich rub shoulders with the under-privileged and new immigrant communities living in nearby housing estates. In the mid-1990s, these concrete warrens presented the police with another problem: turf battles between black, Asian and Somali gangs.

It didn't take long for Page to find his feet and establish himself among colleagues and superiors as a go-to cop when the tough got out of hand. In his own words, he was 'an officer to be relied on'. Being a self-defence instructor helped this image, but it was what happened on Marylebone's streets that cemented the rep Page carried from Essex to the Met.

Oxford Street and its discreet side roads are used by a diverse group of street traders hawking fake or stolen fashion labels, perfumes and electrical goods. There was a feeling among some Marylebone officers that these traders were liberty takers. They conned people but had no fear of arrest because often they were released the next day and back on the streets looking for a new mark.

Page was a willing participant in what he says was a vigilante culture that operated at Marylebone. He recalls going on patrol with a plan to deal with the traders, who upon seeing the marauding police officers would run away abandoning their merchandise on the street. Those not in pursuit would scoop up the spoils for sharing out back at the police station. However, according to Page, other officers got wind of the scam and took it to a new level of audacity. Rather than just steal the fake-designer merchandise, they also 'put a few bodies on the custody sheet'. In other words, they arrested the traders and handed in only some of the gear to be used as 'evidence' against them. The rest was divided up between the police.

Police corruption trials and complaints to the watchdog over the last two decades indicate that such practices were almost certainly common in pockets of the Met, especially among officers in specialist squads targeting armed robbers, lorry hijackers and drug traffickers. However, Page's allegations about Marylebone police station are uncorroborated by prosecution or disciplinary action taken against any officer.

Clearly, corrupt officers like Page were not going to grass themselves up while still serving in the police and colleagues who were not involved in the corruption were unlikely to blow the whistle and become pariahs at work. As for the traders, there was no benefit to be gained from making a complaint.

Even if the Met's anti-corruption squad were called in, Page claims it didn't always spell trouble for officers under suspicion.

For example, on one eventful night duty, an African man was in the cells for a public order offence involving drink and possibly drugs. Such was his level of consumption that the prisoner was put on a round-the-clock watch to ensure he didn't choke on his own vomit.

Around the same time, a junior officer marched a high-class prostitute into the police station for drink-driving. After she was processed, Page recalled that two more experienced officers gave her an escort home. Their timing couldn't have been worse. While they were away, the intoxicated African prisoner was found unconscious in his cell.

Efforts to revive him failed and his death in custody had to be immediately reported to the anti-corruption squad. They arrived shortly thereafter only to discover that the dead man's custody record – a timed log of all police contact – had gone missing. However, a search of the confidential waste bin did lead to the discovery of the prostitute's charge sheet – it had been ripped up.

The canteen talk over the following days was that the dead man's custody record had been 'lost' because checks weren't done at regular intervals. Page and his colleagues were interviewed, but no one said anything to the anti-corruption squad. Indeed, the whole matter eventually blew over.

Irrespective of the accuracy of Page's account, it was not the only time a custody record had disappeared at Marylebone.

On 31 January 1997, 24-year-old Mark McLoughlin died in his cell. The Irish man had been arrested in Oxford Street for being drunk. At the inquest, the police claimed his custody record was lost. The jury heard conflicting evidence from the officer responsible for checking on McLoughlin and his cellmate about the frequency of those checks. A verdict was returned that McLoughlin had died of a methadone overdose, but that police neglect played a part.

£ £ £

The presence of a Black Maria, or any other police van for that matter, tearing around the inner city full of charged-up coppers can twitch the bottle of even the most game.

The Met has been in and out of court for decades trying to defend the actions of officers accused of beating up the arrested in the van and then, sometimes to cover their tracks, having them additionally arrested for assault on the police.

Very rarely do serving police officers talk about what really goes on inside the Black Maria. Rarer still does the same officer admit his own role in kidnap, false imprisonment and assault. However, Page's explanation for his actions won't offend everyone:

> It doesn't take long for you to become very cynical. You see things the general public never will – murder victims, elderly muggings, rape victims, a child sexually abused, or facing death. Anyone who says joining the police doesn't change the way you see society is a liar.
>
> You take on a role. It is a tough life if you are lower down the social scale. There are people out there who don't care what they have to do to get money and they don't care about the police and will shoot them if they have to. Officers get disgruntled over different things. Mainly that nothing's going to be done, that [the criminal] will be out soon and they didn't respect us.
>
> At Marylebone there was a (small) hard core of 'reliable officers'. There was the surface of policing and then another

surface and those officers weren't prepared to stand by and watch the real, hardened criminals who were daily causing misery to people get away with it and there was a concerted effort to target them and make their life a misery.

The 'mobile classroom' was a police van we'd take out and violent criminals with no respect for the law and us as police officers was targeted and put in the van, driven around for ten minutes and 'taught a lesson', then kicked out.

None of them complained. They knew they were violent and got away with a lot of things. And in their eyes, I imagine it was, 'Well it's better than getting nicked'.

Page liked to administer a headlock. He knew about pressure points. One behind the ears was particularly effective.

In one case, a local violent street robber had killed a man in a fight. His reputation grew and his criminality increased. A group of us reliable officers not afraid to confront these people were tasked to do plain clothes surveillance of him and, if the opportunity arose, deal with him.

From the briefing we knew what that meant. Couldn't have been misunderstood. The kingpin was arrested, cuffed and taken to a police cell at Marylebone where he was told, 'Now you are going to feel what a victim of robbery feels like.' He was then kicked out. He made no complaint.

Page had no concern about any internal investigation. The situation on the streets he likened to a 'war' and in combat an officer needs to be assured that others have his back not only on the streets, but also at court and when the internal affairs lot start sniffing around. 'We trusted each other,' he simply explains.

Marylebone was a naughty nick and [I] made it naughtier … You'd have to be naïve to believe it doesn't go on in other stations. These 'values' were shared across the police stations. There is only so much the police can take before they have to look at other ways of dealing with hardcore criminals.

I did fit people up. Yeah I did, but I fit up people who was cunts. The culture was there and I fitted into it … If people think what I've said 'this is an isolated incident', then they are being naïve.

Chapter 3

Road to royalty

As a valued member of the Met's karate team, Page was soon developing friendships with those from other police divisions and specialist squads. Among them were royal and diplomatic protection officers charged with looking after the Royal Family, visiting dignitaries and palaces, including Westminster and the House of Commons.

By summer 1997, Page had been at Marylebone for two years. He was starting to feel he'd had enough of street policing and wanted a new challenge to go with his new responsibilities at home.

'It's a good little number, Paul,' one protection officer told him while offering a day's attachment to Buckingham Palace to see if his face fit.

Page told Laura of the opportunity to move to a new posting. 'I'm tired of dealing with the same old shit every day, love. I don't want to get in a rut and before I know it I've done twenty years dealing with the dross.'

James, their son, was now two and the family had their first home, a three-bedroom property in Badgers Dean, Essex. Laura was looking after James and Thomas whilst child minding for other parents. But it was Page's police salary that secured the mortgage. She welcomed the idea of her man being more out of harm's way.

'I have friends on Royalty through karate who said it was a good place to be. Well paid, no paperwork, no grief, no stress, one or two hours on, and the same off in the canteen or gym,' he continued.

Although looking for a change, the Royalty Protection Department, or SO14 (short for Specialist Operation 14), was not a posting that came immediately to mind. One night duty at Marylebone, he had driven past Buckingham Palace and looked at the SO14 officers on post. 'What a fucking boring job,' he thought to himself. He didn't know until he got there that they were looking back at him thinking, 'What a stupid idiot running round, risking his life for a lot less than we take home.'

Once again, karate would count in Page's favour as the senior management at SO14 considered his application. Having a good reference was important. Page sold well his potential as a self-defence instructor of Royal Protection officers.

Typically confident, he believed it made him a hard-to-turn-down asset. First, though, there was the formality of an interview. But Page wasn't nervous. He told his wife he'd been given a heads-up on some of the key questions.

Part of the interview involved asking candidates to identify a photograph of a royal. A colleague had apparently clued him in about which royal mug shot he'd be shown. He was also told the right response to various scenarios. If, for example, he was on duty and heard someone screaming outside the palace, do not abandon your post. And, no, it was never acceptable to read on night duty.

Page passed selection for SO14. But his transfer from

Marylebone was delayed until 1998, after he had completed a firearms course.

While he waited, the death of Princess Diana on 31 August 1997 was an intense reminder to him and others who were not natural royalists just how much the monarchy still meant to many British citizens. It was also a reminder of how out of touch the Queen and older royals had become in misreading the public mood towards the death of 'the people's princess'. Those who questioned whether Diana really was a candle in the wind did so at their own peril in the run-up to her funeral.

Tony Blair, the recently elected modernizing New Labour prime minister, read the mood right. But he looked too controlling as he jockeyed for the right seat in Westminster Abbey, where Diana's brother gave a speech that took a swing at her in-laws and the media.

For Page, Diana's death was an opportunity to get in on the televised funeral procession. On 6 September, Laura was painting the front door of their new house. The television was on in the background when Page called.

'Hello, love. Are you watching the funeral?'

'Yeah. Why?'

'Look for a police car in the right-hand corner of your screen.' He waited for her to study the TV. 'Do you see it?'

'Yes,' she replied, still unsure what her man was getting at.

'It's me!' shouted Page, as he hung his head outside the driver's window and waved.

Laura had other things on her mind. She was getting married in six days. It wasn't that there was the usual mass of things to do. If only. Her husband-to-be had proposed in a brutally unromantic fashion that could only have pleased a heartless accountant.

Two months earlier, Page had been talking to one of his colleagues at Marylebone at the beginning of their morning shift.

The officer was in a bad mood. He'd just had a row with his wife over who was going to clean up the dog shit in the garden.

'So I said to her,' he told Page. 'I only married you for the tax code, you bitch.'

When the laughter subsided, the officer explained how married couples got tax breaks not offered to singletons and those living together. Page was intrigued by the chance to make money and have one over the taxman.

After his shift, he thought about how he was going to broach the subject with Laura. In the end, he just came out with it.

'Love, we are going to have to get married so my tax code will go down. Do you want to get that arranged?'

The proposal of marriage was not exactly how Laura had imagined. She wanted the special day, meringue dress and high-rise cake. The volatile couple had been together three years now with a fine collection of broken ornaments following silly arguments, mostly driven by jealousy. So slightly heavy hearted, Laura booked a registry office in Thurrock, Essex, which for added romance was next door to a police station.

The wedding was a catalogue affair. Laura's ring, a gold band, cost £29 from Argos. Her dress, from Littlewoods, only arrived on the day of the wedding, while she was having her hair done.

No family member attended the registry office, which also lacked any personal touches. Page had asked his childhood friend Fahim Baree to be his best man. When the registrar announced he could kiss the bride, Laura unexpectedly pulled away from Page's puckered lips.

'I was embarrassed,' she told him later during the reception at TGI Friday's in Lakeside. 'I haven't exactly been led up a romantic path.'

'I know love, but we agreed we'd do it properly when we're flush.'

A few months later, Page bumped into the colleague who had first planted the idea of marriage as a tax benefit. 'Alright?' asked Page.

'No. Not really,' came the reply. 'My wife's leaving me and she's taking the dog.'[1]

£ £ £

Page was not going to Buckingham Palace without any experience of the royal world beyond taking the tabloids. While at Marylebone he attended an incident over the New Year that gave him a telling insight into how royal sexual indiscretions are dealt with by the police and loved by the press.

The incident taught him at least three principles of survival when dealing with the circle of royals, associated peers and their Sloaney hangers on: first, they do not consider themselves like the rest of society so don't treat them as such; second, when senior officers say turn a blind eye, do it; and finally, always remember *Upstairs Downstairs* may well have been off the telly since the seventies but it's alive and well in relations between the police and the Palace. Before going on duty on New Year's Day, Page had a quick catch-up on the gossip from colleagues going home. Apparently there was some hand-wringing among senior officers over whether a suicide had been mishandled.

It wasn't any ordinary citizen who had taken their life overnight. Anne Hills was a 55-year-old freelance journalist from a posh family with a secret past that was the beyond the salivation of her tabloid colleagues.

When Page got home that evening, though knackered, he regaled Laura with details of his bizarre day. One of the dead woman's friends had called the police after getting no reply at Hills's swanky top-floor flat near Baker Street. Through the window the friend had noticed empty wine bottles and blister packets of drugs spread across the table. Officers knocked down the door, but didn't find a body or notice anything else that would indicate a suicide.

When Anne's father was informed he had good reason to suspect the worst having experienced the sad and desperate mood his daughter was in two days earlier. Elliot Philipp knew her flat well and soon found Anne wearing a black dress and stilettos curled up on the roof. She had been dead for some time but looked beautiful, he thought. Philipp called the police. The control room at Marylebone sent Page and another young officer to the flat in nearby Upper Montague Street. As they walked in, the two officers mistook Philipp for someone official, maybe the person who had come to take away the body.

'What's the scenario, chief?' asked Page's colleague, a pen in his mouth.

'My daughter's on the roof. She's dead. Quite dead,' Philipp replied. Outwardly, at least, the 81-year-old retired gynaecologist was calm. His delivery was very clinical and stiff upper lip. Privately, though, Philipp felt his daughter's complicated personal life was a major factor in her suicide.

Anne had taken him to see a production of Tennessee Williams's *A Streetcar Named Desire* two days before. Arguably, the last play a woman in her state of mind should have sat through. The lead female character, Blanche DuBois, is a fallen southern belle. She worries about growing old alone and that her sister will discover the history of promiscuity, which followed a failed marriage to a gay husband who killed himself. Of course, like most secrets it does come out, and before the final curtain falls, Blanche is carted away by the men in white coats.

Philipp gave nothing away as he chatted with Page in the kitchen. But it was obvious to the grieving father that the British press would soon sniff out his loss was no ordinary suicide.

For the last twenty years, Hills had been the mistress of Lord Snowdon or Tony Armstrong-Jones, as he was known before the Queen ennobled him after his marriage in 1960 to her sister, Princess Margaret. When they divorced in 1978, Snowdon, a serial adulterer, met Hills. Legend has it the freelance journalist door-stepped him when pulling together a piece about disability, a subject close to the royal photographer's heart. He had con-tracted polio as a boy. 'I am a journalist and want to do a story about you. But I also want to have an affair with you,' she is reputed to have said. The randy lord needed little encourage-ment and their affair spanned the duration of his second mar-riage to another society beauty.

Hills resigned herself to being 'the mistress'. She had other relationships, some just for sex, but had told her father and friends that she was fearful of being left alone over New Year's Eve. A relationship with her live-in lover was falling apart and Snowdon had his own family commitments. To make matters worse, a national newspaper had just rejected her for a job.

Page excused himself from talking to Philipp and looked for the stairway onto the flat roof to inspect the body. It was a vast space, too high up for someone with vertigo. The body was not immedi-ately visible from the top rung of the stairs. However, behind what he thought was a water tower above an adjacent flat Page eventu-ally located Hills's body. She had drifted into unconsciousness and then death after washing down a cocktail of sleeping pills with alcohol. Page noticed her face was lying on a note. He retrieved it with care, avoiding the mucus that soiled the exposed part. Returning downstairs, Page wondered if the officers who had broken down the front door had actually searched the roof. He was even more surprised when he noticed several sealed white envelopes, which Hills had neatly laid on a piece of furniture. One letter was addressed to an organisation that conducted medical research on donated cadavers. Another was for Lord Snowdon.

Page never read the note he found on the roof. However, it later emerged that she had written of the love for her children and father.

By now, two others had joined Philipp in the flat. He announced that they were going for lunch in a nearby Pizza Hut.

'I'll be back by the time the mortuary people arrive. Don't let them go without me,' he told Page matter-of-factly.

Alone in the flat, the two officers split up and looked around. As Page walked into the bedroom he was struck by the circular bed. After rummaging around, he found a box beside it. Inside were love letters from Snowdon and some black and white nude photographs of Hills. Nearby was a collection of dildos that made Page chuckle at the idea of a sword fight in the turret-shaped bedroom. Nothing in her video collection suggested anything else compromising enough to warrant seizing. Then the phone rang. Both officers agreed it was best all round not to answer. Hills had changed her message for the New Year. 'Hello everyone,' it said. 'I hope you have a lovely 1997.' After the beeps, a mature and very clipped male voice explained that he was unable to see her for some days but they would meet up soon. He ended the call: 'I'm really concerned. Chin up.' It was Snowdon.

Soon after, more senior officers turned up at the flat. Page approached one of them.

'Skip, there's all this personal stuff I've found in her bedroom, love letters, pictures and half a sex shop. We should remove it so the family don't see it.'

'That's not our job,' said the senior officer. 'Put it back and keep your mouth shut.' The police did, however, take away the tape in the answering machine, the suicide note and the sealed letters Hills had so precisely left behind.

As he recounted the story to Laura that night, the thing that puzzled them most was the coolness of the upper classes in the face of such personal tragedy.

'It's the way they've been brought up,' suggested Laura sympathetically. 'You know, not to express their emotions.'

'No, love,' replied Page. 'They're just odd. Had it been one of our kids who topped themselves, we wouldn't be going out for fucking pizza!'

The suicide of Snowdon's lover eventually reached the front pages later that month as 'friends' of Hills opened up. Further details of her last day emerged during the short inquest, but nothing new came out about her affair with Snowdon. Nor were any of the letters read out.

The pathologist had found acceptable levels of the tranquillizer Temazepam and alcohol in her body. However, he concluded it was the large quantity of paracetamol that killed Anne Hills. A verdict of suicide was recorded. 'This was an intended act,' said the coroner. 'It's quite likely this occurred on the spur of the moment. She wasn't happy with her life at the time.'

The *Mirror* had the best exclusive on the tragic affair: 'CHIN UP!' screamed the front page, followed by revelations that this was Snowdon's last words on his lover's answering machine. Only Page and his colleague knew that Hills had never lived long enough to hear them.[2]

Chapter 4

Gripper meets Purple One

On the morning of 22 June 1998, Paul Page slung his 5 Series burgundy BMW around Trafalgar Square and through Admiralty Arch. Cruising down The Mall, the famous tree-lined approach road to Buckingham Palace, the 28-year-old felt relaxed about his move to Royalty Protection. Not every policeman went to work in a 775-room palace that was the seat of Britain's constitutional monarchy.

Page had convinced himself he wanted an easy life away from cracking heads on London's back streets and dealing with 'the dross'. Laura, pregnant with their second son, supported the move. He'd always promised her upward mobility and it didn't get much better than telling friends her husband's new job involved protecting the Queen.

Colleagues on Royal Protection had assured Page he could supplement his £33,000 salary with overtime opportunities while, paradoxically, having more time to spend with his growing family. The extra money would also help realize their plans to buy a bigger house.

Royalty Protection, which is sometimes referred to as SO14, has responsibility not just for the British Royal Family but also visiting diplomats and foreign royals. They also guard against 'obsessives' with a fixation on the Royal Family. Page was joining a 400-strong unit of largely men who are stationed at the main palaces in London, Windsor, Norfolk and Scotland.

SO14 officers are not detectives but come from the uniformed branch of the Met. The unit is split in two: SO14 (1) armed protection officers that wear the traditional Met uniform and are stationed in and around the palaces; and SO14 (2) the armed personal protection officers (PPOs) who are assigned to a particular royal and get to wear the flash suits, Bermuda shorts and dinner jackets at home and abroad.

Page was joining SO14, and would learn during his induction tour that the suit-wearing personal protection officers thought they were a cut above their uniformed colleagues. This didn't overly bother him. As a self-defence fitness instructor he had the power to pass or fail a PPO. And without a fitness certificate, a PPO could guard nobody.

However, it soon dawned on Page during the tour inside Buckingham Palace and through meeting officers guarding various corridors or standing outside a royal bedroom that the unit he had joined wasn't exactly the vibrant mix of young coppers he was expecting. In place of the banter of a busy central London police station there was a stillness and reverence to the weight of history.

'Within an hour I felt like I'd entered the set of *Dad's Army*,' he said. Only Page was in no mood to play Private Pike. Even the preferred choice of weapon betrayed an antiquated approach.

The old guard favoured a revolver, whereas Page told the armourer to issue him with the Austrian-made 9 mm Glock 17 semi-automatic pistol.

In the palace canteen there was no let-up on the serious mood. No one was larking about over a card game or gawping at a newspaper pin-up. Naturally, Page gravitated towards the younger officers and grumbled that the older ones were blanking him.

His first posting was the Garden Gate – a vital part of any Royal Protection officer's duty, he was told. It's the grand entrance to the Queen's personal quarters, which she is often captured on television approaching after driving through the front gates of Buckingham Palace, or BP, as he would now call it.

Colonnade lights on the Garden Gate stay on after Her Majesty leaves the palace and until she returns. Just behind the gate is 19 Post where Page would be sitting for the next few weeks.

All the royals have a call sign by which they are identified within SO14. The Queen is Purple One. 'When the Queen is coming out or into the palace you will be notified through the intercom by her call sign "Purple One". You must have the wooden gates open so she can be driven through without stopping. 'Do not fuck it up because all hell will break loose!' Page was warned.

Fuck what up? He thought. It's just a gate. She approaches in her car, the barrier is lifted and she is driven through. Simple. He was starting to wonder whether moving from cracking heads to opening gates was such a bright career move after all.

One week later, and Page fucked up his first encounter with the Queen. He was doodling, something he often did when bored or musing on a problem. Suddenly, through the intercom her PPO announced: 'One, nine, Garden Gate!'

Page scrambled to open the wooden gates. According to the protocol, the SO14 officer should have both gates open and bolted down by the time Purple One's car approaches and be saluting as she is driven past. Unfortunately, Paul had mistimed Her Majesty's arrival and the royal limo was now at the gate with the Queen and Prince Philip sitting in the back, waiting. Purples One and Two were not amused. The Queen, he recalled, was shaking her head, while Philip stared him out. Even his salute looked comical, he felt.

When the limo eventually passed through the Garden Gate and came to a halt a little down the way near the royal quarters, the Queen's protection officer rushed out of the car towards Page. 'What have you done? The Queen doesn't wait! Don't you know that?' he shouted.

Page wanted to chin the senior officer, but managed to rein himself in. The incident went up the chain of command and Page got another lecture that her Purpleness never waits.

'It's full of weirdos, love,' Page complained to his heavily pregnant wife over dinner that night. 'We were given these maps of the palace to study the quickest route out if there is an alarm. But they wanted me to do it on me own time. Fuck that! I'd rather watch telly in the canteen.'

Laura laughed as her husband got into his stride over the day's events. Page found the change in policing culture jarring. It says a lot that it bothered him that older, some might say more mature, officers actually seemed to take the whole job quite seriously. It may not be frontline policing but there had been a number of spectacular security breaches, in particular at Buckingham Palace.

As early as the 1830s, a boy called Cotton was discovered in the palace gardens and claimed he had lived there for a year. Around the same era another boy repeatedly entered the palace and was finally dispatched to Broadmoor, a secure unit for the criminally insane.

Over 140 years later, German tourists pitched a tent to sleep overnight in the palace gardens thinking it was Hyde Park. And in June 1981, a 17-year-old boy fired six blanks at the Queen during the Trooping the Colour ceremony and shortly before the wedding of Prince Charles to Diana Spencer. The following year, in June 1982, unemployed Michael Fagan penetrated the Queen's quarters while she was asleep. Heads rolled and security was tightened.

£ £ £

Within months of his arrival, a split along age lines was developing among officers at Buckingham Palace. Page was establishing himself with a small group of younger officers. They had given each other nicknames, which reflected the generation gap and attitude to the job in hand.

Page was no longer nicknamed Punchy but 'Gripper' because he had a flat nose from too many battles in the ring; although one colleague thought wrongly it was because he had 'gripped the rail' (stood trial) for some unknown offence before joining the police. Another officer on Page's relief was called 'Monkey Boy'. The nickname caused initial concern when a senior officer heard it casually mentioned over the palace radio system and thought it was a racist reference to one of the few ethnic minority Royal Protection officers. The senior officer, an inspector nicknamed 'Elton John', because he looked like him, soon calmed down after being informed that 'Monkey Boy' was actually white and so-called because he 'was built like a gorilla'. The third member of Page's growing crew was close friend 'Pretty Boy', seemingly named after his love of personal grooming and sun beds.

Then there was 'the Don'. He was an older and trusted member of Page's relief nicknamed after Don Corleone, the mythical Godfather. The Don was a Police Federation representative, which meant he acted for SO14 officers who were in trouble and facing discipline or, worse still, criminal charges. His policing experience outside of the palace together with an ability to smooth over things with SO14 senior management made the Don appear something of a father figure and highly respected by Page and his new crew at BP.

The more *Dad's Army* types also had nicknames but some were more derogatory than others and often used behind their back. One hapless constable was known as 'Fagan', after the 1982 palace intruder, because it was joked among some young officers that he took 'an unhealthy interest' in the Royal Family, when he was just doing his job.

Divisions between SO14 and the Royal Household also vexed Page. He explained:

> There's a class system within the palace and it is very antiquated. You've got the low-level servants, the butlers, the cooks, the cleaners and the handymen and then you've got the middle tier of general admin people. And then the top tier of private secretaries and comptrollers and Lords and Ladies in Waiting. We, the police, were a necessary evil. The Royal Household didn't want us there.

It annoyed Page when colleagues allowed members of the Royal Household to enter the palace without showing their passes. If there was a security protocol then it should be adhered to by everyone, he thought, mindful of his recent dressing down over the Garden Gate.

Page did not like feeling he was on the bottom tier. 'We had our impression of the household and they had their impression of us,' he griped.

During one night duty at the front gates of Buckingham

Palace, Page thought he had a chance to invert the power play. A senior Palace aide approached the gates a little tired and emotional. The aide explained he needed help to recover the briefcase he'd left in a nearby wine bar.

'It's not our remit, sir. We can't leave our post,' Page explained firmly but politely.

'But I have sensitive documents in the briefcase,' the aide urged.

Minutes later the duty inspector was on the phone telling Page to take another officer and drive the aide to the wine bar. Only it wasn't a wine bar, but a gentlemen's club, of the lap-dancing kind.

The doormen informed Page they had ejected the aide. What for was never made clear, but the briefcase was returned and the matter closed. Page would later describe the culture at Buckingham Palace in these terms: 'You cover stuff up, do what you are told, keep your mouth shut and your head down.'[1]

Still, the flexibility with which security rules were sometimes applied to the higher-ups at BP left a mark on Page. He was also struggling with suppressing his copper's instinct for sizing up the streets for suspicious activity. His job was no longer to make arrests but to make sure no one without an embossed invitation or security pass entered Buckingham Palace. What happened outside the gates of BP was a matter for real cops on division, the different areas by which the Met polices London.

One incident brought home his sense of professional emasculation. The BP boys had a marked police car for patrolling the perimeter of the palace and responding to emergency calls from other London palaces such as St James's and Kensington. Early on a Saturday morning, Page was on duty with Monkey Boy in the patrol car. They had clocked a young man slowly motoring past Buckingham Palace. A quick check on the number plate showed the car was registered to a woman. The man refused to pull over and was pursued at high speed around the streets of Victoria. It ended with him crashing into a parked car. When the two SO14 officers dragged him out, he appeared high and had a big knife.

Page thought it was a good arrest and expected a 'nice one' from his superiors. Instead, they considered it 'a depletion of departmental resources', because two SO14 officers were no longer on post. The reaction got up Page's nose. Shortly afterwards he was back on duty patrolling the garden when a superior approached him.

'Did you enjoy yourself on division Paul?'

'Yeah, I did, gov,' he answered enthusiastically.

'Well you are not on division now. We have different rules here and it doesn't entail cavalier attitudes.'

Page was once again biting his lip. He realized SO14 had a wholly unique remit that was not about serving the public but protecting the Royal Family, in the widest sense of the word.

From now on his attitude to being a Royal Protection officer changed dramatically. 'I didn't want to progress my police career. I wanted to progress my financial career.'

Chapter 5

Bubble bath

Paul Page's arrival at Buckingham Palace in June 1998 coincided with the beginning of a boom in the British economy. The New Labour government of Tony Blair and Gordon Brown had won a landslide election one year earlier partly on a promise to be more business-friendly. So the ever-grinning prime minister and his dour chancellor were overseeing a new era of light-touch regulation making London the city where money flowed and big swinging dicks from trading floors and financial institutions across the globe wanted to work and display their gambling prowess.

In this lax regulatory climate two financial bubbles grew – one in Internet tech firms, the so-called dot.com bubble, and the other in house prices. Both were fuelled by the US-led fiscal policy of low interest rates, which had been cut to boost the lagging economy on a gamble that those who believe their house is worth more spend more.

Of course, it wasn't long before the cheap credit-fuelled bubble in US house prices was mirrored in the UK, which continued to froth for nine more years.

Well before its peak, Page traded up to a detached house with front and back gardens on the new, upmarket Chafford Hundred estate near Grays in Essex, the place he had begun his police service six years earlier.

Chafford Hundred was built to feed one of the largest shopping centres in Europe. Lakeside, which opened in 1990, has a special place in the Page love story. It was on a fake steamboat restaurant moored on the man-made lake that the couple enjoyed their first date in the summer of 1993. And four years later they had their austere wedding reception at TGI Friday. The shopping centre and posh estate would continue to feature in many future family dramas.

Laura had only just given birth to their third son, Matthew, when they moved to Chafford Hundred in October 1998. She loved the upward mobility of her new surroundings. It was a huge step up from the 'shit hole' of her Grays roots and the tinned mackerel factory of her youth.

Unlike Grays, nearby Chafford Hundred definitely had a sense of safety, conformity and whiteness to it. The estate was popular with police families and financial workers, who had a direct rail link into the City.

Page had secured a £154,000 loan with Kensington Mortgage Company on his salary alone. The mortgage firm specialized in high-risk customers who the high-street banks might refuse. However, traditional banks and building societies were also starting to abandon their previous prudential ways and offer mortgages that were many multiples of an applicant's income. Page's mortgage was almost five times his police salary and the property was almost twice the average UK house price in 1998.

He could have reduced his mortgage by dipping into the profit from selling the old home in Badger's Dean, or by using some of the money his grandparents had left him. But Page wanted to free up that cash for something else – dealing himself into the dot.com boom.

The bubble in technology stocks was certainly aided by the availability of cheap credit, especially in the US, but another driver was the belief that new Internet technology would solve the world's problems, or at least the need to quicken and ease the flow of money, trade and commerce.

The new economic ethos was one of growth over profits – get big or get lost. So the availability of cheap credit made it easy for start-up Internet companies to float on the stock market before many had earned any revenue let alone turned a profit. Traders, corrupt analysts and tame business journalists did the rest by whipping up a feeding frenzy among ordinary investors who piled into these risky stocks 'before it was too late'. Certainly the initial public offerings made overnight millionaires of the geeky young bosses of companies with little else but an e prefix or .com after their name.

What had started in Silicon Valley and the New York stock exchange was now all the rage in the Royal Stock Exchange in London. The quick profits to be earned from buying and selling tech stocks made ordinary investors like the royal police officer from Chafford Hundred believe he too could be a big City trader.

£ £ £

When Page now came off post at Buckingham Palace, he walked into the canteen like a man no longer uncertain about his role and relationship with the more experienced hands on A Relief. He'd take his lunch over to the television area and ask to change the channel.

'What's on?' an older colleague would enquire.

'Alan Greenspan.'

'Alan who?'

'The chairman of the Federal Reserve and he's about to make a speech,' Page replied as he turned the channel over to Teletext without waiting for objection.

Greenspan had been US Federal Reserve chairman since 1987. International politicians and bankers treated the monetarist like a sage and were persuaded by his total belief in the self-correcting power of free markets. The decision to lower interest rates in an effort to boost the US economy was his and the sage was about to announce a further adjustment. These televised pronouncements moved markets up or down and to a savvy investor they presented an opportunity to make money in stocks and bonds.

Page no longer saw his job at BP in royal protection terms. Security now meant financial security for his family and the labour conditions at the palace were perfect to supplement his police salary with some educated share dealing using the pot of cash he had kept back.

He could often be found in the BP canteen studying the pink business pages of the *Evening Standard*. At home in Chafford Hundred he would scan share sites and chat rooms on the Internet or listen to pundits on Bloomberg and CNBC for analysis of the economic conditions and its impact on the rolling digital strip of share and commodity prices at the bottom of his laptop.

'It's not rocket science, love,' he explained to Laura in an effort to get her signature on some documents. The paperwork was for a joint Halifax bank account he opened on 4 December 1998 to deal in shares.

Page's first foray into the world of stocks and shares was a punt on Halifax itself, which had recently floated as a public limited company. The demutualization of the former building society began with the so-called Big Bang in 1986, a deregulation of the UK financial services industry under Margaret Thatcher. By 1997, Halifax had floated on the London Stock Exchange and was buying up smaller building societies.

Within days of buying the Halifax shares, Page was bragging to Laura that he'd made £800. She noticed how happy and cocksure it made her husband feel. The winnings, which he loved to spend on his family, were also welcome.

Page's punt on Halifax shares was not exactly shooting fish in a barrel, but neither was it intelligent, high-risk trading. What mattered is that it stirred in the 27-year-old a new sense of himself.

He enjoyed his role as family protector, and although disillusioned with royal policing he still believed in the police protecting normal society from 'the dross'. However, the buzz of share dealing gave Page an opportunity to be more of a family provider than his £33,000 salary, even with overtime, allowed.

More worryingly, it also fed an alter ego he was developing as a City trader, albeit one with a police warrant card working at Buckingham Palace. 'I was starting to find my feet with the stock market and that proved more fruitful than doing two days of overtime on a rest day when I was away from my family,' he explained. 'I could earn £300 at a punch of a button in five minutes.'

The first five months of his Halifax statements show that from December 1998 to April 1999 Page earned a staggering £241,530.35 from share dealing. The self-taught trader was mainly buying shares in privatized utility companies, banks, and a lot of tech stocks, especially computer-game manufacturers.

Around this time, Page became friends with a fellow SO14 officer also interested in playing the booming markets. The identity of all the key Royal Protection officers involved in this story are known, but Page would only refer to this man as 'Harry'.

He said they struck up a conversation one day when Page was in the palace canteen studying the business section. Soon the pair were discussing the markets and sharing tips. Before long they started trading together on a laptop Page was now bringing to work. When one was on post, the other was monitoring share prices in his down time.

The story goes that the pair struck big on a tip that came from Harry. A software company was going public and Harry recognized the owner from his previous job body-guarding a senior British politician during a visit to a defence research establishment. The software company was apparently run by a very clever man and was involved in recognition systems used in identity cards and airport security.

'We piled in,' said Page. 'I put in £80,000 and fuck me it went up. But the first four days were the worst of my life.'

The pair would regularly check the laptop but the shares just weren't moving. Then, the digital flicker across the screen started to rise. The bet was coming good.

A month later Page and Harry were sitting in the BP canteen, the glare from the laptop illuminating huge grins. Page said his shares were by then worth over £400,000. Harry had also cleaned up, but not as much as Page, who had secretly gambled more than they each agreed to risk.

The success was not unnoticed by SO14 colleagues. Page liked the feeling. But more importantly, Halifax had been also watching the large balance on his 'sharexpress' account. He came home and told his wife with obvious pride that as a reward for his risk taking Halifax had increased his credit limit to £500,000.

The bank also gave him a personal broker. No longer would Page have to deal with a call centre to place his bets. Having his own broker made him feel superior and smarter than the common punter. He was like the guy at the casino table whose name and favourite tipple were known to the croupier and waitress.

£ £ £

By June 1999, the anniversary of his first year at Buckingham Palace, Page had earned under £40,000 in police wages and ten times that amount from share dealing.

The largest win that year – a staggering £168,204.53 – hit the Halifax account on 10 June, just days before James's fourth birthday.

Although a joint account, it was Page who managed the money. He never let these big windfalls remain in the Halifax share account for more than a few days. Large five and six figure sums were regularly transferred to his other UK bank accounts, which he used to finance further financial gambling but also for immediate and highly conspicuous spending on his family.

Page described his attitude to money as 'easy in, easy out'. He wanted to spend it enjoying life with his young wife and family on weekend trips and eating out. The couple were not natural savers. Their parents had brought them up to respect money, fear debt and avoid credit – the exact opposite message coming from government economists around the world on the eve of the new millennium.

'My parents were the war generation where you saved for a rainy day,' explained Laura. 'I remember my dad would always say "Don't spend a pound if you haven't got a penny." When I was a teenager I'd ask to borrow a pound and he would say this to me.'

The Pages liked to treat their parents. But Laura's mum and dad would often tut at her conspicuous consumption, especially when she dropped in at their Grays council house following a spending spree at Lakeside with the boys dressed in DKNY or Dolce and Gabbana.

'It was a good life we had,' Laura recalls. She was unashamed, proud in fact that her three boys wanted for nothing. 'They always had the latest games and we went on a few good family holidays. But they weren't spoilt,' she is quick to point out.

As a joint account holder, Laura had her own debit card. The Halifax accounts show her spending was not excessive but consistent with a mum of three young boys. At Lakeside she would shop at Marks & Spencer, the budget chain CostCo, First Sport, Toys'R'Us, Boots, Woolworths, Tesco and Safeway, when she could have afforded Waitrose.

'I was not flash,' she said. 'I would only have my nails done every two weeks.' The most upmarket stores she patronized were House of Fraser and John Lewis, where she indulged in the new national pastime of home and garden improvement.

Not for a minute did she fear that one day their bubble would burst. Why would she? The government economists and TV pundits that her husband avidly listened to were all talking up the economy.

Laura loved that residents of Chafford Hundred referred to their property as 'the police officer's house, always with nice cars on the drive'.

Just before a family holiday to Florida in March 1999, Page had bought his wife an A Class Mercedes. She was the first to have one on the estate. Her friends loved it but Laura thought it looked like a disabled car. She told Page to take it back to the dealer. He didn't argue after remembering a previous complaint when he returned a Shogun Jeep because his wife had seen a 'Pikey' family buying the same model. The Mercedes was exchanged for a more suitable model costing £45,000. It made no dent, as Page's incredible financial success from share dealing with Halifax continued into 2000. Between 2 February and 2 March that year he pocketed £577,638. 08.

'It was a very cocky attitude I had. But at the time it was rock 'n' roll,' said Page. His six-monthly appraisals were very short and he wasn't interested in honing his job skills by going on weapons courses and the like when all he wanted was to be a millionaire.

Given his success in a shadow career as an amateur share dealer, it was a curious choice to remain in uniform. But Page explained that although disillusioned at SO14 he still wanted to be a policeman. The camaraderie and new canteen culture at BP made it fun. He also enjoyed the respect of his colleagues and the Royal Protection department who he represented when he won the heavyweight boxing title at the prestigious inter-Met Police Lafone Cup.

Page liked having people around who trusted him and in turn who had his back. His £33,000 police salary represented stability, while his boxing bouts and trading bets gave him the adventure and risk no longer to be found on the beat as a royal protection officer.

One of his most satisfying bets in 2000 was on Abbey National shares, the first building society to demutualize. Like Halifax, Abbey went on a spending spree and bought up smaller building societies and financial services companies until its shares peaked at £14 in 2000.

Page used his winnings in March to take Laura and the boys, Thomas, 9, James, 4, and 18-month-old Matthew for a luxury holiday on the Venezuelan island of Margarita. However, the Caribbean resort was not child friendly, the food was odd, two of the boys had the runs and the general consensus was they should have gone to Florida.

It didn't help matters that Page was frequently disappearing to the hotel room to call his Halifax broker or speak to Harry at Buckingham Palace. Soon he had run up a £1500 phone bill. But there was a silver lining. His broker had just deposited £8885 in the Halifax account. It was a dividend from the Abbey shares.

When Page caught up with Laura in the hotel lobby, she was browsing the expensive boutiques. A large diamond ring with a £1500 price tag had caught her eye.

'It can be the wedding ring I never had,' she implored, reminding him of the £29 Argos special he had slipped on her finger two and a half years ago with a promise to do it properly when they were flush.

'Love, my credit card is maxed to fuck,' Page tried to explain.

'Well, ring up and get them to extend your limit for fuck's sake,' she snapped back.

An international phone call later, Laura was free to shop. She also bought a pair of Gucci sandals.

Yet despite how much Page did what his wife asked, and no matter how good she felt about her own appearance, the green-eyed monster was never far away, waiting to explode. At the hotel pool, Laura was getting worked up thinking her husband was eyeing up the scantily clad and topless Latina beauties. He wasn't. He didn't want to. He wouldn't dare. But when they got back to their room, she let him have it.

The row was so noisy, so Essex and very vicious – keys she threw caught Page in the face – that hotel security let themselves into the room unnoticed. As normal when outsiders interfered in their domestics, the couple united and turned on the bewildered goons. Anyone spending the sort of money this holiday was costing should be entitled to go at it hammer and tongs in the privacy of their room, they rationalized.

Towards the end of the holiday, Laura was still annoyed. She had forgiven her husband but not the hotel. So when her boys demanded chicken nuggets for their tea and the kitchen said 'Que?' she let them have it.

The night they arrived back home in early April, the Pages took the boys for dinner at their favourite Chinese restaurant in Lakeside. Order and peace was restored, for now.

Within weeks, Laura was pregnant again. All Page had to do was look at her and she was up the duff, Laura's mother would joke. But she was happy to be pregnant, and to encourage Page's shadow career as a City trader because the results where undeniable and his behaviour acceptable. She moaned occasionally that he was spending too much time on his laptop watching the flicker of figures and fractions. But at least he was spending the profits on making a home for her and their growing family.

Page envied the City culture that rewarded risk taking, impulsiveness, getting away with it and styling out one's failures. But Laura was reassured that her husband was not one for the out-of-office hours culture of champagne, cocaine and hookers that characterized the City's big swinging dicks. Page was more laptop than lap dance. He had the swagger, the chat and the balls but he kept them for the wife he loved, desired and sometimes feared.

Some of his winnings were invested in a hairdressing business for Laura called Clippers. She was tired of child minding and wanted something more than her boys to nurture and feel proud about. The salon in Grays belonged to her oldest sister, Christine, who had been looking for a buyer for some time. Keeping it in the family made sense, even though Laura had no business experience. As a self-starter himself, how could Page refuse?

£ £ £

The demand for tulips of a rare species increased so much in the year 1636, that regular marts for their sale were established in Amsterdam and other towns. Symptoms of gambling now became, for the first time, apparent. The stock-jobbers, ever on the alert for a new speculation, dealt largely in tulips, making use of all the means they so well knew how to employ to cause fluctuations in prices. At first, as in all gambling mania, confidence was at its height, and everybody gained. The tulip-jobbers speculated in the rise and fall of the tulip stocks, and made large profits by buying when prices fell and selling out when they rose. Many individuals grew suddenly rich. A golden bait hung temptingly out before the people, and one after the other, they rushed to the tulip marts, like flies around a honey pot. Every one imagined that the passion for tulips would last forever … Nobles, citizens, farmers, mechanics, seamen, footmen, maid-servants, even chimney sweeps and old clothes women dabbled in tulips. People of all grades converted their property into cash, and invested it in flowers …

… At last, however, the more prudent began to see that this folly could not last forever … It was seen that somebody must lose fearfully in the end. As this conviction spread, prices fell and never rose again. Confidence was destroyed, and a universal panic seized upon the dealers … The cry of distress resounded everywhere, and each man accused his neighbour. The few who had contrived to enrich themselves hid their wealth from the knowledge of their fellow citizens; and invested it in other funds. Many who, for a brief season, had emerged from the humbler walks of life were cast back into their original obscurity.[1]

49

This brilliant description, by nineteenth-century chronicler Charles Mackay, of the bubble in tulips and the insane betting on the colour of a bulb has great resonance with the froth in tech stocks 364 years later.

Financial delusion and human madness are essential ingredients of a bubble, and like all bubbles the dot.com one had to burst and deluded investors had to take a cold bath.

At the peak of the tech boom in 1999, Page felt he was cock of the walk, a big City trader in police uniform at Buckingham Palace. It was as good as it got. 'I was a 28-year-old Royal Protection officer driving around in a £55,000 Mercedes.'

The only knock to his confidence came following one afternoon nap when he woke from a nightmare so frightening he couldn't even tell his wife. 'I dreamt that I had lost everything.'

The dream started to come true in the spring of 2000 when the dot.com bubble began to burst. Between March 2000 and October 2002, an estimated $5 trillion was wiped off the market value of hundreds of over-inflated tech companies.

Like many ordinary investors, Page's portfolio was overexposed in tech investments. Staring at his laptop in the locker room at BP or at home in his office he started to panic as share prices kept falling. The mask never slipped at work, where he had a reputation to maintain as a successful stock-market player. His Royal Protection colleagues never knew that he was taking a rather cold bath. In contrast, Page's private phone calls with his Halifax broker were increasingly frantic as they watched thousands of pounds being wiped off the stocks he held.

Halifax agreed to hold his positions on certain of them to see if there was a 'dead cat bounce'. In other words, a rally in the shares after reaching rock bottom because savvy investors had started buying them up cheaply which, in turn, gave others confidence to do the same.

The cat bounced a little but Page calculated his losses from the dot.com bubble bath at anything from £80,000 to £100,000. 'We went from 10–15k per month to just wages,' he recalled.

£ £ £

The volume of money that had passed thorough Page's bank accounts in these early Halifax years from 1998 to 2000 was extraordinary. In 1999 alone, he had won almost £1 million tax free from share dealing.

It begged the question: was anyone watching and wondering how a police constable in a sensitive post, earning £33,000 a year, could have six-figure sums – £100,000, £200,000, even £300,000 – regularly hitting his account and then being moved to others?

It turns out that one bank had sent CIB, the Met's anti-corruption squad, a suspicious activity report in 1999 concerning Page's transactions. But nothing appears to have prompted anyone in the force to pull the royal police officer aside and see if he was in too deep.

After the dot.com bubble burst, an academic study of trading patterns in American households found that men had traded more than women and did so 'from a false faith in their own financial judgement'.

Had the Met done its own study of Page's bank accounts in 2001, anti-corruption officers would have found that he was involved in a new and very high-risk form of gambling where false faith in your own financial judgement often meant huge financial losses.

Worse still, Page was now also gambling with other people's money.

Chapter 6

The Currency Club

Page nodded to the SO14 officer from inside his Mercedes as the car-park barrier was raised. He liked the sensation of being noticed at work. This wasn't even his best car. The top end 'his and hers' Mercedes were parked on the drive in Essex. This work one was a 'run-around' he'd bought for £30,000 from his Halifax share winnings. Still, it didn't look out of place among all the diplomatic motors.

Armed officers manned the car-park entrance on The Mall because it is part of nearby St James's Palace, which at the time in 2001 was used for state and ceremonial functions. It was also the London residence of the elderly and not-so-well Queen Mother.

Royal Household staff, diplomats and other dignitaries who couldn't get into Buckingham Palace are allowed to park at St James's, some on-duty SO14 officers too, but not for personal reasons. However, for years there was 'an unwritten rule' to raise the barrier for wives, friends and family members who fancied a spot of shopping maybe followed by a West End show.[1]

Page went straight from the car park to the BP canteen where Harry counselled him about a new betting strategy. Page was in the market for one as the dot.com bubble and bath had taught him an important lesson: never again be so exposed in your investments. Spread the risk across a range of betting opportunities.

In March 2001, two months after the birth of fourth son, Samuel, Page did just that. On Harry's advice he moved from just buying shares to spread betting – a new, tax-free, alternative way of trading on world markets.

Page set up accounts with the two leading spread-betting firms, IG Index and CMC. He maintained the Halifax share account but started spread betting like a man with an insider's knowledge of the volatile world of commodities and foreign currencies, which of course he didn't have.

As Charles Brown of IG Index explained:

Spread betting, essentially, is a way to back your judgement in the financial markets. You can go long or short of a market to profit from rising or falling prices. You simply buy if you think the price is set to rise [going long], or sell if you think it will drop [going short]. The degree to which you are correct dictates how much you win or lose. In simple terms: the more a price moves in your favour, the more money you make; the more the price moves against you, the more money you lose.

CMC's client-relations adviser Gina Plowman put it this way:

A financial spread bet allows an investor to bet on whether the price quoted for a given financial instrument (a share, gold, commodities like oil, bonds and currencies) is likely to go up or go down in value. Their profit or loss is the difference between the price at which they buy and the price at which they sell. Unlike traditional share dealing, spread betting means that investors don't own the physical share, but bet solely on price movements, giving them an opportunity to profit whether the markets are rising or falling.

Making the deregulated stock markets available to common people was a legacy of the Margaret Thatcher era when the Conservative government first sold the privatization of public utilities to the electorate as a progressive step towards a share-owning democracy. The aggressive marketing of share offerings in British Gas, British Telecom and British Rail carried off the trick of getting people to buy a piece of something they had already owned.

Two heavy donors and friends of the Conservative Party, Peter Cruddas and Stuart Wheeler, were the respective driving force behind the spread-betting giants CMC and IG Index.

Cruddas founded CMC in 1989 and would soon boast impeccable royal connections. The self-made billionaire's early life appealed to Page's sense of himself as a self-styled 'cockney wide boy' with untapped potential. The CMC boss came from an east London council estate. He left school at fifteen without qualifications and worked his way up the foreign exchange desks of various banks before leaving to set up the spread-betting company. Through his philanthropy for disadvantaged youth, Cruddas also became friendly with Prince Charles and his father Prince Philip, to whose charities he donated.

In contrast, Wheeler was an Eton- and Oxford-educated banker with a love of gambling and card games – he had apparently played bridge with Lord Lucan and Omar Sharif.

Twenty-four hours before Page opened his first spread-betting account with IG Index, Wheeler had made the largest ever donation to the Conservative Party of £5 million.

On his application form, Page declared his occupation as a police officer earning £33,000 a year with a home worth £120,000 and savings and assets of £180,000. On 15 March 2001, IG Index awarded Page a £20,000 betting limit and wished him every success at the casino of financial markets.

At the time there was no warning to inexperienced punters of the high risks associated with spread betting. That's because when it first started, spread betting was a casino for City professionals who couldn't get enough at work and understood movements in financial markets and currencies.

Fortunes can be won and lost in volatile markets because the price movements are greater. This high-risk gambling is hostage to events in far-off places that come out of the blue, effect supply lines and therefore prices even if only for a few minutes. A dock strike in Rotterdam, a guerrilla attack on a Colombian oil pipeline, flooding in a Chinese sugar-cane factory or a copper-mine disaster in Zambia are all opportunities for the astute City professional. From their swivel chairs they can access market-sensitive information a lot quicker than the man on the street and therefore are able to pile in or bail out more efficiently.

However, it was an inevitable consequence of aggressive marketing campaigns that inexperienced betters, bored of the safer world of share dealing, would soon find high-risk spread betting on financial markets more attractive. It wasn't until after Page was hooked that the regulator told spread-betting firms to carry a warning in its online adverts and introduction packs about the high level of risk, the volatility in prices and the unsuitability for some of this type of betting.

On 22 May 2001, he opened a second online account, this time with CMC. It was a joint account with Mark Joyce, another young SO14 colleague at BP who was more commonly referred to by the nickname Pretty Boy. Six months later, Gripper opened his own online CMC account.

Page bet primarily on movements in the dollar to yen and pound to dollar exchange rates. He was also attracted to the money-making possibilities of price movements in oil and gold.

A boom in commodities had followed almost immediately after the dot.com bubble started to burst in 2000. Reporter Kevin Morrison, who covered the commodities bubble for the *Financial Times* from 2001 to 2007, and wrote *Living in a Material World*, recalls a period when banks made money from selling complex schemes to investors wanting high returns and the more they sold and the higher commodity prices went the more lavish the parties. He says:

> The commodities boom caught the finance world by surprise. Oil went from $20 per barrel to $100 and people thought it would happen to everything else. China was growing at 10 per cent per annum and there was talk of India becoming another China, and the prospect of two-fifths of the world going through the industrial revolution that Britain went through in late 1800s. That got people's attention in the banking world. There was a panic of scarcity that the world's resources would be exhausted by the growth of China and others so prices had to go up.
>
> Commodities suddenly became glamorous. There had been oil-price booms before, but now you had oil, metals, agriculture products, everything was going up. And then there was the gold price going up to thousands of dollars,

well beyond the price that Gordon Brown sold Britain's gold off for in the late nineties.

For a long time commodities was unglamorous. Investment banks like Goldman Sachs and Morgan Stanley were into it. Then all of sudden other trading houses and banks could see the huge amounts of fees that were being earned from buying and selling commodities so they all piled in because they didn't want to miss out.

Finance is like fashion. They were all now saying, 'We've got to be in commodities'. It's the herd instinct and short-sighted greed and envy among the banks. Suddenly they were hiring specialist commodities traders and paying them huge fees. A lot of specialized hedge funds appeared. The banks were selling highly complex commodity schemes to investors on the basis that there was high returns and no risk because prices would keep going up.

But in there was a veil of secrecy around trades. The prices of commodities kept going up and no one knew who was buying and selling. It was not necessarily the end user of the commodity being sold. In fact, there was a lot of speculation going on, talking up commodity prices based on fear. This had a new platform with the explosion of twenty-four hours business channels full of pundits talking up the commodity markets and launching new investment schemes all without any questioning over whether the price rises were sustainable and good for the economy and the man on the street, especially as wages weren't rising commensurately.

For the few doubters, there were mantras: stronger for longer, this time it is going to be different. But the Achilles heel of any boom is it doesn't last. It's all to do with human behaviour: confidence, fear and greed. However, it's important to remember that commodities were part of a greater bubble in cheap credit. Low interest rates also meant people were taking money out of banks and looking for investments with higher returns. This increased liquidity had to find a home, which it did in commodities and subprime debt.

There was an illusion of wealth. People's wages were not going up but they had more money in their pocket.

Page's 'system' for deciding how to spread bet was simple and not that different from what he was doing when buying and selling shares. It's said that when the US sneezes the rest of the world catches a cold. Page was in the Buckingham Palace canteen watching developments in US interest rates policy. Alternatively, he would monitor the New York-based Dow Jones stock market exchange or pundits on CNBC talking up markets or discussing the imminent release of employment figures, budget deficits and other macroeconomic indices.

By the end of 2001, Page's way around the blinking world of digital fractions and figures, his posh cars parked on the drive of his upmarket detached Essex home and the exotic family holidays had all caught the attention of colleagues at SO14.

They knew what he earned as a basic salary and from overtime, which he hadn't been doing much of these days. So it was assumed these chattels were the trappings of a successful player of the financial markets. Could his strutting confidence and apparent Midas touch also work for them, some wondered.

£ £ £

Adam McGregor had come to Buckingham Palace in 2000 with a dodgy past that worried some of his new colleagues for the wrong reasons.

Page first heard the gossip from one of the few female SO14 officers on his relief. The new recruit was said to have broken the unwritten rule of policing by grassing up a fellow officer who was then sacked.

'People on my unit weren't happy,' Page recalled. They convinced McGregor it was acceptable to take a portable TV on his first night duty shift. 'He lit up the garden and ended up falling asleep. The governor came out, but no one activated the ring-round system for him,' Page explained.

The ring-round system was a way officers on night duty could sleep on post without fear of being caught. If a sergeant one night decided to do a spot check of the palace grounds the officer manning the control room at Buckingham Palace would ring to warn colleagues on different posts.

There are two Garden Gate posts to protect the area where the Queen and Prince Philip sleep. Page knew them well from the times he had been on night duty there. 'It was natural for us to go to sleep on night duty and if a senior officer was coming into the garden I would contact the control room because the Garden Gate is alarmed. The control room would ring the officer on post 20 who would ring other posts. Everyone was awake until the governor did his checks and had a little chat and went away, then we'd be back to sleep.'

McGregor wanted to get on at BP and didn't understand why he had been set up. He was told the ring-round system was not for grasses. But McGregor was telling the truth when he denied selling out a colleague. In fact, he had done the reverse and helped out by seemingly corroborating a false account of an arrest outside a pub that had led to a man being wrongly prosecuted. McGregor was subsequently found guilty of 'falsehood and prevarication' at a discipline board for making a false entry in his pocketbook. He was docked £5000 in pay and the other officer was sacked.[2]

Page was prepared to give McGregor a break. He was reassured by the new officer's willingness to help out a fellow officer in need. So with Gripper's endorsement, it was not long before McGregor was allowed 'into the fold' of a group of young Royal Protection officers taking over at Buckingham Palace.

McGregor was grateful for the lifeline. He had already noticed Page's wealth and reputation for making money. When they discussed stocks and shares in 2001, Page appeared knowledgeable. He may not get it right every time, McGregor thought, but generally he was correct about movements in currencies like the Japanese yen.

The following year, McGregor decided he would invest in what Page was now calling his Currency Club. The terms were very attractive and way beyond what any high street bank or building society was offering: a £5000 investment got you a 6 per cent monthly return of £300 in cash. £10,000 got you £600 every month.

To join the Currency Club, a small group of SO14 investors had to deposit an initial stake in one of the spread-betting accounts that Page controlled and gambled with as he saw fit. He guaranteed that in the event he lost, every investor's initial stake would be repaid from his own pot of £70,000. If he won, investors would get their regular returns of £300 or £600 but he would take a lion's share of the undisclosed spoils for himself.

McGregor was in. Why wouldn't he be? It was a sweetheart deal from the Bank of Page. At the time, McGregor was earning £50,000 gross a year from his royal protection work, half of which came from overtime pay. In 2002, he gave Page £10,000 in cash and cheque to bet on movements in the yen, dollar and sterling. At any stage McGregor knew he could have his initial stake back. Instead he chose to roll it over every month after pocketing each £600 return in cash. It was also reassuring to McGregor that the Currency Club had spread to SO14 officers working at St James's Palace.[3]

£ £ £

The first four months of 2002 were a particularly difficult time for the Queen. She lost her youngest sister, seventy-one-year-old Princess Margaret, in February and seven weeks later the Queen Mother died at the age of 101.

Whereas Margaret had a private funeral, the Queen Mother lay in state at Westminster Hall before her flag-draped coffin was escorted on 9 April from central London to St George's Chapel in Windsor Castle.

The two deaths came just as the Queen and Prince Philip began a UK and world tour to mark her golden jubilee, which was planned to end with a June weekend of celebrations at Buckingham Palace. For the first time the palace gardens were to be opened to the public for a series of pop and classical concerts and a firework display.

The preparations at the London palaces were presenting a security challenge for SO14, not least because the nation was already on high alert after the September 11 attack by al-Qaeda the year before.

In this difficult environment, Page got word that Jim Mahaffy, a Royal Protection officer from St James's Palace, wanted a briefing about the Currency Club. BP officers tended to look down on their colleagues from the smaller St James's Palace. Page called it 'the mannequin factory, because it's full of dummies'.

He knew of Mahaffy from the occasional shift all SO14 officers must do at BP. The pair met in May 2000 as the refurbished Queen's Gallery was opened to the public.

Mahaffy, then 38, had worked at St James's Palace since 1995. He'd been a Met constable since 1980 making him one of the more senior SO14 officers. That, according to Page, didn't stop him from getting one of the more unkind nicknames, MAPS, short for 'my armpits stink'.

After 22 years' service, Mahaffy was taking home a good salary of between £2500 and £3000 every month. He and the wife liked to spend their disposable income on foreign travel. He'd heard of Page's reputation in the financial markets and noticed the Mercedes and new house. 'They appeared to be quite affluent,' he said.

Mahaffy had been treasurer of a share club at St James's Palace involving twenty SO14 officers. Each put £50 every month into one account to buy shares in blue chip companies such as British Petroleum, British banks and retail giant Marks & Spencer. They won more than they lost, Mahaffy told Page, but the profits were only in the hundreds of pounds and always split evenly.

In turn, Page explained how his Currency Club spread-betting syndicate would work. He was looking to raise £50,000 capital investment from a group of SO14 officers each putting in £5000. As long as their stake stayed in the Club, each member was guaranteed a cash monthly return of £300. All stakes would be returned within a matter of weeks if anyone wanted out.

'It seemed like a very good return for the money,' thought Mahaffy. He signed a contract joining the Currency Club and wrote out a £5000 cheque from his Virgin account to Mark Joyce, which Pretty Boy then transferred to the CMC spread-betting account for Page to work his magic on the markets.

The Currency Club had arrived at St James's Palace. It was the sort of sub-plot the satirists at *Spitting Image* could have dreamed up as a eulogy for the Queen Mother. The TV puppet show had already cast her as a big drinking gambler with a northern accent and a copy of the *Racing Post* rolled up under the royal bingo wings. A select group of the Queen Mum's Royal Protection officers secretly running a betting syndicate under the palace stairs was a perfect satirical compliment. Only it was true.[4]

£ £ £

Back at BP, preparations for the Queen's golden jubilee were taking shape. Guitarist Brian May had agreed to open the Party in the Park in June with a solo version of 'God Save the Queen' performed on the palace roof with his long curly mullet billowing in the breeze.

Purples One and Two were away on a tour of the UK for most of the first half of 2002. But on the few occasions they returned to BP, the Queen had a right to expect that her Royal Protection officers would have their minds on her safety not the Currency Club.

Page didn't care that he was neglecting his duty. He realized that watching the markets and watching out for the Queen were not compatible. It was intense work, because the foreign markets came online at different times of the day. Sometimes he would not sleep, become 'transfixed' on a particular market and lose money. Conscious of the guarantee he had given Currency Club members, it was all the more important that he recovered the position with more astute betting.

If he was on duty when the US employment figures were

about to be released, Page would get a trusted colleague to cover for him while he hid in the BP locker room with his laptop. If Alan Greenspan was presenting a report on interest rates, others could be counted on to step in while Page watched Teletext in the canteen. One particular Greenspan announcement at the time gave Page and other like-minded investors the economic encouragement to carry on. 'It's not that humans have become any more greedy than in generations past,' Greenspan told the world. 'It is that the avenues to express greed have grown so enormously.'

If he couldn't swap his shift to spread bet, Page would find out who was off duty, ring them up and offer £300 to work his shift. With his real job getting progressively in the way of his shadow career, Page said there were times on duty at BP when he didn't care even if someone were to climb over the wall.

After a while, he didn't even bother to distinguish between making money for the Currency Club and police work. He was mildly bollocked a few times, he said, for using police radios to discuss financial market movements. The most memorable occasion was when the Queen was on her way into Buckingham Palace.

'Purple One. Two minutes' came the call over the radio system. It was her PPO alerting SO14 officers at BP to have the main gates open and barriers up as they were getting near. The call was followed by another pressing announcement over the royal airwaves. 'Er, Gripper, Halifax is up five pence.'

A senior BP officer quickly transmitted a message to all concerned to stop using the radio system for personal business. But it was too late. The PPO had heard it all in his earpiece and subsequently complained. Page was reprimanded.

'At the end of the day we laughed about it, but it was not on,' he said. 'We didn't grasp that we shouldn't be doing it.'

£ £ £

Handing out brown envelopes of cash was now a regular part of Page's rounds at BP and when he slipped over to St James's Palace. Currency Club members were happy with the monthly cash return they were making and spread the word to SO14 officers in other palaces including Balmoral, the Queen's Scottish retreat.

Soon, non-police staff at BP had heard about the Currency Club. Page recalled being on night duty when a royal valet stopped him in the palace grounds.

'Do you know Gripper?' the valet enquired of Page.

'I am Gripper!' he replied with undisguised pride in his voice. It turned out that the valet, a footman and two chefs wanted to invest in the Currency Club. Page said they put in about £4000 in a new six-month deal he was now offering.

'The Queen and Prince Philip will go ballistic,' Page told Laura one night as they discussed how his betting syndicate was growing. He was starting to abandon an earlier policy of turning away officers he didn't like, trust or know too well.

Laura was now more involved in helping with Currency Club business while also running the house and hair salon. She monitored a computer terminal that was linked to various stock exchanges and had got used to having CNBC or Bloomberg on in the background. It was more background noise in a house of four young boys fighting over toys and video games. Page could call at any moment and demand to know the price of a water company share or she would be tasked to call him at BP the moment some financial figures were released. On a rare occasion, Page would ask her to give a brown envelope to an SO14 officer who would be passing by after finishing a shift at the palace.

Police officers were not just cynical but tight with their money,

Page believed. It made him feel good that they trusted him to gamble with large amounts of their cash. It also made him feel good to pay out returns. He felt he was at the centre of a group of officers who all wanted a better life for their families and he was the one who could make it happen, a 'money God', as some apparently called him.

A similar leap of faith takes place every day in the City or Wall Street where young traders are entrusted to gamble other people's money. Michael Lewis, who turned his back on Wall Street for a career chronicling its excesses, put it this way in his book *The Big Short* when describing how, as a clueless recent graduate, he somehow landed a job at Saloman Brothers Bank in the mid-eighties and was soon regarded as an expert:

> The willingness of a Wall St investment bank to pay me hundreds of thousands of dollars to dispense investment advice to grownups remains a mystery to me to this day. I was twenty-four, with no experience of, or particular interest in, guessing which stocks and bonds would rise and fall … Believe me when I tell you that I hadn't the first clue. I'd never taken an accounting course, never run a business, never even had savings of my own to manage. I'd stumbled into a job. Sooner rather than later, someone was going to identify me, along with a lot of people more or less like me, as a fraud.

Page had not hidden from those who invested in him that he was self-taught and unsupported. He was judged by his apparent wealth and the monthly flow of brown envelopes of cash returns. 'There was no me going round with my begging bowl. They were queuing up at my fucking door [to join],' he told me.

However, strangely, Page was concerned that too much cash flying around at BP would attract the wrong attention. 'I was telling people how to spend their money. Don't start putting loads of cash in the bank, get some shopping, bit of petrol, get some new windows, boring stuff you can pay in cash, do up the house nice, get a new conservatory but don't be silly.'

The advice was odd because there was nothing illegal about the cash Page was paying out in brown envelopes. Yet his speech could as easily have come from a Martin Scorsese script where an armed robber tells his gang to spend their share discreetly so as not to attract the attention of the police. In this case, the Currency Club were the police.

Chapter 7

Throne games

One night duty, not long after McGregor had joined SO14 and the Currency Club, he and Page walked gingerly through the dark corridors of Buckingham Palace like two naughty schoolboys with keys to the headmaster's office.

The pair were on a high-risk personal mission which would almost certainly have got them the sack had word of what they were up to reached the Queen. That said, her two Royal Protection officers felt the risk was manageable. It had all been done before. Many times, apparently. Besides, who was around to catch them, unless by the worst of luck an insomniac royal or member of the Royal Household happened to walk by at 2 am?

As Page turned the lights on in the Throne Room the pair felt the weight of history on their shoulders but apparently had no fear of having their collars felt.

Shades of pinks and reds dominate the Throne Room, from the patterned carpets and draped curtains to the centrepiece of this hallowed space, the two 'chairs of state' made in a seventeenth-century style for the Queen's 1953 coronation.

Purple One's red throne sits on a raised pink stage, approachable by three lush carpeted steps. Behind it hangs long red curtains and above is a domed white and gold ceiling and proscenium arch supported by a pair of winged figures of 'victory' holding garlands.

The Queen rarely sat on the throne, except for very special meetings and key speeches to the nation, such as her 2002 golden jubilee address. This symbol of Britain's constitutional monarchy was more commonly used as a setting for official royal wedding photographs; a tradition that started with her own in 1947.

But what would she make of a secret tradition among her Royal Protection officers of using the seat of royal power for goofy family album snaps?

In *The King's Speech*, the dramatization of her stammering father's relationship with Australian-born speech therapist Lionel Logue, there is an imagined scene in Westminster Abbey during a rehearsal of George VI's 1937 coronation.

'Get up! You can't sit there,' said the King, when he saw Logue provocatively slumped on the throne.

'Why not? It's a chair.'

'This is the chair on which every King and Queen …'

Before his stammering patient could finish, Logue interrupts with the memorable line: 'I don't care how many royal arseholes have sat on it.'

From the evidence that would emerge in Page's trial, it appears of late that there may have been more Royal Protection arseholes than royal ones sitting on the throne.

McGregor handed Page his camera and with little or no concern for the accession rights of Princes Charles, William or Harry he went to take his wrongful place as heir to the Throne of England. Before sitting down he straightened his uniform and weapon then struck an ignoble pose as if he was on Elvis's toilet in Graceland.

Snap! All done, back to work. Purple One none the wiser.

'We all sat on the throne and had a laugh,' said Page. 'Fucking hell, mate! If you get a chance to sit on the Throne of England you aren't going to pass it up.'

Page recalled that officers joining BP were naturally keen to be shown around the palace and it was not uncommon for whoever was conducting the tour to allow one of the new boys, there and then, to sit on the throne.

Page also took the photograph of another Currency Club member, this time near the Queen's bedroom, albeit in very disturbing circumstances. The Royal Protection officer wanted a photo of himself holding Page's 9 mm Glock 17 semi-automatic pistol. His own weapon had been taken away following a recent incident on night duty.

The story goes that the depressed officer had been talking to a girlfriend while sitting in his post. He told her he was thinking of putting his gun in his mouth. She talked him out of it and then reported the matter.

Page subsequently accompanied him to a meeting with senior management who decided not to bring in the Met's anti-corruption squad. Instead, the officer had to surrender his weapon, was taken off firearms duty but allowed to work in the armoury booking out weapons to others.

Months later he was told he was being moved off SO14. The officer approached Page when he was on night duty at the Garden Gate asking if he would lend him his gun and take a photo.

Page agreed but it crossed his mind while handing over the weapon that his friend might just go on the rampage or blow his brains out near the Queen's bedroom.

By telling this story Page was trying to convey two points. First, there was a tendency at SO14 for senior management to handle things internally because of the unique nature of where its officers worked and the possible fall-out beyond red faces at Scotland Yard. '[There was] an agreed understanding that what happened at Royalty stayed at Royalty,' he said.

Page was also pointing out that in the four years he had been at BP, by 2002 the culture at SO14 was starting to change. Through recruiting younger or more seasoned officers the balance of power in Page's relief was becoming more daring and less reverential. The new recruits, he said, were coming from public order units or special firearms units. Some were ex-detectives disgruntled with 'working for a living' and had joined SO14 because word got out that it was 'a good platform' for other things.[1]

Page too was changing. With the shift of power among his relief, he no longer felt a need to suppress his cop instincts when coming across public order incidents outside the palace gates.

His experience as one of the instructors in SO14 had also shaped his attitude to work and the rules. All officers carrying a firearm had to have up-to-date blue cards proving they have passed periodic eyesight, firearms and fitness tests. In these early years of the Currency Club, Page was not a heavy drinker. He preferred to go home and be with his family.

However, he described how drinking was a big part of the 'culture' at SO14. He recalled being ordered to pass a protection officer who was still drunk and how an officer with knee damage forged his blue card knowing he would otherwise have failed his fitness test.

'Had he shot someone he would have been unlawfully carrying the firearm. He got caught and it was covered up. He was transferred to another force anyway and although disciplined it was hushed up.'

There were also claims that some SO14 officers were not

loading their guns due to religious beliefs or because they didn't want to be put in the frame for shooting anyone. A new policy was introduced of spot checks and anyone with an unloaded weapon was disciplined, Page recalled.

It was not unusual for officers still drunk from the night before to book out a weapon the next day, he said. Others would be told to sleep off their hangover somewhere in the palace or buy some 'mints and Lucozade'. Any depletion of armed officers on duty had to be avoided.

He further recalled one incident when a senior member of the Royal Household was coming through the security gates of BP. Instead of lifting the barrier, a hung-over SO14 officer accidentally pressed the underground ramp button sending the woman's car into the air. Luckily, only the car was damaged.[2]

£ £ £

The Currency Club was not the only risky financial scheme involving Royal Protection officers in 2002. Details about a controversial 'pyramid'-style scheme called Hearts only emerged seven years later during Page's trial.

According to witness statements of those involved with Hearts, it purported to be about empowering women by inviting them to invest £3000 to get a place on a list. An investor moved up the list by bringing in new people. And when a certain position was reached, it supposedly triggered a cash return of over ten times the original investment.

Schemes likes Hearts are ultimately unsustainable because new investors eventually dry up causing it to collapse, sometimes in recrimination. Those who came in last and are at the lower end of the list find themselves out of pocket while those at the top can make money.

Constable Jamie Ross was one of the young but experienced new BP officers. He recruited for Hearts among business people in Hertfordshire, where he lived, and also among colleagues in SO14, which he had joined from the Met's specialist firearms unit.

Page refused to recommend Hearts to Currency Club members. But Adam McGregor, his mother and other BP colleagues got to hear about it and put around £3000 each into the scheme. Hearts also attracted Royal Protection officers from other palaces too.

Soon, Ross was offering them another more traditional investment opportunity: to buy Kevlar, the synthetic fibre used in body armour.

It was a joint venture with Terry Belton, a salesman also from Hertfordshire. The pair had met and become friends when Ross was responsible for buying the Met's riot equipment. In no time, Ross's wife and Belton formed a company to market a Kevlar airbag restraint to assist emergency services attending crash scenes.

Money for Kevlar from investors poured in. On one occasion, almost £100,000 in cash was handed to Belton in a car park. £15,000 came from McGregor. Another £30,000 came from Watford businesswoman Christine O'Brien, who had taken out a bank loan. She had met Ross though Hearts and said in her witness statement that the Kevlar investment seemed safe because he was a police officer.

However, Ross's SO14 colleagues started to get suspicious when Belton suddenly disappeared to Dubai. At the same time, the Hearts scheme was also failing to pay out the promised returns.

Page and other SO14 officers, who he refuses to name, met to discuss how they were going to deal with Ross. It was decided he would get 'a kicking' in the locker room. Page had also suggested crashing a scrap car through the living room of Belton's Hertfordshire home.

Somehow, however, SO14 managers at Buckingham Palace got wind of the plan and called Page and others to a meeting.

'Do you know anything about a plan to beat up PC Ross tomorrow?' a senior officer enquired. Page and his colleagues shook their heads.

In the end, the attack could not be carried out because Ross was quickly moved to Windsor Castle. An official source with knowledge of these events confirmed there was intelligence of a plot against Ross and said he had been moved for 'welfare reasons'.

McGregor and his mother said in witness statements that they were 'victims' of the Hearts and Kevlar schemes. McGregor also said in the same statement that he never made a formal complaint against Ross but felt his SO14 colleague probably knew more than he had let on.[3]

A senior member of the Royal Household who lost £20,000 in the Kevlar deal asked to remain anonymous because of her position at the palace. She recalled meeting the 'charming' Ross at BP who promised her great returns. However, it was her own 'greed and naivety', she accepts, that led her to pay the £20,000 directly to Belton.

When the returns never materialized she sent emails to the businessman from her palace address and called Ross on his pay-as-you-go mobile. He told her that he too was a victim, having invested £55,000 into the Kevlar scheme.

Eventually, Belton made contact claiming money was arriving from overseas in diplomatic bags. It didn't. Checks by a policeman on her behalf apparently revealed that the Met had previously pulled out of a police equipment deal with Belton and the file had been shredded.

Like McGregor, the senior Royal Household official never reported the matter. Christine O'Brien, however, refused to stay quiet. She made a complaint against Ross but CIB, the Met's anti-corruption squad, took no criminal or disciplinary action against him. Belton, however, was arrested and interviewed. But again, nothing came of it leaving O'Brien unhappy with the quality of CIB's investigation.

Ross told me that Belton had 'hoodwinked' him but declined to answer detailed questions about his relationship with the businessman. Belton didn't respond to any questions.[4]

£ £ £

The Hearts affair was a warning to senior management at SO14 of a problematic gambling culture among its officers. The involvement of businessman Terry Belton could clearly have compromised individual officers and palace security. The way the scandal was hushed up, at the expense of civilian investors, did nothing to discourage Page's running of the Currency Club. Civilian investors were now coming into the scheme contrary to his original intention to keep the betting syndicate to a small group of twenty Royal Protection officers.

The problem was that officers wanted to bring in civilian friends, sweethearts and relatives to benefit from the Bank of Page's incredible returns. Page said he trusted the judgement of his colleagues not to introduce any undesirable elements, but in truth he also needed the fresh cash.

The fall-out from Hearts was a missed opportunity to examine Page's Currency Club. Had anyone from CIB or SO14 done so they would have discovered that Page was hiding a significant problem that his police and civilian investors deserved to know about before parting with more cash.

Page's Halifax accounts showed that since 2001 he was sustaining considerable losses on his share account. That year alone he had lost £200,000. Similarly, an examination of his spread-betting accounts with IG Index also showed troubling losses in 2001.

In fact, just one month after opening the account, IG Index wrote informing Page that he was £2700 in arrears. He had lost £80,000 of Currency Club money in March. IG Index chased but Page ignored them while continuing to bet with accounts in other people's names.

In early 2002, the spread-betting firm won an uncontested county court judgment against Page for £2700. The gambling firm also brought the matter to the attention of SO14. Page promised chief inspector Brian Patrick that he would pay the debt, but never did.

This was the second warning to Met bosses that Page may be a problem. The first was a suspicious activity report a bank had sent to CIB in 1999 about large sums of money going through Page's account. Had the Met looked it would have discovered other hidden losses, which may have led CIB to question whether a growing Currency Club of Royal Protection officers and civilians was such a good idea.

Page's secrecy about his gambling losses mirrored the behaviour of traders during the growing credit bubble. The biggest Wall Street and City traders thought nothing of taking huge gambles with other people's money, hiding losses from their bosses and spending obscene amounts of money on fine dining before returning more than half cut to the office for some afternoon gambling.

Elsewhere, the collapse of Enron around this time also showed how routine such corporate dishonesty had become in the pursuit of profits. Executives of the US energy giant had been hiding huge losses and debts from shareholders through various complex accounting loopholes and tricks, all of which were magicked under the nose of auditors and financial watchdogs.

Chapter 8

ULPD: A firm within the Firm

Page unloaded his five mobile phones onto the kitchen table, washed his hands and enthusiastically started preparing the evening meal. He loved trying out recipes and new techniques learned from the many celebrity chefs who, along with home-improvement shows for the bubbling buy-to-let market, were dominating the winter 2002 TV schedules.

Presentation was important to Page. He finely chopped and arranged food on the plate as if he was competing in *Masterchef* not doing dinner for four young boys with less discerning palates. Laura was glad that her man fancied himself in the kitchen. But as soon as the dishes were done, she wanted a word.

Page had recently been placed on restricted duties following a complaint from Laura's eldest sister, Christine, the one who sold her the hair salon, Clippers. The business went bust a little over a year ago and there was a dispute about money. Christine was taking legal steps to secure a charge against Laura's house. The move caused a rift in the Keenan family and infuriated Page, who was accused of threatening to shoot Christine's husband.

SO14 bosses took away his Glock 17 pistol for three months, ignoring protests from Page that he'd only threatened to beat up his brother-in-law. The incident was not long after Page and others at SO14 had been called in about the planned assault on Jamie Ross over the Hearts scandal.

But this wasn't what was giving Laura a headache. It was the Currency Club. 'We haven't been on a holiday since Margarita,' she protested. 'You're running around with all these mobile phones. I'm rushing back to hand out money. I can't go anywhere Paul, I feel like I'm fucking trapped.'

Page nodded.

'I'm fed up with people coming to the door late at night for their money and waking these up,' she said pointing at the boys. 'I don't want the neighbours seeing this. I don't want this life.'

Currency Club members weren't the only people turning up at their home. There were also red letters from the county court summonsing the couple to hearings over unpaid loans, credit cards, utility bills and hire purchase agreements. 'We were driving nice cars and not paying our bills,' Page recalled. The strange thing was they could have paid on time, but as he left for work Page would tell his wife to wait for the red one.

The couple's crazy attitude was a departure from their early days when Page told off Laura after a debt collector had come to the old house over an unpaid clothes catalogue bill. 'I can't have this love, I'm a police officer,' he had warned, before clearing her debts. Now, in late 2002, a bad credit record was just not something the couple particularly cared about.

With so much free money being thrown at UK customers, debt and moving debt around was normal. As journalist Michael

Lewis observed in his book *Boomerang*, it was a time when 'a tsunami of cheap credit rolled across the planet'.

However, for the first time in their relationship, Laura was the one urging financial restraint when it came to the Currency Club. 'They are coming to you not anyone else. Let's stop it now and let someone else be responsible. Can't we go back to having a normal life?' she implored.

'I can't love, people are relying on me,' her husband replied meekly. Page knew the Currency Club had grown too fast and too big. But he was deluded about his ability in the financial markets and inwardly delighted at being thought of as the Money God of Buckingham Palace. The losses he'd been hiding from his investors and wife were a blip, he reasoned.

'Can't you see what you're turning into? Why has it got to be you?' she demanded to know.

'I can handle it,' Page shot back as the discussion inevitably turned sour.

'You've got delusions of grandeur. You think you are fucking Alan Sugar?' said Laura before storming off.

'I've got a plan to take the heat off, love.'

£ £ £

The Currency Club was already changing by late 2002. Page had recently told his investors that he would be paying their returns quarterly rather than monthly. SO14 investor Jim Mahaffy from St James's Palace was unbothered by the change. Instead of getting £300 every month he was promised £1000 every quarter. Mahaffy could have asked for his £5000 stake back and called it a day. But he didn't, because he was 'making a profit' and happy to leave the betting to Page.[1]

Unknown to investors, Page needed to go quarterly because

he was losing, or not winning enough, and therefore couldn't meet his monthly commitments. Whereas before, when the Club was limited to a handful of SO14 members, he could afford the monthly bill and cover any losses he made from his own stash. But when the Club grew and civilians came in, the monthly bill was around £50,000.

The 'golden rule' of the Currency Club, according to Page, was that members had to be paid returns on time. He knew the repercussions of lateness were enormous for something built on trust. Word would spread and soon they'd be a run on the Bank of Page, with people demanding their stake back under his crazy personal guarantee.

Quarterly returns were a way of 'taking the heat off' him. But Page knew that it was still unsustainable because he wasn't winning enough from spread betting. Some trusted SO14 investors from BP would be good for covering return shortfalls by paying the cash into another investor's bank account. But this was a temporary fix to a deeper problem. He still needed fresh investors to meet the new quarterly payments. However, this growth in investors would only create more financial liability down the line, unless his luck changed.

If ever there was a moment for Page to heed his wife's kitchen advice and get out, this was it. Okay, some investors would have made money, others lost. They all knew it was spread betting. There was no criminal deception; the scheme just didn't work out. Instead, Page gambled that his luck in the markets would change and 'hatched a plan' to cover him in the event that it didn't.

The idea was for members to invest in a property syndicate that took advantage of the twin bubbles in credit and housing. This would be an asset base for Currency Club members that guaranteed their initial stakes against any losses he incurred from spread betting on financial markets.

I wanted to change people's attitude to the greed, get the heat off myself, [of] keep having to perform, keep having to churn out the money monthly, quarterly, but it was day in day out, and to put a structure in place with the investors to come into the property side of things. I did a specimen brochure of sites. The choice is invest directly into one – become a syndicate.

So I opened this company. I've got no, how can I put it, no business sense, about accountancy or anything like that. I didn't profess to be … I didn't know about my responsibilities as a director and really didn't care to be honest with you. It sounds stupid but that was how it was. My first priority was to use some of the money to get a piece of land and build a property. I thought if I could push some of the money into that, it would be a core asset that would be at that time a money maker and the stability against any fuck-ups in the market.

However, no matter how much it is true that Page wanted to put the Currency Club back on a successful footing and earn money for himself and everyone, this was the start of his fraud.

Only much later could he accept this: 'I regret the day I ever expanded it further than just BP,' he told me. 'It was the biggest mistake of my life because greed took over everyone and I was very naive in thinking I could physically sustain as well as mentally sustain what had grown to be something uncontrollable.' In other words, the fuck-up was him.

Greed had certainly blinded Currency Club members to financial logic. None saw the move from monthly to quarterly payments as a warning. At the very least it indicated a cash-flow problem. But any questions, such as they were, Page met with confidence.

He felt comfortable hiding the losses as long as he provided the returns, which, although a struggle, he was still managing to do.

To his investors, the consistency sustained the illusion of success.

£ £ £

One cold late January morning in 2003, Laura opened her front door after a determined knock. Lisa, her twin, hurried in holding her young daughter and an official-looking letter.

Laura was expecting her sister because she looked after her niece while Lisa worked at Next, the retailers in nearby Lakeside. But today her twin seemed agitated. As they walked into the kitchen, Laura wondered to herself if it was anything to do with the £35,000 that Lisa had loaned the couple a few months back.

Her twin, who had dark hair in contrast to Laura's bottle blonde, made no secret that she felt emotionally leaned on by their mum to make the loan. Seventy-year-old Marie Keenan was a hard-working, no-nonsense, tell-it-like-it-is matriarch. Last September, she had let herself into Lisa's house and waited for her daughter to come home to tell her that Laura could lose her house because Page had taken a big hit on the stock market. Lisa was apprehensive about lending the couple money. But she was mindful that her mother had fallen out with Christine, their older sister, for going against Laura. Initially, Lisa stumped up £15,000. The money came from her half of the sale of the house she owned with her former husband. But days later Laura came back in tears asking for more. Page, she said, was in more financial trouble than their mum realized. Laura had asked Lisa not to let on. She agreed and loaned her twin a further £20,000.

No timescale was put on returning the money. But standing in the kitchen with Lisa that cold January morning, Laura was sure this was cause of her twin's agitation. It wasn't.

'I'll get him this time. Look what he's done now,' Lisa said jabbing her finger at a letter from the Inland Revenue and referring to her ex-husband. 'He's only gone and used my name and address for something.'

The letter was a reminder from the taxman that as the recently appointed company secretary to United Land & Property Developments Limited (ULPD) she had certain record-keeping obligations under the law.

The Pages read the letter and started to laugh. Page turned to Laura and said, 'I thought you were going to tell her.'

'No, I forgot.'

Lisa wasn't getting the joke. 'Tell me what?' she asked her twin.

'It's not him. It's us. It's our company.' Laura confessed

Page had convinced his wife over the Christmas holiday that ULPD was the way they could spend more time as a family. Now he had to finesse the situation with Lisa. He told her how he had set up ULPD on 2 January; was its sole director and on company records had listed his occupation as 'police officer'. All true. Then he told a whopping lie. 'I needed to put your name down as company secretary because as a married couple Laura's not allowed to be one.'

Lisa was more worried about her benefits being affected. She was legitimately claiming working tax credit to help single mums back to work.

'Don't worry,' Page assured her. 'You're just a silent partner.' This was another lie. On paper at least, Lisa was a company secretary and shareholder in a new property company. Had the benefits agency and taxman compared notes, it could well have caused her problems; at the very least, the suspension of her tax credits while the mess was sorted out.

'I just need you to sign a few forms to open a business bank account for my company and that's it,' Page told her. 'You don't have no more involvement.'

In March, Lisa went with Laura to open the ULPD NatWest account. She felt 'emotionally blackmailed' by her twin but accepted Page's assurance that she wouldn't have any liability for the firm's debts. However, as joint signatory of the cheques, over the next few months Lisa was called on to withdraw cash if Page was too busy pretending to protect the Royal Family.

Laura eventually took over the ULPD NatWest account in a move that reflected her deepening involvement in Page's affairs. She had also opened an online account with bookies William Hill. Page had his own but would use his wife's for a new betting front – sporting events. Their passwords for these accounts that Page controlled were Gripper 20 and Vogues.

The transition at NatWest from Lisa to Laura was easy because she had already struck up a friendly, almost flirty relationship with the bank manager. If it had been the other way round, Laura would have forced her husband to change banks. But Page was willing to curb his jealousy because the bank manager, he said, was letting them 'get away with murder'.

Financial documents show that over the next few years Page was able to receive or transfer large amounts of cash through his wife's accounts. The manager was not being bunged to turn a blind eye, nor did he have any personal involvement with the Currency Club or ULPD. He was just very accommodating.

'You're going to get me sacked,' he would say when Laura rang up wanting an immediate withdrawal of a large amount of cash, as much as £40,000. Later in the manager's office, the cash between them in a bag on his desk, he would confide in her about his personal life. She listened politely, chatted about her kids then left the bank to hand her husband the cash.[2]

The bank manager didn't know how lucky he was that Page thought he was on side. It didn't take much to set him off and Laura still enjoyed watching it. Page was waiting for her at Lakeside shopping car park. He saw a man say something as she walked passed.

'What did he say?' he asked his wife as she got into the car.

'Oh, nothing.'

'What did he say?' Page insisted.

Laura knew the consequence of telling her husband. 'He said I was nice.'

Page started the car and chased the man until he had him sandwiched against a wall. He offered no resistance when Page grabbed him.

'You fucking sex pest,' Page shouted. And with a copper's instinct, he repeated the false claim to get the gathering crowd on his side. 'He's a sex pest,' he told them.

The penny dropped. The crowd dispersed. Page and his flushed wife drove off.

£ £ £

United Land & Property Developments Limited had no office, no staff, no accounts and no authority to invest other people's money. It was a virtual company that Page had set up for £500 with an accommodation address in London's Canary Wharf, the citadel of the UK financial services industry.

Page said he tried to register ULPD with the Financial Services Authority. The regulator gave him a long form to fill in but it was never submitted. 'I had no chance of getting FSA approval, bottom line,' Page explained. 'I didn't have a long established company, I didn't have the appropriate qualifications, da, da, da.' Nor did he bother with VAT registration or an accountant. Again, he was about to take other people's money for spread betting and for property developments. The separation was essential to avoid accusations of fraud and deception. But Page was more worried about opening up the Currency Club to accountants. 'What am I going to say to them? "I've got this spread-betting operation can you tidy it up for me?"'

In truth, Page didn't want anyone nosing through his bank statements, spread-betting accounts and loose bits of paper on which he noted the names of core Currency Club members and their investments. 'I never told people all the business. No one ever knew, and quite rightly so, no one should ever know all your business, no investor should ever know every single thing that is going on. That's not how it works. If you trust me you don't need to know … My remit was to make them money.'

ULPD, then, was the new front for the old spread-betting operation. Page had effectively set up a hedge fund for cops that retained its core activity of spread betting on financial markets and sporting events but offered a new investment opportunity in property development.

Hedge funds were becoming all the rage in early 2003 after the dot.com bubble burst and banks stopped lending on the same scale to small start-up companies. They filled that funding gap and became a 'shadow-banking system' without the regulation required of a bank. A hedge fund didn't need a certain level of capital to operate; they didn't have to open their books to audits or make declarations to any watchdog. In fact, they weren't required to register in these early days.

Hedge funds managed the money of investors looking for high returns in an era of low interest rates. They might take that money and loan it to a start-up business in return for equity.

They might bet against a company's stock. Another gamble might be on commodities and currencies. The idea being to hedge or off set the fund's exposure by taking long positions (that value will go up in price) and short ones (that it will go down). It's a bit like going to the races and having various options to win money, not just that Red Rum crosses the finish line first.

Hedge funds also benefited from the credit and housing bubbles and from government deregulation since 2000 in another form of City gambling – the derivatives market. These are financial contracts made between traders across the world's markets. The contract derives its value from the performance of an underlying asset, usually stocks, debt, commodities such as oil and gold and currencies. In short, a buyer makes a contract with a seller on how much the price of the asset will change over time.

Ultimately, hedge funds were high risk for high-return financial casinos. Investors never knew or controlled the direction of how their money was invested or gambled. They judged the hedge fund on financial performance in the size and consistency of the returns it paid out. If unsatisfied, they could always pull their stake. In the end, there is no real downside for the hedge-fund managers because they could legally charge commission even for losing other people's money.

Page's ULPD idea was similar in philosophy. But in execution it had two major drawbacks. First, hedge funds and investment banks were not just reliant on human judgement to read the financial markets right. They had also invested millions of pounds in computers and programmers who had written models for ingesting up-to-the-nano-second financial data to determine whether to bet one way or another on a commodity, currency or derivative. In contrast, Page was self-taught, bad at maths and reliant on data that in market terms was very out-of-date.

Second, the way Page managed investors' money was starting to look like a Ponzi scheme – investors deposited money in various bank accounts of his choosing which he then transferred to spread-betting accounts. Quarterly returns were paid from moving around that money between old and new investors.

Charles Ponzi was jailed for running the first eponymous scam in 1920. The simple fraud works like a pyramid scheme, in that earlier investors are paid from later investors' money rather than from the profits generated by successful betting and investments. A Ponzi scheme can run for years as long as there is a regular stream of new investors so that the money coming in exceeds that going out in returns.

£ £ £

Almost immediately after ULPD was set up in January 2003, Page started marketing his company to trusted SO14 Currency Club members. He showed them a corporate brochure with various investment options in property development, incredibly high returns and that crazy personal guarantee of their stake back if all went tits up.

'With the fairly dismal performance of world stock markets over the past few years, many investors have seen the value of their portfolios significantly reduced and in some case have lost nearly all their original investment capital. At this time there is still some weakness with the equity markets although some professional investors would argue that the fundamentals are improving, thus leading to higher interest rates globally,' Page wrote in the brochure's introduction, sounding every bit the pundit he had studied so avidly in the Buckingham Palace canteen.

Obviously there is still concern of continued terrorism issues which could lead to further market setbacks. Equally, investors who choose to leave their money in high interest accounts or savings bonds, which lock in funds for a number of years and penalise you with early withdrawal penalties, have seen a relatively low return with the same period. Again, even with the current pick up in interest rates, returns on your money are still relatively disappointing.

So now let's look at the property market. Over the same period of time homeowners have seen the value of their properties increase dramatically. Many entrepreneurs and building companies continue to profit from the housing market through buying and selling properties on a regular basis as well as specialising in the more lucrative development side of the market where profit margins on new build homes are substantially higher.

At present there are many smaller investors who would also like to capitalise in the property sector but are restrained from doing so due to insufficient funding and/or overall knowledge of the property investment business … With our proven experience, we offer each investor the opportunity to cash in on the property market with no capital risk and achieve excellent returns without the associated problems … Our expertise have [sic] created a sound non risk system of making continued profits for ULPD and our investors.

Making sound business investment decisions is paramount in any company, especially within the property investment sector where there are many pitfalls … Profits can increased [sic] further through development of land for new build housing projects as well as specialist conversions for example barns, stables, dairy blocks etc. Over the last few years interest and development of these particular buildings has soared to an all time high partly due to television and magazine exposures and partly due to their strong profit potential.

Jim Mahaffy from St James's Palace and Adam McGregor from Buckingham Palace were happy to get involved. But the reaction of other Royal Protection officers was lukewarm. There was a sense they were waiting to see how their two colleagues fared before piling in. Page reasoned that many of his police investors wanted to remain in the shadows. Their attitude was, he said, 'I don't give a fuck how you do it as long as it's legal, but we don't want our names on Jack shit'.

Page knew that for ULPD to take off with his police and civilian investors he needed 'a show piece' property to demonstrate what the company could do for them. He had been scouring the Essex countryside for a conversion project he could develop and sell quickly for a substantial profit in the booming housing market.

On 1 September 2003, he made an informal purchase agreement with the owner of three derelict barns on Spurriers Farm in Norton Heath for £450,000. Page had been discussing the idea with finance company Mortgage Guarantee to convert the barns into two-storey homes with three or four bedrooms.

Later that month, after doing its own checks, the company sent Page a formal mortgage offer: £250,000 towards the purchase price and a further £270,000 to be released in stages for building costs over the one-year lifetime of the mortgage. The finance company would charge 1.5 per cent monthly interest on the loan. Its surveyors had estimated that when converted the three barns with land would sell for £1,435 million.

The UK housing market had been frothing since 1998. From 2002 to 2007 UK prices rose 90 per cent, the highest rise within the European Union after Spain. UK banks, building societies and finance companies in 2003 were not just offering many multiples of an applicant's income, they had come up with interest-only mortgage deals and self-certifying mortgages for the self-employed, who didn't have to justify their ability to re-pay.

There was also another type of mortgage on offer for those with a bad credit rating and a high risk of defaulting. The adjustable rate mortgage was one where the interest starts low and then rises steeply. They were also known as teaser loans because low-income families were lured in with the offer of an initial period of low interest rates. The risk was that these borrowers would default when the higher interest rate kicked in. But the banks selling these so-called subprime mortgages were not concerned. Why? Because, for one, they and Alan Greenspan believed that house prices would continue to rise and therefore homeowners would be able to refinance their mortgage when the teaser rate ended as their home would be worth more.

The City in 2003 was the place to be for innovation in how to supposedly spread the risk of selling high-risk loans such as these adjustable rate or subprime mortgages. In an age of low interest rates and cheap credit, large investors, such as pension funds, were looking for higher returns on their money. The banks and hedge funds were keen to feed this need by finding new and more complex ways to sell the bundles of high-risk subprime mortgage debt they were holding.

Welcome to the fiendishly complex world of mortgage securitization. It works like this: In the old world, the high-street bank lending you the money to buy a house expected you to pay them back and were therefore careful to whom they lent. In the new world of derivatives, that same high-street bank making you the loan might sell it on and therefore didn't care about your credit-worthiness or ability to pay them back.

Consequently, the high-street bank now earned huge fees from selling subprime mortgages to risky customers. Often mortgage brokers would be on secret commissions to sell customers these adjustable rate mortgages. The high-street bank earned further fees from selling this high-risk loan to an investment bank.

The investment bank would make even more money by selling the risky debt to investors looking for high returns. First, the invest-ment bank would bundle up the mortgage debt – a process called securitisation – with other types of debt such as credit cards, car loans and student loans into a new type of derivative called a col-lateralized debt obligation (CDO). These CDOs were then sold to different types of investors. Those seeking high returns would buy the high-risk CDOs. Other more cautious investors, such as pen-sion funds with billions of pounds to invest, needed to be assured that the CDO was safe. The investment banks achieved this by pay-ing rating agencies to over-value the CDOs and through this pro-cess some of the most toxic high-risk debt was given a safe rating.

Those CDOs the investment bank couldn't sell were moved off its balance sheet into a front company. The regulator was aware the banks and hedge funds were doing this to create the illusion of a healthy balance sheet, but turned a blind eye.

As there was no regulatory restraint on this process, more and more mortgage loans were sold with no care for their quality or the ability of the borrower to repay. Volume was everything, because more loans meant more fees. And the riskiest loans, such as subprime mortgages, meant higher fees because they carried higher interest rates. This incentivized mortgage brokers to sell more adjustable rate mortgages – subprime loans – to people who either couldn't afford them or didn't need them. The securitization chain was therefore fuelling a huge boom in housing, which together with the credit boom ensured billions of pounds in profits for the banks and financial institutions.

Investors could buy insurance in the event that the CDOs went bad because the people owing the money had stopped paying their mortgage or car loan, for example. The investor would pay a quarterly premium to a company that specialized in insuring it against the debt going bad. This insurance policy was also something that the City could gamble on and to do this a second unregulated derivative market was created called credit default swaps (CDSs).

Speculators and investment banks could now buy CDSs in order to bet against certain CDOs that they didn't own and believed would default. The insurance company would make millions in fees and broker bonuses from selling these CDSs without ever having put aside a large pot of money in case it had to pay out any investor claims. Once again, volume over quality was the guiding principle to ensure huge fees.

And what about the investors? They did not know, because the investment bank wasn't saying that the CDOs they were buying were not good investments but junk, and the bank was secretly betting millions of pounds that it would default.

Through this incredible deception and trickery, in 2003–4 investment banks such as Goldman Sachs, Morgan Stanley, Lehman Brothers and Merrill Lynch earned huge revenues from the process of repackaging toxic debt and selling it as good investments.

After the 2008 financial meltdown, respected *Financial Times* writer Martin Wolf was not alone in describing this process of mortgage securitization as 'a great big national and global Ponzi scheme'.

It was in this general financial culture that Page was able to secure a £510,000 loan offer from Mortgage Guarantee in

September 2003. The finance company was not making the offer to ULPD, as one might expect. It was a personal mortgage in the name of Page and his unemployed wife secured on the barns.

The one-income family qualified for such a large mortgage, despite a bad credit history, presumably on the popular delusion that UK property prices were only going forever up.

But Page still needed to raise the remaining £200,000 to buy the derelict barns.

£ £ £

The owner of the barns had agreed to allow Page to start work on the conversion in October 2003, months before the contracts were due to be exchanged. Builder Paul Ballard, the husband of Laura's sister Jill, was going to oversee the work. Page's brother-in-law was a discharged bankrupt.

Mortgage Guarantee would only release the loan in May 2004. That left Page with eight months to find £200,000 for the purchase price and some start-up cash for the conversion.

Page claims he put £50,000 of his own money into buying the barns. He'd taken out a six-month bridging loan for £30,000 secured against the family home at 2.5 per cent interest. There was also some money stashed away from selling a small property he had inherited from a dead relative.

The remaining monies Page took from police and civilian investors even though the line between the Currency Club's spread-betting operation and ULPD was still very blurred.

Adam McGregor understood this fuzziness. 'As long as I got money back at a later date that was all I was concerned about,' he later explained.

A few months after ULPD was incorporated, Page confided in McGregor about his plan to take time off work (not that he was exactly doing much more than turning up) to convert derelict properties. He claimed he would be funding his new vocation through a lucky consortium of officers.

McGregor was starting to regard Page as a brother. He liked being part of a core group of SO14 officers at BP who he described as 'money-orientated'. He'd already opened his own CMC account in March 2003, which Page was allowed to use. The password was 'Bald eagle', a bird of prey that the receding Royal Protection officer resembled.

It impressed McGregor that Page was diversifying into property and he felt the use of his brother-in-law as the building contractor would prevent any rip-offs during the eighteen-month development period.

After they visited Spurriers Farm to see the proposed site and conversion plans, Page offered McGregor an incredible 20–30 per cent return on any investment. It wasn't a hard sell. Page knew his friend was in for the long term. In fact, McGregor was all in.

'I decided to invest heavily, as much as I could. I considered it to be a very viable opportunity considering what the properties would be worth at the end … I didn't even want a piece of paper, a "contract". It was the fact I trusted him,' he explained later.

The decision to commit so heavily was an interesting one because McGregor had not exactly experienced Page's Midas touch on his Currency Club investment. His £10,000 stake had been gambled and lost with, at best, only £2500 returned.

Nevertheless, over eight days in May, McGregor invested £54,400. NatWest had loaned him £20,000. The same amount came from his pregnant girlfriend, Louise Kilford, who was also a Met police officer. She had taken a loan from Lloyds bank. Most of the investment money was paid into Laura's Clippers account at NatWest and then to Page's CMC account.

McGregor had also convinced his girlfriend's father, Barry Kilford, to invest £30,000 of his pension money from British Telecom for a £500 monthly return. Again there was no contract. What there was, said McGregor, was 'an awful amount of trust'.

In June, McGregor raised a further £35,000 from Barclaycard and his bank, which all went to Page. He later remortgaged his house to free up £30,000 without having yet received any returns. Other money came from running up debt on his credit cards at 0 per cent interest. McGregor borrowed and then cleared the loan by transferring it to another credit company. Once the balance was cleared the same bank would offer him a new loan and so on. He told lenders he wanted the money for home improvements.

Separate to these ULPD investments, McGregor was still feeding the Currency Club's bottomless pit of loss. Between October and December 2003, he put £33,000 into his CMC account for him and Page to spread bet.

In the second week of November, McGregor's brother came over to meet his recently born nephew for the first time.

Robin McGregor, a Royal Marine Commando based at Taunton in Somerset, was awaiting orders to go to Iraq to join the 18,000 British troops stationed there after the US-led invasion in March.

When he arrived, McGregor and Page were sitting around a table covered with plans for the barns conversion. Page had paid £4000 to have them drawn up. The pair enthusiastically described the barn project to Robin, who listened with little interest or disposable funds.

That all changed days later after a call from his brother.

'A lot of my colleagues at SO14 are investing and Paul asked me if you were interested. Are you?'

'What do you think?' Robin enquired.

'I've invested a lot of money. Now's the time to do it.'

'I know property is the thing to be in and the extra cash wouldn't go amiss,' Robin replied.

Days later Page was on the phone offering a 25 per cent return over one year on whatever Robin invested. As he had no savings, he told Page he would see if his bank would loan him £15,000. Barclays, in fact, offered a £25,000 unsecured loan, which surprised Robin given his earnings were so low. Page of course encouraged him to take it.

The next day, 14 November, Robin transferred £19,500 into the ULPD NatWest account, which at the time was only £340 in credit. A few days later Page transferred over £6000 to his William Hill online betting account.

Robin had no idea about the gambling side of Page's operation. So when the police officer called soon after with a new request, the marine was willing to listen.

'Hello, mate,' said Page. 'I was thinking, would you be able to get me into your barracks in Taunton to make a presentation to some of the lads there?'

Robin McGregor was not sold. He was a few weeks from leaving for Iraq and wanted to keep the investment opportunity tight. But he agreed to introduce Page to a fellow marine who wanted to invest.

Meanwhile, Adam McGregor was promoting the ULPD barns conversion to police colleagues in and outside of SO14 over a game of golf while off-duty at Balmoral Castle in Scotland, where the Queen's firm took their summer holidays. On other occasions he would puff the barns project after a round of golf near his Essex home.

In the clubhouse, McGregor pitched the idea to Steve Tree, a sergeant on the Met's Territorial Support Group, which deals with riots. Tree and his wife, also a Met police officer, had just had a child and sold their house leaving them with £60,000 to invest. McGregor took them to meet Page and visit the barns site. The couple was concerned about investing so much money.

'Property prices were going through the roof but there was always a chance of a crash,' said Tree. He could remember the last one in the early 1990s. However, Page reassured the couple that there would be plenty of equity in the barns project when they were sold and offered a crazy return of 30 per cent. Tree was reassured by the involvement of other police officers and transferred £60,000 to ULPD without any receipt or documents.

Such imprudence was repeated time and again by other police investors. Their trust in Page may have been deserved if he could at least demonstrate a degree of record keeping. But there was none, or at least none that he was willing to show investors. And to be fair to him, they weren't asking.

Although Tree's money did go towards purchasing the barns, a lot of other money was going on spread betting and sports gambling with very mixed results.[3]

Page had also asked his Aunty Pat to remortgage the family's Leytonstone home for £150,000, which he said would go towards redeveloping the barns. She loved her nephew and wanted to help him through his financial difficulties. He promised he would keep up the loan repayments but created a wholly false legal financial guarantee for his aunt. It claimed that her £150,000 loan was secured against Clippers Hair Salon and the freehold. But the business was bust, and he didn't own the property.

Even family were now fair game.

Chapter 9

Jimmy's

Constable Mick 'the Don' Hickman approached Page at Buckingham Palace with a serious look on his face.

'Paul, the chief inspector wants to speak to you.'

Hickman was a trusted friend and one of the few older Royal Protection officers who Page looked up to. He was also the interface between SO14 bosses and the officers.

Hickman derived his nickname from being a Police Federation representative at BP. The Federation is the nearest thing the police in England and Wales have to a union. Police officers are not allowed to be in a union. Instead, lower ranks pay a monthly sub to the Federation that covers them for all types of assistance, including legal representation in any disciplinary or criminal matters.

'It's about the council tax,' the Don explained.

Page was none the wiser. 'What do you mean?'

'You haven't paid it mate, and the council have written to human resources. They want to take it out of your job money.'

The penny dropped and Page was straight on the phone to

Laura. 'Love, you've got to pay the council tax, like now.'

'It's not just them, there's water rates as well, Paul,' Laura reminded her husband.

'I'll deal with them fuckers later, just pay the council tax for now, love.'

'And what about the mortgage? We're two months behind on that. I'm not losing the house, Paul, not now, not in my condition.'

'Love, love, just pay the fucking council, I've been pulled in to see the chief inspector. Got to go. Bye.'

As he walked to Chief Inspector Brian Patrick's office across the road from Buckingham Palace, Page began confecting an explanation. It would have to be convincing flannel because almost two years earlier, in March 2002, he had promised the chief inspector to put his house in order after IG Index had contacted SO14 about an unpaid spread betting bill of £2700.

Page was left to honour his word. He didn't and IG Index wrote off the debt and banned him. Chief Inspector Patrick had no insight into how much worse Page's gambling had become when once again he was inviting the constable to have a seat in his office and explain himself.

Only a month earlier on 2 January 2004, Kensington Mortgages had written warning the couple they were £3540 in arrears and had £190,630.14 left to pay on their Hatton Close home after recently borrowing against it. The monthly payment was now £1492. It had just gone up as a new 9.5 per cent interest rate kicked in. Anglia Water was also threatening to take the couple to court over a £400 bill and Page had a dispute with CMC over one of his spread-betting accounts. The company was chasing him for a £15,000 gambling debt. 'What's going on, Paul?' Chief Inspector Patrick enquired politely.

'Well, sir, I've just been so busy at work and at home. My wife's pregnant with our fifth and she's having a bit of a hard time of it all.'

'Look, Paul. You need to sort it all out.'

'Yes, sir. I'm sorry. My wife is paying the bill as we speak.'

Page left the office surprised that he had not been disciplined. He had only recently come off restricted duty over the gun incident with his brother-in-law.

Page rang Laura on the way back to BP. 'Did you get your bottom slapped, then?' she asked sarcastically.

'Not even words of advice. I'm untouchable, love. Maybe they are concerned that too many people will be pissed off if it is stopped. They've never asked me to stop, not once. Stop shouting share prices over the fucking radio and stuff, but not stop doing what you're doing. It was too blatant not to be noticed by very senior officers.'

'So what happened, then?'

'I'm sticking out like a sore thumb now. They want me to reel it in, love.'

'We got a baby coming in three months, Paul. I can't have all this coming to my house.'

'It won't love. I promise.'

Later that day, Page returned home to tell his wife the new plan and how she featured in it.

'I'm applying for paternity leave. It's a piss-take but it means I can concentrate on ULPD.'

'Oh! That's nice, using me as an excuse to get off work. You better pull your weight at home, then. How long they going to pay you for sitting on your arse?' Laura enquired, mindful of the unpaid bills piling up.

'Love, it's unpaid leave. I'll get paid paternity leave when the baby's born.'

'I'm not due until May. How we going to live for the next three months and pay the mortgage?'

'I've got spare cash floating around and if I'm running the syndicate full time and not on police wages then everyone knows they are going to have to sub me.'

'You promised me it was not coming to my door anymore!'

'It won't. I'll still be going to the palace to drop off the dough and stuff.'

Page was not being straight with his wife or himself. The pressure of trying to make money gambling, the property development project and delivering cash returns in brown envelopes while pretending to work was taking its toll on him. 'I was starting to burn out,' he told me.

It was either stop pretending to be a Royal Protection Officer or stop the syndicate. He chose to stop being a police officer. SO14 management didn't object to his proposal. Perhaps it was a convenient way of getting Page out of BP without having to do anything.

A few weeks later on 28 February 2004, Page went on leave, initially for a month. But it was extended for the rest of the year when he claimed Laura needed his help after their fifth son, Harry, was born on 16 May. Laura certainly needed help but Page was too busy building interest in ULPD to give it.

Four days after Harry was born, Mortgage Guarantee paid £250,000 towards the £450,000 purchase price of the barns into Laura's NatWest account. Four days later on 24 May the contracts were exchanged. This, in turn, triggered the release of a chunk of money for the conversion to begin.[1]

Laura had visited the site with Paul in the later stages of her pregnancy with Harry. Her jealousy was out of control. One of the builders had joked that the owner's wife would sometimes appear in a bikini around the site and on one occasion had asked Page for help. Laura went berserk and made her husband swear the impossible – not to visit the site again.

When Harry was born, Laura's jealousy got worse. Watching her husband bashing the phones at home to bring in new investors would send her into a rage if it was a woman on the line. One day in July, Page snapped.

'You're fucked in the head love. You're not in a state to look after Harry,' he told her before getting in his car and driving off with the two-month-old baby. Laura was furious. She rang and rang his mobile until her husband relented and answered.

'Get back here with my son!' she ordered him.

That afternoon, Laura was expecting a visit from the midwife, who found her patient in tears. Laura discussed the situation at home and acknowledged for the first time that she was suffering from post-natal depression and needed support.

Page had moved out to a hotel for a while. That night, he sent a text to the husband of one of their friends telling him to come over with a crate of his favourite beer.

£ £ £

As the Range Rover with blacked out windows approached St James's Palace, the cameras in the control room were apparently turned away so as not to record the scene that followed.

It was the summer of 2004. Page was on leave and doing his rounds. It felt like he was in an ice-cream van. A number of SO14 officers at Jimmy's, the SO14 nickname for the palace, waited their turn to get into his car and left seconds later with an envelope of cash stuffed inside their uniform.

Inside his new mobile office, Page handed out copies of the ULPD brochure and guided officers to a section called 'Advantages to our investors', in particular the part that promised a cash bonus for those who brought in friends and family.

Page 'guaranteed excellent financial returns' of 25 to 40 per cent, far above any high-street bank and the best-performing hedge funds. Anyone putting in serious money was told they would receive a loyalty bonus of an even higher rate of return for signing a second one-year contract with ULPD.

Perhaps the most attractive of all of ULPD's promises was the continued and financially insane guarantee against investors' losses. The brochure boldly claimed there was 'no risk' to investors' capital because in the 'unlikely' event ULPD made a loss on a property, the company would pay out from its own funds.

The brochure described three types of investment scheme. The first was effectively a continuation of the Currency Club: investors gave Page money to gamble and he gave them returns, no questions asked. The second scheme was an investment in ULPD and any other opportunity the company was involved in. The third investment scheme was a straight investment in ULPD for a specific property. The investor was assured they could secure their investment by taking a legal charge against the property into which they had sunk their money.

This was by far the safest option. But strangely, it was also the least attractive to Page's investors. There was little wonder about how ULPD was able to offer such fantastic returns and why in the space of three years they had gone from monthly to quarterly and now yearly.

Page had been desperate to get into officers at Jimmy's since starting up ULPD in January 2003. Jim Mahaffy, the St James's Palace officer most involved in the Currency Club, was the first to invest in the new property venture.

The blurred line between the old spread-betting operation and new property venture didn't overly bother Mahaffy at the time. He kept his original £5000 spread-betting stake with

Page and invested additional money in ULPD.

Mahaffy was promised a 25 per cent annual return on a £15,000 investment. He liked the figures and on 20 February 2003 transferred the money from his joint bank account into Laura's NatWest account for Clippers, her bust hair salon. In June, after getting a £1000 quarterly payment in cash, Mahaffy and his wife transferred another £15,000 to the Clippers account.

The couple believed their money was going to develop a property, but ULPD owned nothing. The Mahaffys signed no contract with the company for this £30,000 investment, all of which Laura transferred to Page's CMC spread betting account.

In August, Mahaffy visited the barns site in Essex, took photographs and discussed a further investment with his wife. 'There appeared to be a lot of profit to be made from the whole thing,' he said. Later that month, at around the same time that they received another £1000 cash return, the couple transferred £10,000, this time to the ULPD bank account.

Although the company didn't own the barns, Page felt able to offer Mahaffy a new deal. The £40,000 the couple had already invested in property plus the £5000 Currency Club stake would be rolled together and a whopping 40 per cent return paid annually. Mahaffy agreed and, in late September, transferred another £25,000 into the ULPD account for the barns project.

Out of the blue, Page contacted him with a very generous offer. 'You are a loyal investor, Jim, so I want to send you and the wife on holiday.' Mahaffy was stunned. Wendy, his wife, was about to turn forty-five in November.

'I've been to Las Vegas. It'll probably cost more than you want to spend so I'll pay the difference,' Mahaffy suggested.

'No, mate. It's on ULPD. Look up BestatTravel online, pick a holiday package in Vegas and then speak to my best mate Fahim Baree, he's a travel consultant there. He'll sort you out.'

Mahaffy chose the pyramid-shaped Luxor hotel with its 120,000 square foot casino. On their return from the mecca of gambling, Jim and Wendy Mahaffy invested £15,000 for a development property in Esher, Surrey, that Page had falsely claimed ULPD was going to develop. The cheque was again paid to Laura's Clippers account on 14 December. No contract was drawn up.

As a token of their satisfaction, the Mahaffys sent the Pages a Christmas hamper. By the end of 2003, the couple had invested £80,000. In February 2004, they went even deeper, transferring another £45,000, once again to Laura's Clippers account. The extra money had come from remortgaging the family home, which had increased in value from £230,000 to £290,000 in the bubble. With their investment now standing at £125,000, Wendy Mahaffy suggested it would be a good idea to get something in writing. Page was happy to oblige; however, the document he provided contained some very odd wording. It said that Paul and Laura Page 'acknowledge receipt of £150,000 paid to us in the form of a loan by Mr and Mrs Mahaffy which will be repaid at a time of their choosing'.

Mahaffy didn't dispute the wording, but was looking for something more formal. So Page scribbled and signed a similarly worded one-page note that was witnessed by an Essex solicitor.

Since the beginning, Page had kept Mahaffy on side by regularly paying amazing cash returns and gifting him a free holiday in Las Vegas. There was, at least in Mahaffy's mind, a beautiful friendship developing between the two Royal Protection officers. The SO14 officer was happy to talk up his investment to other colleagues, hand out ULPD brochures and pass an envelope of cash returns to a fellow officer.

However, by the summer of 2004, when Page's black Range Rover rolled into Jimmy's one more time, Mahaffy was no longer his biggest police investor.[2]

£ £ £

Constable Mark Copley had been at St James's Palace since 1994, but it wasn't until December 2002 that he had his first proper conversation with Page about business.

Copley recalled being in the canteen when he noticed Page scanning the financial news pages and keeping an eye on Teletext. Mahaffy had already told Copley how well he was doing as a member of Page's spread-betting club. It was a far cry from the share club Copley had helped start at Jimmy's.

'Hello, Paul,' said Copley, a small, slightly built man. 'I hear you are interested in stocks and shares, commodities, that sort of thing?'

Page looked up and turned off the Teletext. A property renovation programme was now on the screen.

'I'd like if I had the knowledge and courage to do something like that myself,' Copley continued.

'I've done a few renovations of property, Mark. It's piss easy,' Page replied.

'Oh! Are you a DIYer?'

'No. Fuck no. I've got a brother-in-law who's in the building trade with his own company.'

'That's handy.'

'Yeah, well, eventually I'm going set up a company of my own and take a career break.'

Page had done exactly that when he next saw Copley at Jimmy's the following year. He told Copley about the three-barn conversion in Essex. 'Here's a brochure. I'm looking for substantial investments from SO14 colleagues.'

The pitch could not have come at a more opportune time. Mark and his wife Sufia had a fixed-rate mortgage on their house in Harlow, Essex which was coming up for renegotiation in August 2003. Property prices being what they were, the couple had worked out they could remortgage at a new rate, pay off most of the original loan and borrow £65,000 against the increased equity, no questions asked by their bank.

The couple thought the barns development was a good investment opportunity. In September, Copley told Page he was in. That month, the couple transferred £45,000 to the ULPD account, and on Christmas Eve another £20,000 was deposited.

The Copleys saw themselves as conservative investors. Yet they had transferred £65,000 to ULPD for the barns project on the strength of the plans Page had showed them and without visiting the site, which was only a short drive from their home. They also had no contract with ULPD.

The deal they were promised was spectacular. Page offered the Copleys a 30 per cent return in quarterly payments of £4500 for their £65,000 investment. The couple had also agreed to invest a further £90,000 from remortgaging Sufia Copley's home before she married Mark. This money was a down payment for one of the barns when it was completed.

Strangely, Copley paid most of the £90,000 between March and April 2004 into Laura's Clippers account rather than to a firm of solicitors. Some he also paid directly to Paul Ballard's business account, the discharged bankrupt builder Page was using to convert the barns.

That April, the Pages invited the Copleys to sign a formal agreement to represent their £150,000 investment. Mark Copley drafted the agreement instead of a lawyer. Both couples signed the document, which recognized that the Pages would refund the £155,000 if the Copleys didn't buy one of the converted barns. Meanwhile, the couple would continue to receive £9000 in returns for the remainder of 2004.

Page made sure these were paid on time. It had the desired effect, because the Copleys decided to definitely buy one of the barns. They visited the site and chose Barn C. Scarborough Building Society had valued it at £315,000 when completed. The Copleys resolved to raise the remaining £160,000 through a mortgage.

On 15 November 2004, the couple and their two young children moved in to their new home before it was completed because Page had offered them free rent.[3]

£ £ £

Sikh constable Surinder Mudhar left a career as a structural engineer to join the Met Police in 1994. Five years later, he was posted to Jimmy's, one of the few ethnic officers in SO14 to wear a turban.

One day in September 2003, Mudhar was on duty with Mahaffy, who was boasting about the returns from his investments with a BP officer nicknamed Gripper. 'It's good business,' Mahaffy enthused.

Mudhar was aware the property market was booming and was encouraged that Richard Humby, an officer with extensive buy-to-let interests, was also thinking about investing with Page.

'I'd like to speak to him,' Mudhar told Mahaffy, who set up a meeting at Jimmy's.

Days later, Page parked his Mercedes in the palace and went to the control room, where Mahaffy and Mudhar were waiting. The officer manning the control room continued monitoring the palace security networks while Page launched into his now well-practised spiel.

'I'm going on a career break soon to run my property company, ULPD. At the moment I'm running a syndicate for officers. We're renovating some barns in Essex. Depending on how much you invest with me I'll give you a good rate of return. You can't lose, Surinder.'

Page left the control room to hand out some cash returns and commissions for those who had introduced others to his scheme. Mudhar was interested and assured by the investment of other SO14 colleagues. He took home a ULPD brochure to discuss with his wife of sixteen years. Any investment would have to come from their joint savings account.

'People at work are already involved with Page. He's one of us, Manjit,' Mudhar told his wife.

'But I'm happy keeping our money in the bank. It's safer,' she replied.

'Yes, but we can earn more money out of property than just letting it sit in the Halifax or Barclays savings account.'

'I'm worried we will lose it, Surinder,' she told him.

Mudhar reported to Page that his wife still wasn't sure. Gripper left it a few days before coming to their house to pitch her the property scheme. He arrived in his flash car carrying a laptop, the brochure and architectural plans for the barns.

'Are you going back to the police after your career break?' Manjit enquired after the introductions.

'No, not at all. I'm doing so well,' Page replied.

Manjit explained that their savings had been put aside for their two young children's education, wedding and for a house. She said her husband had been saving since he had started working at seventeen.

'Manjit. I understand you need to be sure but it's as safe as houses. ULPD will cover your investment. Listen, I was talking to an estate agent down in Surrey, there's a property there I'm interested in developing in Esher. This agent says to me the property, when done up, will either go to Arabs or footballers. He let slip that Chelsea's Jimmy Floyd Hasselbaink was interested in the same development.'

The Mudhars were impressed with Page. However, they decided to start small and transferred £5000 to the ULPD bank account on 25 September 2003. Page had offered a 20 per cent net return of £1000 in a year. Mudhar was one of the few who had a contract. But the couple had invested without visiting the barns site.

Over the next two years, the Mudhars would put in a further £80,000 under a contract in which Page offered increasingly incredible rates of return from 30 to 90 per cent. They took out various bank loans, cashed in their premium bonds and dipped into the Barclays joint savings account. The money was transferred to ULPD or Laura's NatWest Clipper account.

However, on two occasions they handed Page £20,000 in cash. The couple met him by a golf club off Junction 3 of the M25, half way between their homes.

The Mudhars were also interested in buying a property they had visited in Orpington, Kent. Page claimed that ULPD was going to develop the bungalow, which suited Manjit as she was suffering from rheumatoid arthritis. The involvement of the Copleys in a similar arrangement made the couple feel safe and protected. 'I was happy to invest as other colleagues were involved and I trusted their views,' said Mudhar.

In time, he would allow his Barclays account to be used to transfer syndicate money to other officers or receive cash from

111

complete strangers. He appears to have taken a small cut with Page's blessing for the service.

The couple were sufficiently impressed with Page and his operation to recommend 'the great opportunity' to a close family friend who had a large amount of cash after recently selling his house.

Randhir Suri, an accountant nicknamed Pinky, was earning low interest on the money. After being faxed the ULPD brochure from St James's Palace, he decided to invest £70,000 in Page's various schemes on the promise of up to 30 per cent returns. Some money was transferred to Laura's bank account without a contract or receipt, simply because he trusted his friends. Suri raised other money by taking a home improvement loan from the bank.

Gripper and Pinky did meet once at a pub in west London. He came away thinking Page was a 'good salesman' and trustworthy because he was a policeman. Pinky was happy to give Page money to gamble on the stock market and property when he saw thousands of pounds coming back to him in returns.

The Mudhars were not left out of ULPD's apparent largesse. Gripper, who sometimes referred to Mudhar by his SO14 nickname, 'the Turbanator', also rewarded his police colleague with a free family holiday to Florida.[4]

£ £ £

'It was like a circle of money coming in and coming out. I could click my fingers and someone would put fifty grand into a total stranger's fucking account on my say-so. To me one hundred grand became nothing,' Page recalled.

Between 2003 and 2004, the first two years of ULPD's existence, he had taken an estimated one million pounds from police and civilian investors. This did not include the £217,000 that Mortgage Guarantee had started releasing for the barns conversion since May 2004. Not all of the finance company's money went to his builder brother-in-law for materials and labour; some of it was diverted to the spread-betting accounts or recycled to pay returns to investors.

Page realized he had to widen ULPD's property portfolio, or at least the illusion of one, if he was to attract more investors. There simply wasn't enough money in the barns for everyone.

That month, a Kent-based estate agents put Page on their list of buyers looking for properties with a £900,000 to £3 million price tag. Page also started putting in offers for properties while trying to negotiate multi-million pound loans from specialist finance firms.

In July, a £1.1 million offer was put in to develop an Essex scrapyard into Berwick Hall. In November, Page offered £1.2 million for the Esher property – 33 Meadway – that he had already mentioned to the Mudhars and Mahaffys.

His own finances were in a parlous state. He had to sell the family Leytonstone home inherited from his grandparents and force his Aunty Pat, who lived there, into rented accommodation. His grandfather would have turned in his grave that the inheritance was frittered away.

As for ULPD, it hadn't even filed any accounts. The problem was none of the finance firms he consulted would lend him the money because he wasn't able to show them passable financial accounts. Thus, the search for new investors had to continue using the old lures.

Page told me that by 2005 his betting and property syndicate had spread beyond SO14 and into other Met specialist squads (Diplomatic Protection Group, Anti-Terrorism, Special Branch

and Firearms); east London police stations (Limehouse, Dagenham and Romford); and other forces (Greater Manchester,
Hampshire and Avon and Somerset).

He said SO14 officers going to Balmoral via Stansted Airport
would drop by at chez Page for cash returns to take to fellow
policeman in the Scottish police who liaised with SO14 officers
protecting the Queen's castle.

'I was responsible for a machine that was churning out lots of
money and it was responsible for people working in highly sensitive areas. It was mega money. Sometimes in my house I'd have
one hundred grand laid out on the floor. It was that bad. It got
to the stage where we had police convoys, I shit you not, full of
money.'

Chapter 10

Gripper Airways

Their friendship began as toddlers at an east London nursery in the early seventies. It ended almost forty years later in a south London courtroom; two broken men squaring up in front of the jury until anger and betrayal gave way to tears and white flags.

Fahim Baree and Paul Page were born within a month of each other in 1971. They grew up in Leytonstone, forever in each other's houses when they weren't hanging out with their gang. Page felt so comfortable around Baree's family that he called Mrs Baree 'Mum'.

The British Muslim family was aware that young Page hadn't exactly had the best start in life. His paternal grandparents had brought him up since he was six-months old because his mum and dad weren't able to look after their only child. That's all the Baree family knew but it was enough to take the young boy into their hearts.

Page's grandfather, a successful building contractor, had ambitions for his grandson. He encouraged Page to study and hoped one day he would join him in the building trade, possibly as a draftsman or surveyor. But they both knew that Page was not cut out for academic study. Sport was his thing, especially karate. His grandfather encouraged Page to a black belt at thirteen. Baree remembers his best friend was 'well liked' at school and college and even 'revered within the community as doing very well for himself' through karate.

'I knew his grandparents better than his mum and dad. My mum and dad were very close to his grandparents. I called them Gran and Grandad, it was that kind of a relationship,' Baree recalled during a long interview.

The two boys shared a love of cars. They were the first to get licences and motors and saw themselves as the dominant person-alities among their friends. But Page had an edge with his skill in martial arts. He recounted one incident when, as late teenagers, the pair had fought over some real or imagined lack of respect.

Mrs Baree, a social worker, would on occasion intervene and asked them to make up after one particularly serious fall-out. But the pair maintained a solid friendship thereafter, despite going on very different career paths, one a travel agent, the other an officer of the law.

Baree clapped Page at his passing-out parade for Essex Police in 1992 and drove him home with his proud grand-mother and Aunty Pat sitting in the back seat. But he saw a change in his friend, and not for the good, when he became a policeman. Before he joined the force Page had kept his licence clean, didn't drink, take drugs, gamble or throw his weight around. 'He was that clean, squeaky,' Baree said. He believes his best friend's mind became 'polluted' by what he saw in the police.

Baree was alarmed at the style of vigilante policing Page was learning at Essex and later in the Met.

When he got into the police and started training other coppers, then he got a bit of a big head and he told me little stories about what they used to do in the back of the van. No one knew about it apart from the guys who done it. That was his self-justice. As soon as he got in the force and started to do all these things, they just brainwashed him. Seriously, some stories he was telling me about murder [scenes] and what he had to do, and the bodies, I think it [gave] him more hero status, he wanted it.

Page outgrew Essex, says Baree. 'He didn't like policing the beat at Grays. It was just scroats, Gypsies, nothing of interest to him. He wanted more big-time stuff.

Baree was best man and keeper of the £29 Argos ring when Page wed Laura in 1997. The travel agent was also married with young children. The two couples would hang out, although according to Laura she didn't get on with Baree's wife. There was a competitive edge between them, she said, and Laura liked to flaunt her Mercedes and 'Louis' (Vuitton) when they socialized.

Baree was impressed by his friend's move to royalty protection in 1998 but took his money-making schemes and share trading with a pinch of salt. Two years later and Page was regularly faxing Baree at work with information on property for sale.

It became more apparent that he was trying to be more like a sorcerer, 'I can do this, I can do that', but it didn't click until he started working and all his money came out and he was driving around in this Range Rover and Porsche. Then my interest picked up and I thought 'He's got to be doing something right.'

So when Page mentioned in late 2002 his idea to set up a

property company and develop some derelict barns, Baree was intrigued. The plan was viable and exciting in a booming property market, he thought.

At the time, Baree believed his friend was a successful spread better. He had no idea about the losses and Page didn't explain the true reasons why he needed to set up the company or admit that he was starting to burn out. To Baree, the new house in Chafford Hundred, the 'his and hers' Mercedes on the drive, the exotic holidays and a prestigious job guarding the Queen were all signs of substance and success.

The pair drove around Canary Wharf looking for an office for ULPD. The financial centre was booming with testosterone-fuelled trading in toxic mortgage-backed derivatives, followed by jeroboam-sized lunches, cocaine and hookers expensed as 'research'.

Bankers saw no dark cloud on the horizon or any conflict about making money from selling a product, which at best they must have known was unsustainable in the long term. The Ponzi-type scheme worked liked this: an investor would be offered a high-yielding mortgage-backed derivative by the same bank or hedge fund that was secretly betting in another market that the toxic product was likely to default.

The type of men and women celebrated by this banking culture were those with balls big enough to hide huge losses from their bosses when gambles didn't pay off, wipe their mouths and get back into the casino to quietly recover the position.

As he drove his Mercedes through Canary Wharf with Baree next to him, Page also felt like a big swinging dick. He had the swagger, the chat, the confidence and trappings of wealth. He too had been let loose with other people's money without any training whatsoever. He too saw no looming dark cloud or ethical issue about how he was using investors' funds.

Instead, Page saw a financial culture that rewarded those taking short-term risk without regard to long-term consequences. In a booming financial market, it is said that traders feel divorced from reality, immune from risk. As Page had already admitted, at this point in his life £100,000 was nothing.

'Are you in?' the street-smart cop with more front than Buckingham Palace asked.

'Yeah,' said his best friend. 'I'll help you out. Give me a title, give me a job, some kind of pay, I'll come work with you.'[1]

£ £ £

Legend has it that in 1993, Rita Sharma set up BestatTravel (BAT) to escape a dead-end McJob. Rahul, her husband, resigned his job as a chartered accountant to help 33-year-old Rita run the new firm specializing in 'affordable luxury holidays for the discerning traveller'.

Today BAT employs over 70 people in its central London call centre and headquarters. The Sharmas are the sole directors and equal shareholders in the company. It is their main asset, although through clever property investment their fortune in 2003–4 was estimated at £95 million, earning them their first presence on the *Sunday Times* Rich List.

Their entry among the richest 1000 people in Britain and Ireland said: 'The Sharmas have resisted City entreaties for a flotation at £60m. They have shrewdly invested in bricks and mortar, so we add £35m for their homes in India and the south of France, their luxurious central London mansion and other property interests and assets.'

The couple shared rankings with *Gladiator* director Sir Ridley Scott, *Dragon's Den* entrepreneur James Caan, Pink Floyd co-founder Roger Waters, Rolling Stones drummer Charlie Watts and former Take That singer Robbie Williams. They are also stars among the British Asian business community and through BAT donated to the Conservative Party.

Fahim Baree was a trusted senior travel consultant at the firm. He liked his job but was heavily attracted to the idea of working with his best friend.

In early 2003, Baree helped design the ULPD brochure and agreed to be named as the financial director in promotional material. He was not registered with the watchdog, nor did he have his name on any official company documents. There was, however, a verbal agreement with Page that he would receive a 1–2 per cent commission for every investor brought into the business and a higher rate of return on any money he invested himself.

The opaque arrangement suited Baree. He didn't want to resign from BAT until he could see how ULPD performed in its first year. Page did not see this as disloyalty. After all, his other 'lieutenant', Adam McGregor, was furiously selling the new investment opportunity to his family and police friends. So much so, that by the end of 2003, McGregor had brought in over £180,000, a lot of which went into the CMC spread-betting account that Bald eagle had opened for Gripper.

Baree started to change his mind about investing in ULPD when in September that year Page showed him the £510,000 mortgage documents on the barns. He was also aware that the official evaluation suggested there was almost £1 million profit to be made from flipping the property.

Baree worked in an open-plan office and sat next to Anjam Khan, his manager and friend. Khan could overhear the enthusiastic phone calls with Page. It wasn't long before Baree gave him the sales pitch.

'He's a childhood friend of mine that runs this company, ULPD. He's a police officer at Buckingham Palace. I might leave and make some money.'

But Khan wasn't interested. 'All my money's going into doing up my 'ouse,' he told Baree in an even broader Essex accent.

By early 2004, Baree still hadn't decided whether or not to leave BAT. Instead, he opened up a new hub of purely civilian and mostly British Asian investors inside the travel company or connected to it through Khan. By the end of the year this new hub had invested £240,000 into Page's scheme.

The first to invest was Bimal Lodhia, a 38-year-old Ugandan-born Asian. He had arranged Khan's mortgage and did the same for Baree.

Lodhia had only been a mortgage adviser since 1999. Before dispensing financial advice he'd worked in a chemist dispensing over-the-counter health products. The property boom had been kind to Lodhia. When Baree came to see him he was living in a big house in Chigwell, Essex, with a Mercedes outside and the trust of many in the local Asian community.

Lodhia was interested in meeting Page and seeing the barns development. He spoke to his friend Paresh Solanki, another mortgage adviser with even less experience, who he knew from insurance work.

Baree drove the two men to meet his partner. It was also Baree's first time at the barns. Page was waiting in a Portakabin, his alternative office to the Range Rover now that he was officially on leave from BP.

Solanki was impressed by the amount of work going on. 'This is a family business,' Page told him as they walked around the site. 'It's me, Fahim and my brother-in-law. I've taken a break from royalty protection to get into the property game. A lot of police officers have invested in me, including senior ones.'

Solanki had made money in the housing boom since 1999 by buying and selling investment properties, so he knew what was possible, even in such a frothing market. The deal Page was offering him – 25 per cent return – he accepts was 'phenomenal' by any standards.

However, Solanki says that he had no idea about the spread-betting side to Page's operation when he and Lodhia invested. Court documents show that none of the £240,000 invested in 2004 by them or on behalf of others went directly to ULPD.

Lodhia gave Page £20,000 in April 2004. In June, Solanki persuaded his brother-in-law to give him £15,000 for a high-return, short-term unspecified investment. Days later, Solanki invested £20,000 of his own money, which he paid into Page's Woolwich building society account. A further £25,000 investment in September went to Laura's Clippers account at NatWest.

Solanki said he received 'substantial' cash returns in brown envelopes from Page and Baree for these investments. He also earned a 10 per cent commission for introducing two other investors in 2004.

The more significant of the two was Mubasher Hussain, an IT consultant in his early thirties, who ended up investing £133,500. The money was raised through a £50,000 remortgage and raiding his ISA and Tessa savings accounts, he said. Hussain also 'cleared' his wife's bank account to invest in the scheme that Solanki, his 'trusted' financial adviser, had brought to him.

Hussain met Page in June 2004 and originally agreed to invest £30,000 for an annual 25 per cent return. He denies having any idea about spread betting until well after all his money had been handed over. 'At the time the property market was booming. I wanted to get into property. I was dealing with a policeman … There were a lot of police officers involved in this. It was a good investment,' he later explained.

Hussain's first investment was transferred to Page's Woolwich account. The second investment had an altogether different routing. Hussain transferred £20,000 to the Barclays account of SO14 constable Surinder Mudhar. The St James's Palace officer then transferred this money to Laura's Clippers account.

Hussain used Mudhar's bank account on two more occasions to invest a further £35,000. However, the court documents show that 'the Turbanator' kept most of this money because it appears Page had told him it was the return on his own investment.

The willingness of police officers to allow complete strangers to use their personal bank account to transfer large sums of money was an extraordinary and foolish feature of this story.[2]

£ £ £

By summer 2004, the money-go-round was impressing Fahim Baree, now a key lieutenant involved in dropping off brown envelopes. He said he believed the Pages had bought the barns outright and then borrowed against it to fund the conversion. Yet he also said he didn't know exactly where his best friend was getting the funds to pay cash returns. He told me:

> He would give me money to pay people off every month, [I] didn't question where the money came from, all cash … Being a novice in that area, I thought, okay well if he is going to get money for the barns [from Mortgage Guarantee] he can pay investors off in that way. Because the land that he bought was only £500,000 and the end value of it

was £1.4 million … So I could see obviously there was a big wealth pot there and I assumed that was where the returns were going to be … From that point [ULPD] seemed like a machine that could actually work.

On this account, Baree wasn't alarmed that the conversion budget would run out if his best friend continued to use it to also pay investors their returns. More details of what Baree knew emerge from looking at his actions between August and October 2004.

Although still not ready to resign from BAT and join ULPD, Baree decided to invest his own money with Page. In August, he remortgaged the flat where he lived with his wife and two children and gave Page £30,000 in cash at a BMW garage. There was no contract just a promise of a 33 per cent annual return, which Page said he would double if his best mate brought in more fresh blood.

Two months later in October, Baree opened a CMC spread-betting account for Page to use. Asked to explain this, he told me:

I set up the account for the purpose of Paul to hedge against it. I'd never used the account. He needed an account to hedge against … He told me he needed three or four accounts to hedge against so that one would go deficit, one would go plus, so he would make money. I didn't know the ins and outs.

Baree said he initially thought the spread betting was separate from the property side of ULPD.

'In my head it was a separate thing he was doing. It didn't click to me to think that he's using, well, okay, yeah, it's

124

obvious if he's taking 30 grand one day and making 40 grand the next, that money's got to be used for something. It's not going be used in the building trade. So yeah, obviously, naivety was there at the beginning. But when you think, hold on a minute he's taken, I mean, I didn't even know he'd been taking money off other people, but then the next day he'd say, 'I've made 40 grand off the markets'. I thought 'How did you do that? Where's the capital come from?' He goes, 'So-and-so has given me, invested'.

Page needed Baree to open the CMC account because other spread- and sports-betting accounts had to be closed down after sustaining losses. Page couldn't use his own CMC account because he was in dispute over a £15,000 debt. The year before he had closed down his joint CMC account with SO14 constable Mark 'Pretty Boy' Joyce after losing £35,600.[3]

The William Hill accounts had also been closed down after sustaining losses. The records show Page bought casino chips worth £173,000 and lost £88,000. He had also lost on the two William Hill accounts opened in his wife's name.

Baree didn't know about the losses on these other accounts. But like McGregor, he opened a CMC account for Page and knew his best friend was spread betting while taking investors' money for ULPD. Baree also allowed investors to put money into his Halifax account, which he then transferred to CMC for Page to gamble. The investors didn't know.[4]

£ £ £

The Queen's Flight is the name for the fleet of VIP aircraft at the disposal of Purple One and the Royal Family. After a merger with the Royal Air Force in 1995, the fleet was renamed No. 32

(The Royal) Squadron based at RAF Northolt. Purple One and The Firm can charter executive planes to fly the world at an hourly rate picked up by the taxpayer under a royal travel grant allocated by Parliament.

Goldman Sachs, the investment bank earning billions from a derivatives-based scheme that was driving the world economy towards a crash, flew its executives, tame regulators, pocket politicians and key investors around the world in a fleet of private jets fuelled by greed and irresponsibility.

Royal Protection officer Paul Page, another degenerate gambler, thought he too should offer key investors a chance to travel the world for 'free' courtesy of 'Gripper Airways'.

ULPD's bespoke travel company, BAT, made the arrangements mostly through Fahim Baree and later Anjam Khan. Plane tickets and hotel bookings were generally dispatched to the palace pigeonholes of key SO14 officers, although apparently some would collect the envelope from BAT's West End offices.

Las Vegas, Florida, Tel Aviv, Paris, Dubai, Thailand, the Caribbean and Australia. No destination was too far, no hotel too ritzy for the select group of investors who Page needed to keep sweet.

'It's on the house. We're flush. He's been a good investor, never moaning,' Page would tell Baree, when authorizing the booking.

Page convinced himself that when people gave him money it was his to do with as he saw fit for the greater good of the syndicate. The idea behind the holidays, he told me, was to 'build up fierce loyalty – I'm looking after you, you look after me'. This type of loyalty bonus was an extension of the secret commissions system he paid those who brought in new investors or who allowed their bank accounts to be used to transfer money around the syndicate.

But in reality, the holidays were also a lure to foster trust and the illusion of success and profit in his scheme. The holidays, like the commissions, were not free but paid for from other people's money.

Baree said Page never rewarded himself with 'free' holidays. However, it frustrated him that his best friend rarely paid on time for others. It was 'like pulling teeth'. Sometimes, Page would even ask Baree or Khan to front the payment on their credit cards.

But it was not just 'free' bespoke holidays on Gripper Airways that Page offered his key investors. There was also a bespoke executive car company that Page used as another investment sweetener – something for the weekend, from a Mini to a Bentley, to please the little lady in your life.

It was in August 2002 during the Currency Club era that Page first started doing business with Arrow Hire in Cardiff. The business was personal. Page was losing a lot of money and had to sell the 'his and hers' Mercedes to raise cash. But he also needed to maintain the illusion of success for his SO14 investors who were used to seeing him in a flash car.

Page leased a Range Rover, which became the new mobile office from where brown envelopes were dispensed out of view of the palace security cameras.

His investors would continue to think that the Range Rover and later a Porsche belonged to the Money God. Instead, they were paying over £600 per month for each vehicle parked on Page's drive, as well as his mortgage and those utility bills he chose to settle.

Craig Gunn, Arrow's director, knew nothing about the ULPD business. He thought Page was an affable good customer, especially when he started to hire cars for syndicate members. They got on well, despite Page's habitual lateness paying the hire bill.

But the policeman made up for this by providing a very unusual service to Arrow Hire.

According to Gunn, the local Welsh police were not always interested when he reported a missing car. Detection wasn't that difficult because the cars had trackers fitted to them. But the local police considered recovering the vehicle a civil matter, he said. On two occasions Gunn turned to Page for help retrieving first an Audi and then a Porsche in London.

The Audi convertible was somewhere in the south of the capital. Page said he asked two police colleagues on night duty to keep an eye out for it. When it was spotted, Page turned up with policeman-turned-freelance-repo-man Adam McGregor. Page then called the telephone number on the hire contract and introduced himself as a police officer.

'You've got a short window before this goes beyond an informal resolution. They just want the car back.'

The man agreed and left the Audi as instructed at the car park by Leytonstone tube station with keys under the back wheel.

The story of the Porsche Cayenne was a more complex repossession. Gunn had been in contact with the hirer, who claimed the car was up north. The tracker showed it was in fact parked in east London.

Page picked up McGregor and located the car near a garage in Ilford. A warrant card was flashed and the men inside the Porsche were persuaded it was in their interests to walk away.

McGregor later admitted in court that he had gone with Page to 'locate some cars'. His general loyalty had been rewarded with a 'free' Saab Cabriolet from Arrow Hire. To McGregor it was a 'thank you' for investing his family's savings in ULPD.[5]

In fact, Bald eagle had gone further in 2004 than Page could ever have imagined. McGregor had opened up a third hub, this time of civilian investors, from the Bristol area.

Page was still the controlling mind of the whole ULPD syndicate. But the system of lieutenants and commissions he created meant others had their own incentives and responsibility for bringing in investors who he had never met but whose money he was happy to take.

In short, going into 2005 his hedge fund was taking on a life of its own which made Page's fraud a lot easier to continue, especially as no one in SO14 management appeared to be paying any serious attention.

Chapter 11

The corgi that didn't bark

'Holy diversionary tactics, Batman!' said Robin, watching a group of their men create a disturbance outside the main gates of Buckingham Palace.

'To the side of the palace, Robin,' said the caped crusader, leading the way. Batman scaled the smaller perimeter fence, then propped the ladder against the main palace wall and started to climb as armed SO14 officers approached.

'Holy show-ups, Batman! You've breached Buckingham Palace security and beaten all these jokers in uniform.'

'Watch out, Robin! They're behind you,' Batman warned as he edged his way along the ledge towards the famous main balcony from where The Firm wave on royal wedding days.

The Boy Wonder had by now beaten a hasty retreat and was speaking to the assembled media. 'We are ordinary guys and if we can get in there, anybody can,' he told the BBC.

SO14 officers had decided not to shoot Batman because he did not appear to be a terrorist. Doubting his super power of flight, however, they moved a crash mat under the ledge while he unfurled a banner. It read: 'SUPER DADS OF FATHERS 4 JUSTICE. FIGHTING FOR YOUR RIGHT TO YOUR KIDS.'

The stunt on 13 September 2004 by activists Jason Hatch (Batman) and Dave Pyke (Robin) was one of the most memorable security blunders at BP since Michael Fagan gained entry to the Queen's private quarters twenty-two years earlier.

That Purple One was away on her summer holidays at Balmoral Castle when the Dynamic Duo struck mattered not. The security breach was enough to force Home Secretary David Blunkett to make an emergency statement to Parliament that evening.

Tory MP David Davis, his opposite number, put the incident in perspective. 'It beggars belief that we have had four major breaches of security in a year. When the threat from terrorism is at an all-time high it is worrying that episodes like this can still take place,' he told the BBC.

In June the year before, comedian Aaron Barschak set off alarms at Windsor Castle when he gate-crashed Prince William's twenty-first birthday celebration dressed as Osama bin Laden, just a few weeks after the invasion of Iraq.

Barschak scaled the perimeter wall and gained entry to the private party, where nearly all of William's family was present. SO14 officers thought he was a fancy dress guest until he interrupted the Prince's speech to ask for a kiss.

Lax security and gate-crashing palace parties was not the preserve of publicity seekers and activists with a serious point to make. According to Page's defence-case statement, some SO14 officers in his syndicate would fix it so friends and family could gate-crash palace garden parties.

The court document said:

Some police officers had given extra perks to some loyal investors whereby it was arranged that the investor and one guest would be 'spirited' into royal garden parties by these officers. These persons were not invited guests of the Queen nor were they subjected to the strict vetting procedures undertaken on genuine guests. They would bypass the usual long queues and were escorted through various security posts before being left in the grounds of the palace with bona fide guests. Additionally, they were given the mobile number of an officer if any problems occurred and briefed with a cover story.

The security review into the breach at Windsor Castle concluded in August 2003 that there had been a 'series of errors' for which a few minor heads took the brunt and the bosses at SO14 survived. However, Met Commissioner Sir John Stevens said the report was a 'grave wake-up call'. He had assured the Home Secretary that 'significant lessons' were learned.

Except, in November, the *Mirror* splashed the results of its two-month undercover investigation at Buckingham Palace. Reporter Ryan Parry had got a footman's job with false references in the run-up to the state visit of US President George W. Bush.

The Met commissioner launched another review and suggested that the SAS could do penetration testing of the royal palaces while his officers gathered intelligence on publicity seekers and royal obsessives. Vetting procedures would also be tightened and a new royal security coordinator, an ex-SAS brigadier, was appointed who reported to the Queen's private secretary and liaised with the head of the Royalty and Diplomatic Protection Group, Commander Peter Loughborough.

SO14 was the only unit in the Metropolitan Police with a lord in charge. Loughborough, the 7th Earl of Rosslyn, is a hereditary peer. His seat, Roslin Castle in Scotland, was created in 1801 for his great ancestor, a Lord Chancellor.

The Castle includes Rosslyn Chapel, which was made famous by Dan Brown's *The Da Vinci Code*, published in April 2003, just as Loughborough was about to take over at SO14.

Brown's blockbuster recycled various conspiracy theories about Freemasonry and the Knights Templar. These included that the Catholic Rosslyn Chapel is the secret resting place of the Holy Grail because Loughborough's ancestors were direct descendants of the secret union between Jesus and Mary Magdalene.

More historically accurate are the following facts: Loughborough succeeded his father in 1977 and two years later, aged twenty-one, took his seat as a hereditary peer in the House of Lords. Perhaps his youthful modernity chimed with New Labour because the party allowed him to escape its cull of hereditary peers in 1999.

As well as being a senior policeman, Loughborough is active in the second chamber as a cross-bencher, which means he is neither a member of the governing party or the official opposition, but has the unelected potential to shape or influence legislation.

The Eton-educated peer read Latin American studies at Bristol University. He joined the Met in 1980 and transferred to Thames Valley Police in 1994, where he was the commander for his old Eton stomping ground. After returning to the Met in 2000, Loughborough was sent to study criminology at Cambridge University. A year later, in May 2003, he was appointed head of SO14 at the age of forty-five.

Loughborough is married with two sons and two daughters, one of whom went on to play Kate Middleton in a US TV film of her blossoming relationship with Prince William. He is said to speak the Queen's language, which no doubt came in handy when he had to explain why only one month into his new job her son's birthday party was gate-crashed by an Osama bin Laden lookalike, and how the Dynamic Duo had gained entry to Buckingham Palace in September 2003.

Of course, Purple One had no idea about another scandal brewing under her nose: Page and his out-of-control Ponzi fraud and the SO14 culture of greed and gambling that was also undermining her security during the war on terror.

But then neither, apparently, did the new head boy at SO14.

£ £ £

The warnings were there, six of them between August 1999 and November 2004, when Loughborough was well into his job. But no one in SO14 at a senior level put it together and asked the right questions.

Since 1999, there had been two complaints about Page's unpaid spread betting and tax bills, the last one in January 2004; two suspicious transactions reports from banks, the last one in August 2004; the gun incident with Page's brother-in-law; and the Hearts scandal when an officer had to be moved to Windsor Castle to prevent Page and others beating him up.

In his defence-case statement, Page gave a flavour of the culture at SO14 that he had in part inherited and helped change. It was hardly a picture, reinforced by newspapers, of an elite squad of SAS-trained police officers ready to confront a new terrorist threat.

> Those within Royalty Protection were stationed there for limited reasons. Some were lazy and did not wish to work hard so therefore enjoyed the slow pace of the squad until retirement. Others had just had enough of policing and were clearly frustrated with the legal system. Some wanted

the 'down time' for studies to progress through the ranks by preparing for police exams. A further common feature was officers using their time to make money from other business interests outside the police.

The prevailing attitude within the 'Royalty Protection Department' was that it was a licence to print money for officers. Thousands of pounds could be earned on overtime for doing very little. All these factors made the system very close knit and officers wanting to join would be 'vetted' by other officers before their formal interviews. This exercise would entail the potential departmental recruit being invited to spend a day with departmental officers. If they were not deemed popular they would be 'blackballed'.

When [I] was at Royalty and went on leave an agreed understanding with most at the Department was that 'what happened at Royalty stayed at Royalty'. That was not restricted to investments with [me].

The way SO14 handled Page's requests for extended leave suggests further mismanagement on an epic scale. He was allowed to go on a sham parental leave request in February 2004 but managed to stay off work until his fraud collapsed three years later. Page had given all kinds of spurious reasons to continue his unpaid leave yet no one queried it. 'All kinds of strokes we pulled to get me out of there for a long period of time. My file was dropped down the back of the cupboard and I did disappear off the radar,' he said.

£ £ £

Page had certainly disappeared off the SO14 radar, but the Complaints Investigation Bureau (CIB), the Met's anti-corruption squad, had finally picked up on his activities in November 2004.

The squad was set up in 1993 to secretly examine the levels of corruption in the force following high-profile scandals, including the murder that year of Stephen Lawrence.

Anti-corruption chiefs believed there were two types of corrupt officer – the 'meat eater' and the 'grass eater' – and two types of corruption – those who were 'bent for self' and those who were 'bent for the job'. The meat eater was largely bent for self, in that he was driven by a corrupt opportunity to make a pound note. But he was also an effective policeman, a leader of men and someone who knew how to bend the rules and play the justice system not only to his advantage but also to fit up criminals when the evidence was lacking. In contrast, the grass eater was a follower who went along with corrupt practices for a pound note but also out of some sense of misguided loyalty.

In 1998, when Page moved to SO14, the Met announced to Parliament that it was launching a campaign to root out up to 250 meat eaters in its ranks.

However, by October 2004, CIB had only managed to convict a handful of corrupt officers. My book about CIB, *Untouchables*, was published that month and revealed that the squad had cherry picked its cases, ignored or protected some corrupt officers while others were unfairly crucified, and covered up corruption allegations including those involving a detective on the Stephen Lawrence murder inquiry.

In November, when concern about Page first reached anti-corruption detectives, the squad had been renamed the Directorate of Professional Standards (DPS). Within the DPS is a covert department called the Intelligence Development Group (IDG), also known as the 'Dark Side', which runs undercover officers, handles informants and sets up stings to test officers' integrity.

The IDG had received intelligence about large amounts of money moving through Page's bank accounts. Detective Sergeant Jim Wingrave, a financial investigator, was tasked to look at 'large electronic transfers from third parties and gambling transactions in respect of a Barclays Bank account held by Page'.

On 16 November, he presented an interim report to SO14. It identified nine transactions totalling £236,000 between May and July 2004 as being a 'cause for concern'. Some of these were payments to William Hill and there were two £60,000 payments to Page from a married police couple (Steven Tree and his wife) and a BAT investor (Mubasher Hussain).

The report also noted the Pages had £22,000 worth of county court judgments against them. The majority, over £18,000, was against Page's name. He had also defaulted on bank accounts, loans, credit cards, hire purchase and vehicle agreements going back to September 1997, the very time he was successfully vetted for SO14.

Wingrave's inquiries at William Hill identified three accounts, two held by Page, one by his wife, which had amassed almost £40,000 in losses. These, however, had been paid off but Wingrave was alarmed at the volume of money being gambled. He recommended that while he continued his inquiries, SO14 should conduct a risk assessment on Page's 'potential vulnerability to corrupt approaches that may seek to take advantage of his financial situation'.

SO14 had not carried out any risk assessment of Page by January 2005, when Wingrave returned with his boss, Detective Inspector Gino Lupo, to update a very senior Royal Protection officer.

In fact, by January, SO14 had, through its actions and inactions, unwittingly helped Page continue his fraud. First, that month Page was granted another six months unpaid leave without any questions asked. It looked suspiciously like some of SO14 management were glad to get him out of the palace.

Had someone followed up on Wingrave's report they would have discovered that CMC had recently won a county court judgment against Page over an unpaid £15,000 gambling debt and the spread-betting firm was placing a charge on the family home, where the mortgage was already in severe arrears.

Second, and worse still, Page had been allowed by senior Met management to register ULPD as an outside business interest in November 2003 without any oversight of the company and its dodgy director. In all likelihood, had someone from the Met done simple checks on ULPD they would have discovered that it was a ghost company and a vehicle for Page's growing fraud.

This, then, was the situation in January 2005 when Wingrave and Lupo met with the second most senior officer at SO14 after Lord Loughborough.

Chief Superintendent Peter Prentice had spent thirty-one of his thirty-nine-year police service in the Royal Protection Squad and had risen from a sergeant to chief superintendent in 1998, the same year Page joined SO14.

According to a DPS intelligence note of the meeting, Lupo carried out the briefing. He told Prentice: 'Whilst there are no criminal or discipline concerns at present, there are welfare concerns around PC Page with regards to his gambling addiction and that upon his return to Buckingham Palace from his career break he would have access to a firearm and confidential SO14 intelligence.'

Prentice says he made a note immediately after the meeting. He wrote: '[Met Police] notified of large amounts of money passing through bank account of PC Page. This would appear to be associated with his business activities in building development. The [DPS] investigation reveals considerable activity by PC Page in loans and credit applications and large amounts of money being exchanged with William Hill.'

Prentice concluded that 'in view of his financial dealings he should not serve in a unit which could bring embarrassment to MPS or leave the officer open to inappropriate approaches from outside influence or persons'.

However, Prentice was retiring in three months. He does not appear to have briefed his successor when he left on 11 April. Instead, he put his handwritten note in a brown envelope marked 'CONFIDENTIAL' and placed it in Page's SO14 file. An official later attached a yellow sticker marked 'RESTRICTED' to the brown envelope.

Remarkably, SO14 did not think it necessary to investigate Page's spread-betting and property syndicate to find out how many other SO14 officers were involved, vulnerable and needed warning that their Money God was a man of straw. Nor did anyone make any welfare visit to Page.

On 29 March 2005, DS Wingrave submitted a closing report to his bosses at the DPS. A senior anti-corruption officer signed off the investigation with the words 'There is no evidence of any wrongdoing' and recommended the file be 'put away'.

Page had already taken approximately one million pounds from police and civilian investors. Over the next two years he would take at least two million more before his fraud collapsed in a spiral of alcohol abuse, degenerate gambling and violence. One of his investors would even contemplate having him kidnapped or murdered by a hit-man.

Part II

Bust (2005–2014)

Chapter 12

Grand designs

A few days after sacking Paul Ballard, his brother-in-law builder in charge of the Essex barns site, Page got the workforce together to appoint a new foreman.

It was early April 2005 and after eighteen months the three barns were still unconverted, and the £217,000 construction budget from Mortgage Guarantee all spent. The slow progress against continual outgoings convinced Page that Ballard was fiddling things and buying cheap materials. The finance firm shared his unhappiness about progress and had already loaned an extra £120,000 to complete the works with little effect.

Page exploded at Ballard when he learned that the taxman was also now chasing him for £17,000 in unpaid employment contributions for the builders working on the barns site.

'I fucking warned you about taking the piss,' Page told his brother-in-law. 'We are so fucking behind and you are using the men to do other work.' Ballard denied fiddling the development budget, but Page sacked him anyway and stormed off with the accounts – the irony of feeling short-changed and betrayed clearly escaping him.

This was now the third serious fall-out with a member of Laura's family since 2002. First, there was the threat to shoot or beat up the husband of her sister, Christine. Then came Lisa, her twin, who was still angry at being duped over ULPD and the failure to repay money.

Addressing his workforce in front of the unfinished barns that April afternoon, Page was over £700,000 in debt to Mortgage Guarantee and had just come off the phone pleading for an extension on the repayment plan. He sacked some of the builders he believed were moonlighting for Ballard and turned to the others and said: 'You've all got to pull your weight.' Adding: 'And you, Dave, are now running the show.'

Dave Newman had only been working on the site for one month. He got on well with Page and in part shared his concern that money did not appear to have been spent on materials. Walking around the site, Newman seized the opportunity to ask him about a rumour among the workforce.

'Is it true you're a copper, Paul?'

'Yes, mate, I'm Royalty Protection at Buckingham Palace.'

Newman was impressed. He too wanted to join the force, but wondered to himself why Page was developing property and not protecting the Queen.

The new foreman had also bonded with Adam McGregor, who on occasion came to the site with a camera to show potential investors around. Newman became one of McGregor's golf partners and fitted a kitchen for Bald eagle as a thank you from Page for bringing in the new hub of Bristol-based punters.

Page had confided in McGregor about some of the problems at the barns and asked him for another £35,000 for building materials. McGregor in turn asked his older brother to take out a £19,000 bank loan. He also prevailed on his mother to give him £16,000, most of which she withdrew on her credit card at lunchtime. Her largesse was rewarded with use of a 'free' Saab courtesy of Gripper's car-hire connection in Cardiff.

The spring of 2005 also saw McGregor's brother, Robin, return from the Iraq war. The injured Royal Marine was concerned to learn from Page that Ballard had been sacked and there was a labour shortage to finish the job.

Before going to Iraq, Robin had borrowed almost £20,000 from his bank to invest in the barns. There was no contract because he trusted his brother. But Adam McGregor still hadn't told him that Page was also an avid spread better.

The marine was on sick leave when he contacted Page in April. Earlier in the year he had been evacuated back to the UK after an Iraqi special forces soldier accidentally shot him. Months of rehab had helped Robin rebuild muscle and start walking again. But his financial situation was worrying him. As well as the money invested in the barns, he and his girlfriend had also bought a house with a loan from the Marines for first-time buyers before he left for Iraq.

Page had not paid Robin any return on his initial investment but had the front to ask for a £3000 loan for one week for which he offered to pay £500. Robin understandably thought it was in his interest to help complete the barns and borrowed the money with ease on his credit card. Page did pay the return on time, but then asked for a further £1000. Again, Robin obliged, but this time Page didn't pay.

By summer, Robin was feeling fitter and offered to work for free at the barns doing some plumbing, his job before becoming a marine. Within days of being on site Robin was very concerned for his family's huge investment, now standing at almost £250,000.

'The operation is a farce,' he told his brother and Page.

The discovery alarmed Robin further because before he went to war he had introduced fellow marine Lee Howarth to Page. Howarth then brought in his father and sister, who were prison officers.

Page was offering 60 per cent returns on a two-month investment. The Howarth family ended up investing £22,000 in 2005, all transferred to Laura's bank account.

Lee Howarth's younger sister had just bought a house so she was able to borrow more money from her bank to invest in the barns. But when the return wasn't paid she had to borrow from her family to pay back the second loan.[1]

£ £ £

Jimmy's officer Mark Copley had moved his wife and two young children into one of the unfinished barns in November 2004. It was at the same time that the anti-corruption squad had started investigating Page's financial activities. But no one from the squad came to warn Copley before effectively shelving the financial inquiry in March 2005.

By summer, the Copleys had decided they definitely wanted to buy Barn C, despite concerns about the quality and safety of the work, in particular the kitchen wiring.

Scarborough Building Society had valued their barn at £315,000. In conversation with their solicitor, the couple tried to explain the unusual financial arrangement they had struck with Page around the purchase. On 3 August, the solicitor wrote expressing concern that the Copleys had already paid a £155,000 deposit directly to Page and said he would have to refer the matter to the building society, which was offering them a £160,000 mortgage. In the same letter the solicitor asked for details of how and when the deposit had been paid.

It was a very unorthodox transaction. The Copleys had paid cheques into the bank accounts of Laura and her brother-in-law, Paul Ballard, the recently sacked builder, rather than to ULPD. When the solicitor heard this he warned the couple they had 'no legal protection' and the so-called contract, which wasn't drafted by lawyers, could be worthless.

Matters escalated when Scarborough's money-laundering compliance officer phoned Mark Copley expressing concern about discrepancies in the figures supplied. There was a suspicion that the size of the deposit paid to Page had been inflated by £45,000.

It hadn't, but Copley put down the phone and composed an extraordinary letter to Page. The money-laundering compliance officer, he wrote, wanted 'details of the amounts we moved to you, when and the account numbers [and] the contract details. I think they suspect that we are using dirty money as part of the cost of the barn and the "extra" £45,000 is dirty and you are laundering it into the deal.'

Copley then asked if they should give Scarborough copies of the contracts for the £155,000 deposit or whether Page wanted them 'changed at all, or backdated'. In a further extraordinary paragraph, Copley wrote that the two policemen needed to 'tell the same story' to the banks and authorities if it was Page's intention to put £45,000 from another deal through the barns one.

Page was already stalling the Copleys over selling them the barn. He didn't address the letter but played for time, as ever, while trying to get the other two barns finished for sale so he could pay Mortgage Guarantee and some of his favoured investors.

The Copleys remained on side for the rest of the year. In fact, Mark Copley was an enthusiastic advocate of the project to other officers from Jimmy's.

Richard Humby had only been at the palace for a few years. He had come there from the river police and before that had been at an unremarkable south London police station.

Richard and his wife Beatrice were enthusiastic players of the property market with several buy-to-let flats in the Kent area.

He recalled receiving reassurance from Copley in early 2005 that the Essex barns were the real deal. Humby said it gave him the confidence to sign an initial contract with Page that was witnessed by their Jimmy's colleague, Surinder 'the Turbanator' Mudhar.

Humby put in £20,000 for six months with a 30 per cent return and £15,000 over one month at 15 per cent. Although an experienced buy-to-let developer, he did not find these types of returns on property to be too good to be true. Page, he claimed, had assured him the returns would be paid from ULPD's rental income on the properties it owned and 'other bits and pieces'.

Humby steadfastly maintains that he never knew spread betting was behind these high returns. However, he did no due diligence to see if ULPD owned any properties, which it didn't, nor did he visit the barns before releasing the money. He was also happy to transfer the £35,000 to Laura's NatWest Clippers account and Fahim Baree's Halifax account, who then transferred £12,750 of it to CMC, although there is no evidence that Humby knew this.

Soon after paying returns on these initial two investments, in April Page arranged to come to the Humbys' home to pitch a new development opportunity in Esher, Surrey. It was the same one he had talked to Mahaffy and Mudhar about the previous year. One of the selling points Page used was to claim that the property was sought after by a Chelsea football player and others, such as Ashley Cole, lived nearby.

In the Humbys' kitchen, Page produced a ULPD brochure featuring the Surrey property, Meadway, as a 'magnificent 6000 sq ft residence set in one of Esher's most sought after private roads'. He spoke confidently of plans to develop the property into a six-bedroom cottage called Ivy House.

'When it's finished, Dick, ULPD will be able to sell it for £3.25 million. This will leave a net profit after capital gains tax of £771,000,' he said.

The Humbys didn't take long to bite and invest £100,000 without visiting the Meadway site. Humby relied on the word of another police officer who went there and told him, 'I don't know how Paul does it, it's a great site, there's a crappy bungalow to be pulled down, the site is big and looking at the rest of the houses down the road they must cost millions'.

The truth was the owners of Meadway had recently, in principle, accepted Page's upped offer of £1.3 million but no finance company would give him a mortgage so a few months later they pulled out.

The Humbys were promised a 40 per cent return on the £100,000 investment over a year. No solicitors were involved and the money was once again transferred into the bank accounts of Fahim Baree and Laura.[2]

It hit their accounts a few days after the Windsor wedding of Prince Charles to Camilla Parker Bowles on 9 April.

£ £ £

Key investor James Mahaffy, from Jimmy's, seemed to be curbing his enthusiasm for Page by the beginning of 2005. It wasn't that the cash returns on his £125,000 investment weren't coming his way. Far from it. Brown envelopes had been frequently trousered in the almost three years he had been involved with

Page's spread betting and property syndicate.

But when he asked for all his money back in January, Page was momentarily floored. 'Fucking MAPS,' he cursed under his breath. Mahaffy's nickname, short for 'my armpits stink', was not one he used to the face of such a major investor and introducer.

Page pulled up £15,000 in cash, no doubt from some hapless new investor, and promised Mahaffy another £30,000 would be transferred to his bank account by the time he returned from a holiday in the Maldives.

It wasn't, and Mahaffy called to complain when he got home. Page mollified him with another £15,000 cash envelope. It was enough for him to feel he could ring up Mahaffy on 1 April, the day he sacked Ballard, to ask for more money.

'I'm in the shit, Jim,' Page levelled with the sun-tanned Royal Protection officer. 'I need money to pay building bills on the barns.'

Mahaffy relented and gave him another £20,000 in cash. It was the last money he invested.

The next month, Mahaffy's world fell apart when Wendy, his wife, became very ill. He thought she might die. Sitting by her hospital bed, Mahaffy took a call from Page offering a new investment opportunity, a flat for Mahaffy's son. He declined because all his efforts were on his wife's recovery.

Wendy did get better over the summer and Mahaffy promised to get the rest of their investment back. However, Page was elusive and full of excuses. Mahaffy sent emails telling Page how 'very pissed off' he was getting, but curiously signed off one angry email 'Jim x'.

Page was moved enough to give Mahaffy another £5000 and offered to fit an expensive kitchen for 'free'.

'Why don't you just give him the fucking money,' Laura shouted at her husband when he told her that the Mahaffys had accepted the kitchen offer.

'They've been on the look-out for a new kitchen and I need to get MAPS off my back. I don't have all his fucking money.'

Laura cared because it was her best friend's husband who was going to fit the kitchen.

Like 'Gripper Cars' and 'Gripper Airways', 'Gripper Kitchens' had the desired effect of stopping Mahaffy from pulling out in 2005. Yet despite his reservations since January about Page's schemes, Mahaffy continued to act as an introducer. Three new Jimmy's officers invested over £190,000 following Mahaffy's advocacy.[3]

Gerry McCallion had only been in SO14 for a few months when he first heard about Gripper. In January 2005, Mahaffy told him that Page was looking for new investors and introduced them when the Range Rover rolled in to deliver brown envelopes. McCallion and Page spoke briefly at Stable Yard, where the changing of the guard takes place. Page said he would visit him at home.

On 27 January, Page arrived in his Range Rover with a Louis Vuitton briefcase full of architect plans for the Meadway development in Esher, Surrey and sales material for various properties in Stratford, east London.

'I'm looking ahead of the Olympic bid,' he told McCallion pointing at the Stratford bumph. The location for the 2012 Olympics was due to be announced on 6 July. 'So if we get it, I'm quids in with all the properties I've bought in Stratford. In any case, with the property market the way it is I can still sell them for a profit.'

Of course, Page and ULPD didn't have any other properties other than the heavily mortgaged and financially troubled barns development. But McCallion didn't know that when he agreed to invest £30,000 for one year at 25 per cent.

Page explained he would have to transfer the money to his wife's Clippers bank account. McCallion was unaware that Clippers had gone bust, but he was one of the few policemen to ask why his money was not going to ULPD.

'It will speed up the transfer and won't flash up with the bank. I use Laura's hairdressing business account to spread out the amount of money I'm dealing with,' Page replied. 'We've got a bank manager on board,' he added for effect. 'He's part of the set-up.'

Throughout the sales pitch, Page's mobiles were constantly ringing. McCallion noticed that sometimes he would check the number and ignore it or answer and promise to call back.

'If you come on board, mate, you'll get holidays as a reward. My friend from school is sorting that out,' Page continued. 'I personally will deal with my police investors as family. Others will deal with outside investors.'

McCallion bit and joined the high-yield family, investing a total of £68,000 in 2005. The chatter about the returns, cash bonuses, holidays and kitchens was enough to lure McCallion's girlfriend, a physiotherapist, to also invest £50,000 for three months at 20 per cent. The money came from selling her house.[4]

McCallion's contract was signed and witnessed by another new colleague from Jimmy's who Mahaffy had also introduced to Page during one of his visits to the palace.

Duane Williams recalled Mahaffy telling him that his relationship with Page was good. There was no mention that MAPS was thinking of asking for all his money back.

When they met, Page lied to Williams that he was able to offer such high returns because he was going to make a large profit on the barns. 'At that time there was a lot of property programmes on the television encouraging people to venture into the property development world and what he was telling me seemed plausible,' Williams explained. 'The investments made sense to me at that time when house prices were going up and people were making money on property'.

Williams declined the safe investment option of a 15 per cent return once the barns development was completed in favour of an unsecured 20 per cent return paid quarterly. He thought such returns were not unbelievable because in 2005 the TV schedules were full of programmes such as *Under the Hammer, Location, Location, Location* and *Moving Abroad*. The media, he said, were pushing up house prices.

Like others, no legal advice was sought before investing and no visit was made to any site. As with Humby, Williams said he relied on the word of other Royal Protection officers.

Over several months in 2005, Duane Williams transferred £35,000 to Clippers, Fahim Baree, Anjam Khan and a Bristol investor's bank account. Only one small payment went to ULPD. He also gave Page some cash. Some of the money came from his daughter's account. Some was borrowed as a car loan from the bank.[5]

Finally, there was Phil Williams, a veteran of Jimmy's since 1994. To him, Page was a good laugh and a bit of a wide boy, which explained his nickname 'Gripper', a police officer who Williams thought had once gripped the rail – stood trial – for an unknown offence.

In January 2005, Williams had a pile of cash to invest after selling his house and moving in with new wife Linda Jolly, a financial analyst. She loved property programmes, especially *Grand Designs*, the reality show that film couples developing a dream home in a unique style.

Later that month, Williams was on duty when he spotted Page parking his Range Rover at St James's Palace. Gripper was delivering a cash return to an officer but stopped to whet Williams's appetite about Meadway, the Esher bungalow development he pretended to own.

'There's going to be a state-of-the-art gym, swimming pool, tennis court and security gates to keep out the riff raff,' Page enthused.

Williams later got a brochure from Mahaffy, which he took home to discuss with his wife. It was exactly the sort of development they were looking to get involved with and invested £10,000 for six months for a 25 per cent return.

Every so often, Williams would see Page at the palaces and ask him how the grand design was going. He came to learn that Gripper had a catchphrase: 'Things are going good.'

After six months and not a return in sight, Page was still able to persuade Williams and his wife to invest another £28,500 for one year at 30 per cent paid quarterly. This time the contract declared that the money would be invested in ULPD, the property company with no viable property, no accounts and no funds.[6]

£ £ £

Laura was strapping four-year-old Samuel into the Range Rover when one of the mothers from the local playgroup approached her with some good news. The two women shared a love of clothes and an opportunity had come up to indulge their passion for haute couture.

'A friend of my husband is willing to lease us his shop in Grays with no deposit or rent for the first few months while our boutique finds its feet,' she told Laura.

A week later, in early August 2005, they took the shop and

went on a spending spree to decorate and buy stock. A candy-floss sign in gold went up outside announcing the imminent arrival of Wicked Wardrobe.

Laura splashed out £90 per roll of gold and pink wallpaper, £1000 on an antique wardrobe, a burgundy chaise long with gold painted wood and hangers made of crystal beads to match the crystal chandelier. Her favoured clothing suppliers were Love Sex Money and Coronets and Queens.

Page had voiced his reservations about Wicked Wardrobe's location – Grays was hardly an up and coming part of Essex where genuine Versace, Prada and Armani was flying off the rails. He was also doubtful of his wife's business head, which was a bit rich for a man so deluded about his own financial acumen.

That said, Page knew his wife needed a project of her own, beyond their five boys and running his errands. Even he could see their relationship was under great strain. She was reluctantly more involved in ULPD business as sole signature for the company's NatWest account and Page was sending her to various M25 service stations to drop off cash when he was too busy or avoiding his clients.

Laura got to know many police and civilian members of the syndicate and resented most of them. They got the money in brown envelopes while she had to put up with an absent husband or one who might as well have been because he was so obsessed with gambling while at home. 'I was growing to hate the TV being on all day and that music for CNBC or Bloomberg,' she told me.

For the first time, her husband was starting to appear desperate and pathetic to her. When he lost, which was often, he would become depressed and ask if her mum could lend him some cash. Laura had even taken to hiding money in a handbag in the wardrobe, until Page found it one day and without any sense of irony called her 'a devious little cow'.

He had begged her to open two accounts with bookies William Hill because his were too much in debt.

'No. You're not getting me into more shit,' she told him.

'Go on, love. You've got to,' he pleaded.

She relented, he set it up and Laura got to choose the password – Vogues. To keep her happy, Page part-funded Laura's Wicked Wardrobe dream to be in the fashion game. He knew his wife had a history of bad credit and spending more than she earned. In fact, a debt collector was chasing an old online shopping bill and court costs while the couple set up the new boutique. Yet despite the strains on their relationship, they were emotionally dependent on each other and still bonded by family, loyalty and love. They had 'gelled' from the moment they met, Laura told me. And as the relationship grew, she realized that her jealousy was an anxiety that Page would go off with another woman, when in fact he had no wandering eye and was very protective of anyone disrespecting their bond.

She still liked goading him into proving his love and he liked to beat his chest for her. One incident they relished telling testifies to their crazy love.

Laura adored her Range Rover. Page teased that she had 'pimped her ride' by adding chrome wing mirrors, a chrome footwell and a chrome strip down the side.

One sunny afternoon on the way back from Wicked Wardrobe, Laura was talking on her phone as she drove round a Lakeside roundabout. One of the council workers on the island shouted at her: 'Get off your phone, fucking cunt!' Laura was incensed, stopped next to the island, wound down her window and asked him calmly: 'Who you calling a cunt?'

'Get off the phone!' said the worker, standing his ground.

'Fuck off Elvis! Laura replied having noticed his big black glasses and quiff. With that she drove home.

Page sensed something was up when his wife walked in. 'What's the matter, love?' He asked.

'Someone called me a cunt.'

'Where?'

Page jumped into his car with red mist in his eyes. He scanned for the Elvis lookalike as he approached the roundabout. Easing his car into a lower gear, Page drove onto the island, through the flowerbeds and stopped.

'Who called my wife a cunt?' Page asked of the council workers. This was no time for solidarity and Elvis was soon pointed out.

'I'm sorry,' murmured the King.

Page persuaded him that his next best move was to get on the phone and apologize to his wife. He dialled the number and handed Elvis the phone. Apology delivered, Page reversed over the flowerbeds on his way home.

£ £ £

Wicked Wardrobe opened in August 2005. It was around the time that Page had gone to Royal Protection officer Richard Humby's house to explain 'his system' for making money.

'Because the property side is doing so well, Dick, I'm going to dedicate my time to the financial markets. Let me show you how it works,' Page offered.

Humby was intrigued and switched the TV over to Teletext. Page explained how he hedged his bets by going long and short in the financial markets.

'Take oil and other commodities. I've got a broker and we

have triggers in place to prevent losses.'

This self-portrait of well-informed, measured gambling with a broker angel watching over his shoulder to ensure the sweet smell of success did not go to his head was as far from the truth as Page could get. He was, in fact, so desperate for money in the summer of 2005 that he'd even applied to return to SO14.[7]

'[I needed] to get back into the markets and make some big money quick, which went wrong,' he told me.

'How wrong?' I asked.

Page explained that he had access to three or four online casinos in which he lost £100,000 of ULPD money. Some of it was learning a new roulette technique. 'I was taking the piss,' he said. And how.

An analysis of his betting record just days after giving Humby the masterclass gives a frightening picture of what a sad, degenerate gambler on a massive losing streak Page had become.

A sleepless Sunday morning on 14 August saw Page, frozen in front of his laptop screen, staring at a virtual pack of cards. It was 1.21 am and time for a game of Internet poker. Betting in multiple currencies, he lost $3000 in two hours. At 3.13 am Page emptied his account and bought chips worth $10,250. Further losing hands over the next thirty minutes left him $3500 down. But the award of a £10 bonus from the online poker company brought him back to the table for a final losing bet before he joined Laura in bed at 3.49 am.

After a few hours' sleep, Page was up for the Sunday afternoon premiership clash between Arsenal and Newcastle. Thierry Henry was making his first appearance as captain of the north London side. The bookies were offering 5–2 on Arsenal. Page bet the balance of his account, £5414. He won £2165 with ten minutes to spare before the Chelsea v Wigan kick-off. He bet the lot on the London team, and won again.

Feeling his luck had changed, Page waited for the boys to go to sleep before returning at 11.21 pm to the online poker table with $1000 in chips. It hadn't. He lost a few small hands and decided to buy more chips, this time in sterling. Further hands were lost but at least he was only a few hundred pounds down by 1.32 am. A £10 bonus kept him at the table and he decided to buy $16,600 worth of chips with the remaining balance of his account. He lost a few more hands before switching back to sterling chips. The currency may have changed but not his luck. He'd lost just under £1000.

At 1.57 am, Page decided to bet on US basketball. He hedged bets on two games and lost £2801. Time to quit and go to bed.

However, he hardly had time to digest his Monday morning breakfast before he was back at the poker table. By midday he'd lost $1000. By 3 pm he had lost the £3200. But a £1000 injection from his Solo debit card and Page was back betting, only this time on cricket. He backed England to beat Australia. They didn't, leaving £7 in the pot.

After a few hours off, at 8.03 pm Page transferred £2000 from his Solo card to his online betting account and treated himself to a long poker session. But by 2.40 am on Tuesday 16 August he was potless.

Page's gambling with other people's money was not that much different from some investment bank traders and hedge-fund managers in the financial casinos of Wall Street and the City. The first round of losses is hidden on the justification that the positions will be recovered the following month. When they are not, the deceit gets bigger until eventually the losses are so great and the lie so embedded that there is no way back, only a gambler's delusion that it could all be put right with the throw of the dice. 'I'm in so deep, what have I got to lose,' they tell themselves.

The hope that the position can be quickly recovered is not illusionary, but rare. A 26-year-old Morgan Stanley commodities dealer returned well lubricated from a three-hour lunch and racked up a $10 million debt over ninety minutes, which he then hid. Luckily, he managed to recover the position the next day with his bosses none the wiser.

More common in these times was the activities of a small group of traders at Swiss Bank UBS who, for several years and without authority, had gambled tens of millions of pounds of clients' money on foreign currencies and precious metals, then hid the losses. The scam was not picked up internally or by the asleep-at-the-wheel watchdog.

On 12 September 2005, Mortgage Guarantee wrote to the Pages warning of a 'serious overspend on the [barns] project which together with the overrun on time is causing great concern'.

The finance company had no idea how much worse Page's grand design was about to get.

Chapter 13

Winter of discontent

'I want you to follow the dough back into London,' Page told Adam McGregor.

It was Sunday 16 October 2005 and the two men were waiting for the representative of a major civilian investor in a retail car park in Beckton, a regenerated part of east London's docklands.

McGregor had recently transferred out of SO14 and was back on the beat at nearby Dagenham police station. Although no longer in Royalty Protection he was still a key lieutenant in the syndicate. In that role, Page had asked him to provide police protection for a large sum of money that was too big for one brown envelope. The cash was for Rahul Sharma, the co-owner of BestAtTravel (BAT).

Anjam Khan, Sharma's employee and agent in the transaction, was expected any minute. His boss was waiting in his central London office for the money. The police escort was Page's idea to impress the multi-millionaire.

McGregor was on duty in a marked police BMW with a colleague. Page had parked his leased Porsche convertible next to them. In a carrier bag on the front seat was £35,000.

Khan, a small overweight 40-year-old with big tinted glasses that covered most of his face, arrived in a new BMW X5 jeep. He alighted to greet Page and then McGregor, whom he knew.

'Here's the dough for Rahul,' Page said, handing over the thick package. 'Adam is going to escort you as far as the Limehouse tunnel.' Khan felt comfortable with the idea. McGregor had recently driven him to pick up his X5.

The three men got into their cars. Page turned right onto the A13 back to Chafford Hundred. Khan and his police escort turned left towards London. Within minutes the police convoy was in the shadow of Canary Wharf. McGregor flashed his lights as he turned off at the entrance to the tunnel. Khan continued under the Thames emerging on the approach road to the Tower of London and central London.

On his arrival at BAT in Whitfield Street, Khan handed Sharma the cash and watched his boss deposit it with great relief in the company safe.

£ £ £

The tsunami on Boxing Day 2004 started as a massive subsea earthquake in the Indian Ocean and ended up wiping out fishing villages and exclusive holiday resorts along the coast of Indonesia, Sri Lanka and Thailand, killing over 200,000 people in its wake and destroying the livelihoods of many more.

The natural disaster also had a financial effect on the UK travel industry. Companies such as BAT took a hit in cancellations, which caused a cash-flow shortfall that Sharma estimated was around £100,000. He and his wife Rita, the boss of the

162

company, were in India over that Christmas, which was also affected by the tsunami.

Rahul Sharma had quietly watched Anjam Khan and Page's best friend, Fahim Baree, talk up ULPD to his staff and their friends. By October 2005, almost £500,000 had been invested and large cash returns delivered to the circle of British Asian investors and financial advisers linked to his two employees

As the first anniversary of the tsunami approached, Sharma confided in Khan that the business was still suffering a cash-flow shortfall. He discussed investing in Page's scheme and was attracted by the prospect of quick and high returns. Days after his forty-seventh birthday on 2 October, Sharma told Khan and Baree they were to be his agents in a large short-term investment he was going to make using company funds.

Page had always wanted to bag the Sharmas as major investors in his syndicate. He believed that Rahul Sharma really didn't care if he was getting returns from dog racing or property, as long as he got them.

£50,000 was transferred on 7 October from BAT's NatWest account to ULPD. Sharma was expecting a 20 per cent return in one month. But the financial director asked for no security, never visited the site, nor did he talk to Page before releasing the company funds.

Sharma continued to think there was nothing funny when Khan delivered £11,000 in cash just twenty-four hours after his initial investment. The BAT director did what Page had hoped and five days later transferred another £110,000 from the company account.

While Page was feeling good about bagging such a big mark, Sharma was having a major wobble. 'I didn't really know what we were getting [into],' he explained later. However, he knew enough to know that he had gambled the company's money without telling his wife.

A distressed Sharma told Khan and Baree they had to get the money back. Page was annoyed at the news, but was willing to play the long game. He transferred £70,000 back to the BAT account and found £35,000 in cash. This was the money he arranged for McGregor to escort in a police car from Beckton to the Limehouse tunnel on 16 October.

The long game worked. Three days later, Sharma changed his mind again and reinvested £100,000. On the bank transfer form he put 'cash for trading'.

A few weeks later, Page gave Khan another huge cash return for his boss, this time £25,000. With the risky investment going so well, Sharma now felt compelled to tell his wife about the golden goose that could help get them out of their financial problems.

Unfortunately, Rita Sharma didn't see it that way. She was furious with her husband. The more she learned about the unsecured investment, who Page was and the police escort he had provided, the more concerned and angry she became with Rahul. Had her husband done any due diligence before investing he would more than likely have discovered the CMC charge on Page's house, the huge mortgage on the barns, the overspend on its development and poor quality of the conversion.

In no uncertain terms, Rita told her husband to get all the money back. Rahul put it more diplomatically during Page's trial when he said: 'My wife and I were both under pressure, it was company money.'

Rita was also annoyed at the involvement of Page with five of her employees. Most of them Khan and Baree had introduced. One, Jitendra Mandalia, thought investing in the barns was 'money for nothing.' He was offered a ridiculous return of £6000 in two weeks on a £10,000 investment. Although he felt it was all 'too good to be true', he nevertheless transferred the money to ULPD from the joint account he had with his wife.

Dharamendra Patel was a different story. He felt encouraged to invest within days of learning on the office grapevine that his 'clued on' boss had put in a six-figure sum. Patel invested £30,000 by bank transfer to ULPD. He said he put 'cash loan' on the bank transfer form on Baree's advice.

Shit, they say, tends to roll downhill, and after the dressing down from his wife, Sharma made it very clear to Khan and Baree how important it was to him, and them, that Rita got her money back.

Page realized the long game had failed, so he reverted to type and lied. He told Khan that his boss's money was waiting for him at Wicked Wardrobe. When he went to pick it up on 14 November Laura wrote out a cheque for £104,000. Khan noticed that it was signed by Laura's mum and drawn on her bank account not ULPD's. Given the general unorthodox nature of how money moved around the syndicate, Khan made no issue of it and left for the office with the cheque.

Days later, Sharma went ballistic when it bounced. 'Get Page on the phone now,' he ordered Khan, who dialled the number and passed his boss the phone. Page was not scared of Sharma and gave him a ready excuse with a promise that the cheque would be honoured if presented once more. As a sweetener, the next day, 18 November, he also gave Sharma £10,000 in cash.

The cheque bounced on.

£ £ £

The BAT sales manager, Anjam Khan, was not just a bagman for his boss, Rahul Sharma. He was also a key investor in Page's syndicate.

Khan had initially resisted Baree's attempt in 2003 to get him to invest with his cop family friend. He was Baree's boss and earned £4000 per month plus commission from flight sales. All his money, he told Baree, was tied up developing his own Essex home with swimming pool.

Baree mentioned ULPD again in 2005 and Khan met Page at a café in Lakeside to hear the sales pitch and review the ULPD brochure that Fahim had helped draft. He walked away from the meeting thinking the policeman was 'convincing', the money easy and that he would invest heavily. 'I didn't question it. I thought it was easy money. I didn't give a toss,' he said. Between April and October 2005, Khan put in £115,000 of his own money, £40,000 from his two brothers and another £45,000 from a friend.

His first two short-term investments of £30,000 at 25 per cent were transferred to Baree's account, who put it into the CMC account he had set up for Page. Khan said he was unaware of this.

Given the proximity of the two Asians, it seems almost inconceivable that they did not know that spread betting and the barns were inextricably linked.

Khan started to deal directly with Page and received £40,000 in returns by July, although a cheque for that amount had initially bounced. It didn't stop him from investing £50,000 in August by transfer to ULPD, for which he was expecting a whopping 44 per cent return by the end of the month.

The return didn't appear, but Page renegotiated the terms promising Khan that if he rolled over the money until Christmas he would double it.

In the meantime, Khan took a Dubai-based friend, Sanjay Luthra, to meet the Royal Protection officer at the barns. Luthra thought it all looked 'very nice' and agreed to invest £45,000 in

September to help complete the conversion. The investment was short term, again with a promised huge return of £12,500.

Three days after Luthra had invested, Khan invited his older brother over to meet Page and Baree. Saeed Khan was an estate agent doing well in the housing bubble. Anjam talked up the barns investment and Baree guaranteed that if anything went wrong he, personally, would pay back Saeed from his own money.

Saeed was still sceptical but his brother, Baree and another BAT investor followed up the meeting with a call pointing out they were all making money. Saeed felt pressured to invest but eventually transferred £20,000 to ULPD, almost half of which was raised as a loan on his Egg credit card. He never went to the barns.

Khan's other brother, Pervez, also invested £20,000 a few days later and brought in his wife's uncle. Retiree John Ayling was worried about investing his pension money. In his witness statement he recalled how in October 2005 Pervez and Anjam Khan had asked by phone for £25,000 to buy some land and promised him £1500 back in six weeks when it was sold.

Ayling claimed in the same statement that during the phone call he was also told that 'police officers and judges had already invested'. Certainly the police had but not the judiciary. The next day, he transferred the money to ULPD. However, by the onset of winter 2005 the Khan brothers were getting increasingly anxious about their investments. Anjam felt Page's syndicate may be going 'belly up'. When he eventually managed to contact him to complain about the lack of returns, Page told a big lie. He claimed to have £600,000 credit in a CMC account, which the spread-betting company had frozen over a misunderstanding. In truth he owed CMC money.

£ £ £

Fahim Baree was the only investor on the inside at both BAT and ULPD. How much he shared with others is open to question. However, his own financial folly inescapably came home on 4 November 2005 when a letter from CMC arrived at Baree's house saying his spread-betting account was now almost £38,000 in deficit.

Baree had opened the CMC account for Page thirteen months earlier. He regularly received emailed statements showing Page's trading activity and notification that the gambling debt was unpaid. But he said he didn't pay any attention because Page insisted it would be reversed with his next win.

The November letter, however, was different because for the first time it threatened legal action against Baree if the balance wasn't cleared in seven days. Page agreed to cover the CMC debt. But Baree wanted more than his word. He had seen how Page operated with other investors. Ringing in his ears was his best friend's favourite phrase when investors got angry, which was getting more frequent. 'Change their nappies. Make sure they are all fresh for tomorrow. I'll deal with them.'

But of course Page never did, leaving Baree to take increasing flack, especially from his BAT colleagues and now from his boss Rahul Sharma as well.

While Baree never dreamed Page would shaft him, he wanted to make sure there was something in writing indemnifying him from the CMC debt. Page provided an undated letter to that effect, which wasn't worth the paper it was handwritten on. Baree told me he had no idea until much later that the barns had been bought with a huge mortgage. Up until this point he believed the Pages had bought the barns outright and then borrowed £250,000 against it to fund the conversion.

Baree had earned some returns and commissions but his initial stake was still in the syndicate by November. He said:

Ultimately I was waiting for mine like all the people who'd put in thirty thousand. Ultimately their dividends were coming at the end of the year, or quarterly or [Page would] say, 'Look, if I don't pay you this dividend just roll it over'. So it would be rolling over with some who never got anything. I got something out of it, which I gave back in two months. There was some very happy people, very happy people. For a period of time they would think the sun was smiling out of Paul's mouth. He couldn't do a thing wrong.

But by the winter of 2005 that time had long passed.

£ £ £

Laura Page was very surprised to hear such a distressed voice on the end of the line when she answered the home phone that day in early November.

'Is that Laura?' enquired the sobbing female caller.

'Yes. Who's this?' she responded.

'It's Beatrice Humby, Richard's wife.'

The Humbys had invested £180,000 in Page's syndicate since January. They'd done so without proper due diligence, not even a site visit or the involvement of lawyers. Richard Humby, an officer at Jimmy's, had simply piled in on the recommendation of his colleague Mark Copley and Page's promise of an incredible 40 per cent return by the end of 2005.

The couple had a small buy-to-let empire of properties on the south coast but were getting concerned about the lack of return from their substantial ULPD investment. Page had been ducking

Humby's texts and calls since September. When he did respond, invariably it would be with a short text playing on the death of a relative, his great uncle, or some exotic medical condition.

Humby had sent a condolence card and was still willing to give his fellow SO14 officer some leeway. But his wife, who was not bonded by the brotherhood of policing, had other ideas. Beatrice had lost all patience with Page and also over one stone in weight from the stress of feeling he was conning them.

When she rang Laura in early November, Beatrice was sitting in her car. Through the tears, she explained how the situation with Page now meant she was taking anti-depressants.

After mollifying Beatrice, Laura rang her husband convinced that the woman on the end of the phone was suicidal; although Beatrice would later claim that she was laying it on thick to gain sympathy and get their money back.

'I've just had that Beatrice Humby on the phone, Paul. She's told me she's drunk a bottle of wine and is going to drive into a wall.'

'For fuck's sake! I don't think Dick's told her the full fucking story. I'll ring him right away, love.'

Humby agreed the three of them should meet in south-east London to straighten out the situation. A few days later, Page arrived in his Porsche. He came with what he hoped was a reassuring lie that their money was safe with ULPD and some bank statements as props to falsely reinforce it.

Page admits he went there to deceive. But he maintains that Humby was also 'in the shit' with his wife for investing money without her knowledge. The couple flatly deny this.

In any event, Beatrice was not buying Page's spiel. She listened as he tried to seek her sympathy about his own personal problems and why he never picked up the phone.

'If I'm honest, me and Laura are also going through a bit of a difficult patch,' he said. 'And like I told Dick before, it didn't help when I had that spider's hair in me eye.'

Page did keep tarantulas at home, but Laura was still the scariest thing in Hatton Close. One day, during feeding time, he'd managed to infect his eye with one of the spider's hairs. He was certainly in need of hospital treatment but it was taking it too far to claim this was why he had ducked so many of Humby's calls.

Beatrice had heard enough. She was feeling sick just listening to the lies and excuses.

'I don't believe any of this,' she shouted at Page. 'You know what you are?'

'No. What am I?' Page fired back, realizing the game was up.

'You're a bent cop.'

If this had been a karate match, Beatrice Humby's words were a knockout blow. Page was floored but seething with rage. There are very few things that strike at the heart of a police officer's psyche than being called corrupt, especially by another officer's wife.

'A tax dodger, yes. But a fucking bent cop? You cunt,' he thought to himself as he gathered up his bank documents. Beatrice watched with some satisfaction as Page screeched off in the Porsche.

When he got home, Page told Laura about the meeting. 'How dare she fucking accuse me of being bent?' he exploded. In Page's polluted mind, his actions may have amounted to sharp financial practice but not criminality and certainly not police corruption. A bent cop is one who sells out the force or his colleagues to criminals for a pound note, he believed.

Laura shared her husband's outrage, but for different reasons. The Humbys had been on a free trip to Bruges by Eurostar and received returns, like all the other greedy whingers. They knew what they were getting into, she thought.

That night, Laura rang Beatrice and expressed in the least diplomatic way she knew how that she was never again to speak to her husband like that. Beatrice shot back that Page had sworn at her and been threatening.

But Laura wasn't buying it. As she later explained to me, 'He don't talk to women, because if he did I'd stab her and him. You know what I'm like!'

Beatrice Humby was not going to be intimidated. For a few days after the meeting it seemed that the wives had taken over what the husbands had started. Beatrice would sometimes call Wicked Wardrobe and put the phone down or have her say.

'Are you going to back up your husband's claims, then?' she asked during one call.

'You rude bitch,' Laura replied then hung up.

The Humbys were determined to find out what had happened to their money and hatched a plan based on a less confrontational strategy.

On the morning of 7 November, the couple drove to the Pages' house. Beatrice had a tape recorder in her handbag. The plan was that she would go in first while her husband parked the car.

When the bell rang, Laura looked out of the bedroom window to see a forlorn Beatrice outside. As soon as she opened the front door, her unwanted guest burst into tears. Laura, still in her nightdress, gently ushered Beatrice into the sitting room. Both women were surprised at each other's appearance.

'You look quite younger than I expected,' Beatrice said with tears streaming down her unmade face.

'You look like you've lost weight,' replied Laura in a sympathetic tone.

'Is your husband in?

'No, he's out.'

'I need to know what has happened to our money,' said Beatrice, clutching her handbag and a tissue.

'You should take that up with your husband,' replied Laura with a little more steel in her voice, but not enough to appear abrupt or rude.

At that moment, Richard Humby walked into the sitting room. Laura felt his manner was cocky and didn't take to being asked to put the kettle on.

The three of them sat drinking tea. Beatrice did most of the talking and felt Laura was being sincere when she promised to do what she could to get some of their money back.

'I know how you feel. I will sort it out for you. I'll get the money back, half of it before Christmas. I can't promise the whole amount. I would rather just pay everybody off.'

'I don't mean to be rude but can we have that in writing please?' Beatrice asked.

'I'll ask Paul when he gets back,' Laura promised just as the phone rang again. 'It doesn't stop. I'm sorry. I've got to get that. It's probably for him. He's so busy at the moment.'

When Laura returned she confirmed it was her husband on the phone.

'I tell Paul, "Don't offer holidays just pay people their money". I take the brunt of the phone calls. I don't have a problem with people turning up at the house but I do have a problem when people are rude to me. I have my own business now, which is going well.'

The Humbys had wrung all they could out of the encounter and left shortly. The secret tape recording did not yield any incriminating admissions or clues, just an earnest agreement by Laura to help.

At 10 pm that evening, Beatrice received an email with Page's repayment plan. It promised £50,000 on 30 November and

173

£67,000 in January. The Humbys were told they had already had £43,000.

Beatrice immediately pinged back an email disputing the figures. Her husband read the exchange with deepening concern. He later said this was the moment he knew he and his wife were 'in a lot of trouble'.

At the end of November, Page met Humby in a motorway service station with the first instalment. The £13,000 cheque was well short of what the email had promised and was drawn on the bank account of Laura's mum.

When it bounced, Page told Humby it was because his affairs were now under investigation by the Inland Revenue and the taxman had frozen his bank accounts.

It was a variation on a theme of false excuses he had been developing over the winter. Other police investors were told that monies he had invested with Baree in Dubai were also frozen because of new banking vigilance around terrorist financing of UK-based jihadists.

Phil Williams was another Jimmy's officer Page was letting down in November. Williams and his financial analyst wife were fans of the TV programme *Grand Designs* and had invested almost £40,000 in a scheme to develop the Esher, Surrey bungalow site, Meadway.

Page, however, had failed to turn up at a motorway layby to hand Williams his first return. Instead, he called to apologize, blaming his no-show on a dead relative. In the same breath, Page offered to make it up with a free Gripper Airways holiday. The couple decided on Egypt and Page gave them Baree's details at BAT.

However, shortly before their departure near Christmas, Williams received a call from Baree to say the trip was cancelled. Page, he told the couple, had gone AWOL without paying for the holiday package at the cut-off date.

£ £ £

Dave Newman, the foreman at the barns site, slid down his window as he approached St James's Palace one evening in early December. He was running an errand for his boss who'd told him to mention his name when he got to the palace gate.

'I'm a friend of PC Page,' Newman informed the SO14 officer standing guard. 'I'm here to see PC Surinder Mudhar.'

Newman waited while the officer located the Turbanator. Minutes later he was waved through without any checks of the car or what Newman was couriering: a tightly wrapped, thick brown envelope for Mudhar.

The delivery was Page's response to family pressure on the Sikh officer to get back the £150,000 invested since 2003. £20,000 of it Mudhar had borrowed from his bank at Page's request who promised to pay the interest, but didn't.

The Sikh officer was not a confrontational character but had recently called Page at home to ask for his £20,000 back. It was Laura who answered the phone. She sensed the despondency in Mudhar's voice and told him that her husband was out but would soon be getting over £800,000 into his account.

There was no large imminent injection coming in December. But Page was telling the truth when he rang Mudhar to explain how 'a man called Dave' would shortly be dropping off some money at Jimmy's.

As Page was bouncing cheques all over the place and, in the Internet gambling world, was regarded as something of a busted flush, it wasn't obvious from where the £20,000 was coming from. He claimed to me that the tightly wrapped brown envelope sent to St James's Palace came from Essex gangsters wanting to invest in the ULPD syndicate through a mutual contact of Khan's. There is no evidence to corroborate Page's claim and Khan flatly denied it.

Mudhar was unaware where the money came from when Newman handed him the brown envelope inside Jimmy's. The courier was also clueless but impressed by his regal surroundings. St James's Palace is not open to the public but used for official functions and the offices of some of the most important royal households. Clarence House is also inside the palace grounds and was the home to newly remarried Prince Charles and his two sons Princes William and Harry.

'Is anyone famous in the palace tonight?' Newman enquired.

'Cherie Blair is here,' Mudhar responded, 'and one of the princes.'

'The wife is going to love that. Can I use the toilet before I head off?'

'Of course,' said Mudhar, pointing out the way.

On his way home, Newman rang his wife to tell her all about his unusual royal errand.[1]

Mrs Mudhar was less impressed with the evening's events. She wanted the rest of their investment and was tiring of Page's latest excuse that his mother was ill.

One cold December morning, the Mudhars made an unannounced visit to the Pages' house. There was no answer so Surinder made door-to-door enquiries, which confirmed that the family had not gone away.

After a coffee break at the local Sainsbury, at 8.45 am the Mudhars returned to Hatton Close and knocked again. This time Laura answered the door.

'What the fuck are you doing here?' she said loudly.

'We've come to speak to Paul to get our money,' replied

Surinder, a little taken aback by Laura's stance.

'You can whistle for it.'

'What would you do if you were in my position?' Surinder asked.

'I wouldn't get in your position,' Laura retorted. 'Now fuck off!'

The curtains in the cul-de-sac were twitching. Surinder didn't want to make more of a scene so the couple returned to their car and left.

Later that day, Page called Mudhar at home.

'Hello, Paul,' he said putting the call on speakerphone so his wife could listen.

'Why are you coming around to my house, Surinder?'

'Because I wanted to see you.'

'What about?'

'I need my money back, Paul. I don't believe all the excuses, the tax investigation, your mother's illness.'

'You won't be getting your money now. You'll have to wait like the rest of them. You shouldn't fucking insult my wife,' Page told him.

'I didn't, Paul. She was the one swearing at us. Calm down, Paul. Please.'

£ £ £

In the run-up to Christmas, Jim Mahaffy and his recuperating wife received a new kitchen without knowing that Page had paid for it from investors' money. It was Gripper's alternative to paying back the couple's entire six-figure investment.

The value of the kitchen was in dispute. Wendy Mahaffy claimed it wasn't worth more than £10,000. Page said the granite surfaces gave it a £28,000 price tag.

Regardless, it still left the Mahaffys wanting the rest of their

177

money. They too had tired of Page's silence or excuses. Like Mudhar, Jim Mahaffy had paid an unannounced and emotional visit to Page's house where Laura, once again thrust into the front row, assured him he would get what was coming to him.

In early December, Mahaffy emailed Page. 'I don't know what you are up to but not talking is not good,' he wrote. 'It's about time you spoke to me face to face. You keep telling me the money transfer is done and nothing turns up. You agreed to pay back £120,000. I'm going to be forced to do what Wendy has been wanting for months and seek legal advice.'

Page responded on 9 December. He promised things would be 'sorted'. They weren't and he went silent again. Mahaffy had already consulted a solicitor to look into the bona fides of ULPD. None could be found, so he placed a charge on the Essex barns, making the couple the second in line after the equally concerned Mortgage Guarantee.

Page's ostrich act towards his key investors was a big mistake. Mahaffy's charge on the barns had a ripple effect on other officers at Jimmy's. They too began reaching for lawyers to recover money they now believed Page was hiding from them. A period of recrimination was about to begin and some investors would try to strike private deals with Page. Like penguins desperate not to miss out on a feeding frenzy, one by one they had jumped into choppy waters and now they were jostling each other to get back on the slippery rocks.

In 1841, Charles Mackay described the phenomena in *Memoirs of Extraordinary Popular Delusions and the Madness of Crowds* when discussing the end of the tulip bubble:

Confidence was destroyed, and a universal panic seized upon the dealers … The cry of distress resounded

178

everywhere, and each man accused his neighbour. The few who had contrived to enrich themselves hid their wealth from the knowledge of their fellow citizens; and invested it in other funds. Many who, for a brief season, had emerged from the humbler walks of life were cast back into their original obscurity.

Journalist Michael Lewis observed the same phenomena in his book *Liar's Poker* about 1980s Wall Street's casino capitalism:

Investors do not fear losing money as much as they fear solitude, by which I mean taking risks that others avoid. When they are caught losing money alone, they have no excuse for their mistakes; and most investors, like most people, need excuses. They are strangely happy to stand on the edge of a precipice as long as they are joined by a few thousand others.

Mahaffy had heard on Jimmy's grapevine a false claim that Page's father had died so he decided to leave any further contact until after Christmas.

On 28 December, he drove to Page's home. Mahaffy rang the bell, but no reply came. A short while later, Page emerged at a small side window.

'Can I come in, Paul? We need to talk,' Mahaffy asked softly.

'I can't open the door, Jim, there has been a burglary of the keys. Laura will be back in a few hours' time.'

'I'm going to solicitors, Paul. I don't believe you anymore.'

Mahaffy drove home and composed with his wife an 'or else' letter to Page which he resolved to hand deliver straight away. A few hours later, as he parked in the cul-de-sac once more,

Mahaffy spotted Laura at the front door. She looked very stressed and very angry. 'It's a holiday, Jim. Why are you coming here? Leave us alone!'

'I need to speak to Paul.'

'He's not well. He's lying down. He's got a headache.'

'What about my money?'

'The account's been frozen, Jim.'

'If I can't talk to Paul I'm going to solicitors,' Mahaffy responded waving the letter in his hand. But Laura slammed the door, so he slipped it through the box and left.

Laura let her husband have it. He was in the sitting room watching television and drinking another can of Stella Artois. 'Oi, Walter Mitty?' She shouted, using her new nickname for Page. 'He said he's going to lawyers. I can't have this, Paul. Not another year of this shit.'

'I know love. I'll change his nappies. It'll be fine.' But inside, Page knew his confidence had gone and Laura could sense it too.

'I was losing the plot,' he told me. 'I had one more game in me, that I can turn things around, that I had the command and respect of my peers.'

Not Mahaffy. When he got home he emailed Page that legal action was the next step in the New Year.

Had Page been honest in 2005 and admitted the scheme was insolvent, he was right in thinking there was still enough loyalty, stupidity and greed among investors to try and rescue the barns or at least give non-believers a realistic Christmas repayment plan, as would be the case in any company insolvency.

Instead, Page chose lies, evasion and fraud throughout the winter of discontent. Like Shakespeare's Richard III, he was 'determined to prove himself a villain'.

Chapter 14

The Bristol connection

The end of 2005 saw the third hub of investors from Bristol fare no better than the Royal Protection officers and BAT boys.

The same pattern of misplaced trust, reckless greed, deceit and recrimination was also a feature of the West Country arm of Page's operation: large sums of money had been invested in various of his schemes without due diligence; some of which investors had transferred to the bank accounts of complete strangers with no questions asked; returns beyond the dreams of avarice and financial logic had been offered and not met; and money was being secretly siphoned off for hopeless spread betting and sports gambling.

At the centre of the Bristol connection was Steve Phillips, a thirty-something catering company salesman married to a police officer's daughter. He became Page's Bristol agent and was responsible for bringing in his family, friends and then a group of business contacts that together invested £400,000 since January 2005 and ended up losing most of it.

It was Adam McGregor who introduced Phillips to Page. The catering salesman had come to London in January 2004 to see McGregor's police-officer girlfriend, an old family friend of thirty years or more from Bristol.

It was no coincidence that Page turned up at McGregor's house in his Range Rover and the three men went to the barns and other sites Page claimed he owned or had interests in. Phillips was further impressed when McGregor showed him proof of his own substantial investments with the fellow SO14 officer.

'Any investment you make, Steve, I will cover with the equity in a flat I own in Cheshire,' McGregor told him. 'We can also offer you returns of 25–30 per cent.'

Phillips had spare cash to invest from a recent property sale but asked for time to think about it. Weeks later he was on the phone striking a verbal agreement with McGregor to invest £25,000 for one year at a 30 per cent return.

Phillips said he was 'mainly' putting money into the barns development. The clue to what else he invested in perhaps lies in what his friend McGregor did with the £25,000. Phillips wired it to McGregor's bank account, who transferred all of it to the CMC account he had opened for Page.

A year later, in February 2005, Phillips was back at McGregor's home where he received a cash return of £6000 and a cheque for £26,500 from Laura's NatWest bank account. The catering salesman was weeks away from getting married to Nicola, the daughter of a retired Avon and Somerset Police chief inspector. She had recently remortgaged her home and had spare cash to invest. The couple made the fateful decision not to bank the £26,500 cheque but reinvest with Page. They put in an additional £13,500, increasing their investment to £40,000 at 30 per cent over six months.

Nicola didn't know in what they were really investing. Page, however, knew that her husband was hooked. He saw him as a soft-touch country bumpkin to be rumped for cash. The Bristol connection was also a way of getting his irate London investors off his back.

Page was soon on the phone to the newly-weds asking if they knew any locals also willing to invest. With gusto, Phillips approached family and friends using his salesman skills but no ULPD paperwork to punt the exciting opportunity to 'make some money'.

His cousin Paul Phillips worked at Lloyds Bank and was impressed by the returns that the Bank of Page was offering when compared to his own financial institution. The royal policeman was so desperate for cash that he offered to cover the monthly repayment of a £20,000 loan he encouraged Paul Phillips to take and also to pay him a 25 per cent return in six months.[1]

The cousin considered these terms 'too good to miss' and took out two loans online. He happily transferred £20,000 to ULPD and recommended the investment to a bank-worker colleague and others who put in a further £26,000 at 20 per cent. One of them had also borrowed from his bank and was promised that the monthly repayments would be taken care of by Page.

By the summer of 2005, Steve Phillips considered himself an 'employee' of ULPD. He retained his salesman job but had negotiated with Page a 10 per cent commission for bringing in others.[2]

It was not just property schemes that Page punted to Phillips. He also approached his new lieutenant with an investment opportunity supposedly involving a Premier League footballer. Phillips was content not to know the details. He felt the investment was 'strange' but asked his mum for £10,000. She stumped up the cash on the promise of an amazing £2600 back every month.

Page was working the same line on a few Jimmy's officers. He'd told them that an unnamed African Blackburn Rovers player needed £400,000 to complete a mortgage or financial deal and there was money to be made from the short-term loan. Why a footballer who earned more money than God and worked less would need a bridging loan made no financial sense at all.[3]

Steve Phillips was also happy to involve his sister, Leanne, in yet another strange request from Page. This time he wanted to use her Lloyds Bank account to receive £10,000 from a complete stranger – an innocent investor – and then transfer it to Laura's ULPD bank account. Phillips convinced himself that Page was simply seeking a way of avoiding bank transfer fees. Leanne was happy because she was promised £250 for the service. However, because her account was overdrawn only £9000 was available for onwards transfer. She called Page with a little nervousness to tell him the situation.

'Don't worry about it. Keep the grand. Just make sure you withdraw the £9000 and put it into Laura's account,' he told her. What to Leanne must have looked like the generosity of a successful gentleman businessman was really a desperate mask for Page's degenerate gambling and fraud.

Like lieutenants McGregor and Baree, Steve Phillips was also treated to a holiday courtesy of ULPD's bespoke travel agents. The couple had wanted to go to Hawaii but because Nicola was now pregnant they couldn't fly. Instead, they took a long weekend at Disneyland in Paris by Eurostar. Nicola recalled running out of money during the break. 'Steve rang up and spoke to Laura. [She] said, 'No problem', and transferred £500 into our account.'

After Paris, Page took Phillips in a convertible Mercedes to show him a number of sites including Meadway in Esher,

Surrey. Page also signed some blank ULPD receipt of funds forms and legal contracts and encouraged Phillips to seek investment for the development back home. The contract contained the following wholly misleading sentence: 'ULPD Ltd confirm that there is no risk to investors' capital and guarantee to pay the agreed returns as stated.' Phillips left for Bristol confused about whether Page actually owned the Esher site, but appears to have made no effort to check for himself before punting it to friends and neighbours.

He told his father-in-law, the retired Avon and Somerset police chief inspector, about the possibility to make money. Page met Jeffrey Thomas during a family trip to Bristol that summer. He showed him various development plans and gave a very confident pitch to the old copper. Page knew from Phillips that Thomas had a rental property for sale and was considering investing some of the profit in his development scheme. So he pulled out all the stops and put in an offer for the house in Laura's name.

Meanwhile, Phillips had persuaded his wife to use a £20,000 bank loan for a loft conversion to invest with Page for a very short term at 20 per cent. The money was transferred to the bank account of Anjam Khan from BAT, no questions asked.

Page had promised to cover the monthly interest payment on the £20,000 loan. He also invited the couple to London for another all expenses paid weekend. They drove down in a Porsche Cayenne, which Page had given to Phillips for three months courtesy of Gripper Cars. Part of his job was to look for development opportunities in the West Country for which he was promised an extra £500 for every site visited.

In London, the couple stayed at a golf hotel near to Lakeside. 'Page paid for everything,' Nicola recalled. 'We had en suite rooms, champagne when we arrived, and they took us out for a meal at a floating Chinese restaurant, which Laura paid for in cash, which she carried in her handbag. I recall this because when she opened the bag it was full of cash.'

Page, of course, wanted something else in return. Phillips agreed to open a CMC account in his wife's name for Page to use. Phillips couldn't open it in his own name because his credit record was poor at the time due to a problem with a previous girlfriend.

Page told them it would help to move money around the syndicate. The fact that spread betting was blazoned all over the application form they had filled out and unmissable on the regular emailed statements apparently didn't make the couple question this absurd claim.

Phillips said Page had claimed that the CMC account was a 'tax-free account he could put money in for me to access to give people their money back or returns which he would top up so I didn't have to go to him for money … I never did any transactions that weren't directed by him. I didn't know how the online CMC account worked.'

Nicola Phillips added:

As far as I was concerned this was some sort of Internet banking account that Paul knew about. It was something to do with the stock market and Paul said he would build up the money and Steve could access it. As far as we were concerned this was all above board and fine. I didn't have too much to do with the account. I knew Steve saw that money was going in from the statement we received. We did see the money going in but then it would disappear.[4]

The twenty Bristol investors who ended up investing £400,000 were never asked by Steve Phillips to transfer their money straight to CMC. Court documents show that some of it was transferred to his HSBC bank account, which he then sent to the CMC account in his wife's name.

Phillips had recently offered his uncle, David Jones, a 25 per cent 'family rate' of return if he invested with Page. Jones didn't want to use his voluntary redundancy money from his old job as a factory worker so he took out a £20,000 personal loan from Tesco. On the form he said the money was for home improvement because he suspected that if he gave the real reason – to make money from a Royal Protection officer's syndicate – his application would have been denied. The money was wired to Fahim Baree, who transferred it to the CMC account he too had opened for Page.

Jones was none the wiser. However, almost immediately he received a £5000 return, which dissipated any latent concern. Page also offered him £250 to allow money to go through his Lloyds TSB account and onto ULPD. He agreed, no questions asked. Then came an amazing offer to make £2000 on a four-day loan. At the time Page dangled this carrot, Jones's wife was dying of a brain tumour. The couple had saved a 'nest egg' of £8000, which Jones transferred to the ULPD account, again without any contract.

After weeks and not a return in sight, when Jones finally started digging around online he discovered that certain ULPD documents had not been filed with the official register, Companies House. Immediately, he alerted his nephew that he now believed the whole thing was a con. Phillips tried to reassure his uncle, but Jones thought his nephew didn't want to believe it was all going wrong. In the end, Phillips promised to speak to Page, who mustered faux fury at the suggestion of criminality and said he would ring his agent's uncle to protest. But Jones was in no mood.

'You're a conman,' he told Page down the phone.

'No, I'm a legitimate businessman,' the policeman replied.

'Then why haven't certain company rules been followed?'

'The matter is in hand,' said Page.

'Paul, I know you are a cop.'

'Listen, mate, you know nothing and I could find out all about you in twenty minutes.'

Detective Sergeant Mark Davey of Avon and Somerset Police's Serious & Organized Crime squad had started to take an interest in Page's scheme after a tip off from Steve Phillips. The Bristol agent had not turned supergrass and Sergeant Davey was not about to arrest Page for fraud. On the contrary, the detective and his wife had decided to invest their joint savings with the Royal Protection officer who they believed was on sabbatical.

Mark and Elaine Davey were friends of the Phillips. The two wives worked in the same local government social services centre and Mark had served with Nicola's chief inspector father at Thornbury police station. The Daveys were looking to move house and were persuaded to use their £10,000 seed money sitting in a Nationwide cash ISA account for a three-week investment in ULPD at 15 per cent. Sergeant Davey thought this was a lure to make a more long-term investment but was apparently happy to use the opportunity for a quick buck, reassured that other Phillips family members were investors and Page was a fellow policeman. That said, when they handed over their seed money the couple had never met Page, had no contract and saw no paperwork specifying which ULPD property was yielding such incredible returns in the short term.

As 2005 drew to a close and no money appeared, Davey asked Phillips for an explanation. He was told the ULPD bank account had been frozen because of an Inland Revenue inspection. Like other Bristol investors given the same excuse, another Page invention, the Daveys agreed to wait.

The entire Bristol hub had no idea that the London end of the operation had collapsed, or that there had been a major fall-out between Page and the Royal Protection officers and boys from BAT.

Phillips was equally unaware and had taken a day's unpaid leave from his catering sales job to drive to London in December on the understanding that Page had money to pay returns. Phillips waited all day only to be fobbed off by phone that one of the BAT boys would transfer the money. It never arrived.

Days before Christmas, he returned to London and collected a cheque for £30,000 from Laura that was drawn on her bank account. Before cashing it, he wrote out five cheques to a select group of out of pocket friends and family in Bristol.[5] They all bounced because the £30,000 cheque was no good. Page simply explained it away by claiming he had to use the funds for another matter.

Page was playing on Phillips's greed and willing. He needed to deceive his West Country lieutenant that all was thriving in London in order to sucker in new investors for gambling money and to pay token returns to some of his old ones: a classic Ponzi fraud.

£ £ £

When Page heard the doorbell ring that February morning in 2006, he was too hung-over to worry. With resignation he shuffled in his dressing gown to the front door to find Gerry McCallion, a Jimmy's officer, staring at him.

'Hello mate,' said Page with false bonhomie.

'Hello, Paul. You're a hard man to reach. Can I come in?'

Page ushered McCallion in while trying to remember the lies he had told him.

McCallion and his girlfriend had invested £118,000 over a one-year period that was now up. Page had lured them in with talk about the development in Esher, Surrey and property near the Olympic site in east London, neither of which he owned. On the plus side, his drink-addled brain remembered personally delivering one brown envelope with £1375 in cash to McCallion's house and giving Mahaffy another £3500 to hand over at Jimmy's.

McCallion wasn't used to seeing Page in such a dishevelled state. The Money God was normally suited and booted when rolling into St James's Palace in his black Range Rover. McCallion couldn't decide if Page was depressed or hung-over.

'You look rough,' he told him.

'Yes, mate, I know. I've been out on the tiles with a possible investor; he's an Arab from Dubai. He's thinking of putting in two hundred and fifty grand, Gerry.'

'Look, Paul, me and the girlfriend, we are concerned about our money. She's invested £50,000, all her savings from selling her house for Christ's sake.'

Page nodded.

'People at work are also extremely concerned. They need to hear it from you that their money's safe. There's all sorts of rumours flying around,' McCallion added.

'Like what?'

'Like that as well as us lot at Royalty, two soldiers in Africa have invested fifty grand each.'

'Look, Gerry. Lots of other investors' money is coming in. Not just the Arab. Tell everyone at work their money is safe and everything is going well. It is, mate. Trust me.'

McCallion left with an uneasy feeling. He passed on the message to mutinous colleagues at Jimmy's but when nothing changed, weeks later he returned to confront Page with Phil Williams, another concerned Royal Protection officer.

This time no one was home. But the pair bumped into an officer from the Met's Special Escort Group, the motorbike outriders and drivers that protect politicians and dignitaries. Page had arranged for him to collect a return but hadn't shown up.[6]

Laura was getting used to seeing men parked in the cul-de-sac outside the house. On her way out or back from the school run, shopping and various errands for her husband she would nod at the occupant, or on occasion offer to bring them tea and biscuits. But the surveillance detail had usually come prepared with flasks and Tupperware of their own.

Laura was starting to worry about her husband's excessive drinking. It had started during the 2005 winter of discontent. Like the music from CNBC business news, Laura had come to dread the sound of a beer can being opened. If it was early in the morning, Page would wrap a tea towel around the can hoping his wife upstairs was too stupid to recognize the unmistakable sound.

Before leaving the house to take the kids to school and play group she would secretly count how many cans of Stella were in the fridge or in the crate next to it.

'How many have you drunk?' Laura asked her husband when she returned.

'I've only had one.'

'You liar! There was five or more in the fridge.'

'Alright. You caught me out. So what? Don't treat me like a fucking kid,' he spat back.

Page's capacity for deception was no longer just hiding gambling losses from investors. He was also hiding his descent into alcoholism from his wife. Initially, he came up with the idea of putting the empty beer cans at the bottom of the crate to give the impression it was still full. But Laura got wise to that. It was only when she persuaded him that the kitchen needed redoing that his most successful hiding place was discovered.

Laura had asked the husband of her best friend Kelly to put in a new kitchen. Those ingrates, the Mahaffys, had one, why not us, she thought. When the old fridge was pulled back to start the work, over one hundred crushed cans of Stella fell to the floor. There was also a bottle of vodka under the bed.

£ £ £

Page had been trying to return to work at Buckingham Palace since his official extended leave period came to an end in late July 2005. He wanted to be a paid SO14 officer again because the syndicate was collapsing around him and, with no savings, he needed the wages and security.

However, unknown to him, SO14 management had decided to cut Page loose but leave him in police limbo, a Royal Protection officer without a palace to protect.[7] The decision was a strange, cynical response by SO14 to the March 2005 report by anti-corruption Detective Sergeant Jim Wingrave of the Met's DPS.

Wingrave's four-month covert financial inquiry had discovered prolific gambling, prolific losses, large sums moving through officers' bank accounts and a concerning amount of county court judgments against Page and his wife for unpaid bills. His report recommended to SO14 management that their boy may not be guilty of criminal wrongdoing but should be risk assessed because of a 'potential vulnerability to corrupt approaches that may seek to take advantage of his financial situation'.

Wingrave was engaged for the remainder of 2005 on a terrorist inquiry after home-grown jihadists bombed the London transport network on 7 July. With no pressure from the DPS to follow through on his report, SO14 decided to put as much distance as possible between the palace and Page's syndicate. No steps were taken to consider his welfare or that of the other Royal Protection officers involved with him. The fraud ran on while it was quietly decided that Page would never return from his extended career break to Royalty Protection.

In January 2006, Wingrave met with Chief Superintendent Steve Grainger, the second in command at SO14. The anti-corruption detective was back on the case and wanted to clarify information about Page's relationship with Jimmy's officers Richard Humby and Surinder Mudhar. Wingrave later recalled in court that Grainger had told him there was no further information to be given. That was probably true, because no one at SO14 appears to have investigated further.

The same could not be said of the Ministry of Defence (MoD) Police, whose officers guarded sensitive military establishments. MoD plod, as it is known, was concerned about a complaint from a new recruit. Mike Tinsley, a former SO14 officer, had claimed he lost £135,000 in Page's syndicate.

All defence installations were on high alert after the terrorist attacks the previous year and the MoD was concerned about the vulnerability of its staff to compromise. On 27 February 2006, a MoD police official contacted the DPS to ask about Page. Wingrave went to see the official. 'Tinsley doesn't want to make a criminal complaint,' he was told. 'He's content to go down the civil route to recover his money. But are you investigating Paul

Page? Because if you aren't, for whatever reason, we will,' the man from the MoD explained. Tinsley was one of four former SO14 officers now serving with the MoD police who had been involved with Page's syndicate.[8]

Wingrave assured the MoD official that the DPS was on the case and shared some, not much, information about Page. Control of the investigation, however, was to rest very much with the Met's anti-corruption squad.

Wingrave set about making further inquiries about the Tinsley matter. It turned out that in February Tinsley's wife had obtained a court order against Page for £22,231 and £71,000 against Laura as charges on the barns.

The Tinsleys had also taken to turning up unannounced at Laura's shop, Wicked Wardrobe, in the afternoon.

'You can't sit here all day,' Laura told them, as if their presence would put off passing trade, when the business was weeks away from shutting down.

'Yes we can,' replied Susan Tinsley, 'and when we leave we'll come to your house.'

True to their word, when Laura got home the Tinsleys were parked in the cul-de-sac.

'You can't come in. I've got to give my kids their dinner,' she told them.

'That's all right we'll wait in the car. All night if necessary.' A bright glow emanated from their BMW as the couple watched television, drinking tea and eating sandwiches.

Surveillance of the Pages, however, was not for Jim Mahaffy. He had warned Page at the end of 2005 that he would go down the legal route to recover his £112,000.[9]

On 26 March 2006 the pair had a remarkable email exchange on the matter in which a belligerent Page warned that if Mahaffy didn't cease and desist with his 'silly court action' the royal house of cards would come tumbling down. 'I ask you to put it on hold for your colleagues' sake. If you insist, my backers' money will be used to fight you in court all the way and your colleagues [at St James will have to attend court] as witnesses.' Page added: 'Don't forget all the cash in envelopes. £80,000 over four years. Have you declared that to the taxman? I've got witnesses to back that up. I wonder who?'

The email was another gamble and exaggeration by Page. Mahaffy had only received a little over £30,000 by this time. But Page believed, and with some reason, that his colleagues at Buckingham Palace would hold the line and not wash their laundry in court. It was only the mannequins at Jimmy's who were bottling it, he thought. But Page had no intention of defending himself publicly in a courtroom. He hadn't contested one of the many county court judgments for unpaid bills and was not about to start now. Besides, he had no defence and would only be leaving himself open to possible criminal proceedings.

Mahaffy was unmoved by the threatening tone of Page's email and placed a charge on the barns and the Pages' family home. Also in line were police couples the Copleys (who lived in one of the barns) and then the Tinsleys.

All this activity had reached the covert intelligence-gathering arm of the Met's anti-corruption squad. The Intelligence Development Group, known by the rest of the force as 'The Dark Side', had received details from a victim of Page's fraud. The intelligence was passed to bosses at the DPS, who decided on 20 April 2006 that it was time to launch a formal operation codenamed Aserio into Page's activities.

Wingrave was sent to brief Lord Loughborough, the head of SO14, because the operation had the potential to impact on his command and possibly embarrass the Queen.

For that reason, Operation Aserio should have been referred to the new police watchdog for supervision. The Independent Police Complaint Commission (IPCC) had been set up exactly two years earlier to quell public concern about the police investigating themselves. However, although a civilian element ran the IPCC, its investigators were largely former officers, many of whom had come from the Met's DPS.

Even then, the DPS didn't see the need for the limited external accountability offered by the IPCC and instead shut them out. There was precedent here. The watchdog was effortlessly pushed aside in July 2005 when an innocent civilian, Jean Charles de Menezes, was shot dead on the London underground on suspicion of being a terrorist.

The failure to refer Operation Aserio to the IPCC ensured that this highly sensitive investigation into fraud at the royal palaces remained an internal matter for the Met and SO14. The DPS would liaise very closely to ensure it remained that way.

Page, however, was aware within days that the anti-corruption squad was looking at him. An unnamed SO14 officer, he said, had tipped him off.

£ £ £

Four days after the launch of the corruption investigation Operation Aserio, on 24 April 2006, Jimmy's officer Richard Humby rang Page. Humby secretly recorded the conversation.[10]

'Hello, Paul, Richard.'

'Hello, mate.'

'I haven't pestered you much because I couldn't see the point and I haven't sent any shitty texts like I know you have received.'

'I've had to change my mobile so many fucking times it's unreal. But on a personal basis I've had a shit time with health problems with family, but on a business side things are looking very upbeat in the coming weeks, mate.'

'Really, Paul? All I need to know is, I mean, I gave you a hundred grand last May and you've given me twenty back on it. I know you promised me forty. I know things have not been good.'

'I've had two particular dickheads who are causing me major problems and I have had to sacrifice my own shit for your well-being and some of the others. I've had to rest and not go to court and kick off because I couldn't have everything exposed, but that is something I will deal with once I'm back on top, which will be very soon and I will deal with it harshly. Mahaffy, he's fucking done me up. But he's not the one I'm talking about. Tinsley, that's the one. That cunt will pay because he has more or less jeopardized it for all of us. Now, I don't want to keep anyone's money, you know what I mean?'

'Mahaffy bores the shit out of me,' replied Humby. 'The only person I speak to is Copley, who tells me there's blokes who need paying down at the Barns.'

'Well, they've been paid. No. They've been laid off. Don't take any notice of that.'

'I know you've spoken to Lenny [Thiel, another SO14 officer who had moved to the MoD Police] and he talked about paying people back at the end of the month.'

'Without cutting my throat we are looking good. Look, I'll be honest with you. I've burnt a lot of paperwork mate, as you can probably appreciate, because of being paranoid my door's being fucking kicked in.'

'Yeah.'

'I burnt a fuck load mate. But you know for all the reasons, thinking that it was all gonna go mega, mega tits up. So I need bank details from you and I can give you full and frank dates, erm, and amounts of money that will come to you.'

'I don't want any hopeful figures. I believe you spoke to Lenny and said you can't promise the interest rates.'

'No, not immediately. What makes sense is that I start filtering out the money as soon as my balls are out of that vice.'

'I don't know how much you owe people, it must be quite difficult to calculate. If you said, "Look, Richard, I can't pay 40 per cent on that hundred grand, I can only pay 10 per cent", I wouldn't be fucking crying, Paul.'

'I appreciate what you are saying. I mean once I get myself back on my feet I can, erm …'

'If you give me 10 per cent I'm not going to slag you off or think you're a cunt, because that's 6 per cent more than I'd get in the bank. I mean you've put a few grey hairs on my head, Paul!' Humby added, laughing. 'You know, my marriage is fucking sort of on the rocks. Well, that's an exaggeration, but things have been a little difficult. You know it's not good when your wife thinks you're a cunt. So I'm asking, Paul, for complete and utter clarity with me.'

'Now there's things that obviously I'm not forthcoming with, which isn't in my interests to do so. You know I've got problems with Dubai money.'

'I'm on a mobile, Paul, that's why I didn't phone you from my home number.'

'I'm on my landline so I won't go into too much detail. Once we get over this, you are one of the people, and I'm not just saying this, but I've appreciated their common sense and patience. Because I've had headless chickens about my feet that have caused me fucking major grief. Had they kept their nerve they wouldn't be getting a kick up the arse when this is resolved. I'm very reasonable, but it's not helped that people have lost faith in me. Now, I can appreciate people's concern, their frustration, and I've got to base it on the fact that I had a fucking history of good business for a long time.'

'That's why I went into business with you and invested quite a lot of money. I heard you had a good track record, I asked certain people and they said, "Yeah, he always come up with the dosh'. And you know what you offered in interest rates.'

Mahaffy had recently told Humby that Page's name was not on the official Land Registry records as the owner of Meadway, the Esher property in Surrey that he had punted to both of them. Humby used the call to inform Page that Mahaffy was telling everyone the money had been 'spunked on gambling'. Page tried to lie his way out of it by claiming that while there was another company on the Land Registry, he had put £550,000 into the Esher property. Then came this whopper.

'But I don't gamble, Dick. I don't gamble on anything.'

'Well, gambling on the oil markets is a gamble, innit? I know you got your trigger stops on your computer,' Humby replied, recalling the quick guide to spread betting that Page had shown him on his television one afternoon.

'I've got four accounts, mate, and you hedge. You buy on one and you sell on the other, then you don't get killed.'

'Copley said you are not the sort of bloke that's gonna lose a million quid fucking gambling on the oil prices. But the bottom line, Paul, is when are you going to pay? We are majorly concerned Paul, and Lenny probably more than most, him and Surinder. I mean, I'm a little bit more sort of philosophical about it.'

'My mum's seriously ill and I can't help her if I can't get this resolved. Now in the coming fourteen days you will start to see money flowing.'

'I know from a personal point of view my contract is worth something but from a legal point of view I don't know what.'

'I haven't disputed this crap in court. Because would you really want me standing up in court telling all our business. I certainly don't, you know what I mean, because that would blow things out the water. Now, I've got away with shit by the skin of my teeth, and I shit you not on this, but I've been lucky. But I've made sure, as things are gradually coming to the point where we gonna get paid out, I've got things lined up that are totally legit and that are in people's own names and I'm just taking a cut from them.'

Page felt his blarney had reassured Humby enough to be able to suggest a new property deal on the up-and-coming south-east coast of England. He knew Humby owned rental properties in Margate and Herne Bay. But the Jimmy's officer was no longer willing to be the chump and said all his money was tied up with Page.

'I do need to start seeing some money, Paul. I've got rents coming in, but unfortunately I mean rents coming in and my police wages don't, I haven't got my fucking security blanket any-more and I feel cold, you know what I mean?'

'I am not gonna to say a word to any fucker about who is get-ting what. I'm gonna make sure that I look after you. Mahaffy's gonna be picking up crumbs after everyone is sat there full. I'm sorry but he's fucking cunted me.'

'Every time I speak to him he's fucking slagging you off. And I'm thinking, "Well, hang on, I've only been in this caper a year with Paul and you've been in it five years plus and you must have done pretty well over the years, otherwise you wouldn't be near him".'

'He ain't hard done by, he's had his money back. He's not like you. That's your cheese, mate, you know what I mean? That is one fucking cunt, 'cause he's greedy, mate.'

'Basically Tinsley and Mahaffy, you are gonna put them to the bottom of the pile?'

'Tinsley's jeopardized us all in what he said in the court letter. He does not give a fuck.'

'Well, basically, he said you're a fraudster, Paul.'

'Well in certain terms, yeah. What do I do, Rich? The tax office has got its hand up my arse at the moment. Also, I'm shitting myself about the DPS.'

'Are you going back in the Job [the police], Paul?'

'I had a board for the airport, mate, I mean I rolled up in a fucking Carrera, mate, and people like go, 'Who the fuck is that?' I thought I'd stick out like a sore thumb. I should be coming back for six months to sort out my tax and pension.'

'What, Royalty?'

'I'm not coming back to Royalty. I was going to go Diplomatic Protection Group just to hide for six months and then fuck off. I'm getting my businesses sorted at the moment. I've got a car business as well. I've got a Bentley 930 if you want one of them for the day.'

'Let me tell you how bad things are in my house. I had to run down to the auctions and buy myself a second-hand Honda Civic!'

'Fucking hell! That is bad, mate.'

'You know this tax investigation? You needed to show a bit more clarity to people.'

'I spoke to my solicitor, do not tell any fucker, because I said to him, like, you know I told him that I was running an unofficial investment club, that's what I called it. And when I started going into detail that's when he said to me, "You know, you could be looking at time". I don't know if I told you that.'

'You did.'

'The last thing I was gonna do was give anyone copies of any fucking investigation. Imagine what old Mahaffy would do. He'd fucking stick it on his forehead and run around Jimmy's. Not only that, fucking DPS would have been on me like a fucking rash, mate, and then I'd be nicked for bringing the Job into disrepute or whatever, do you know what I mean?'

Page asked Humby not to tell anyone else except two former SO14 officers who had gone to the MoD Police.[11] Humby said Surinder Mudhar was turning up for work at St James's Palace looking 'like something off the mortuary slab'. Page promised to call the Turbanator who, he was told, looked 'suicidal'.

But there was something else on his mind. 'It's gonna be like lions to the fucking, you know, I'll be the Christian, there'll be hundreds of lions come out wanting a piece of meat. So I'll be careful who I give what to,' said Page.

'I won't breathe a word. If you transfer money to my account it's between you and me. I'll wait for another fortnight, Paul.'

'No worries.'

'Take care, Paul.'

'Take care, mate.'

Beatrice Humby, Richard's wife, had agreed to wait for their 'cheese'. But after several weeks, when it was clear Page had lied again, she rang him at home.

Laura answered the phone and Beatrice got straight to the point about the money. Before long the women were going at each other until Page took over the call and said he would be only too happy to pay her a visit.

'Are you threatening me?' Beatrice asked. 'You and that wife of yours don't have the balls to come and sort me out.'

Beatrice hung up and immediately called her husband at work. 'The Pages are screaming down the phone about paying us a visit,' she told him. Richard Humby knew his wife could press people's buttons. 'Look,' he said reassuringly, 'don't worry, it's probably bluster, an empty threat. He's a policeman, he's not coming round in a menacing way.'

But Beatrice was not convinced. 'I told him he doesn't have the balls to come and sort me out,' she said. 'What are we going to do?'

'Don't worry. Just ignore it. Let's wait and see if any money does come, if Paul comes to his senses. Any more problems call me at work.'

In the afternoon, Page called Humby at Jimmy's. 'I need to speak to you, Dick,' he said.

'Well, I need to speak to you. I'm tucked up with something. I know you spoke to my wife this morning, Paul, and I'm not particularly happy. Call me in ten.'

Page agreed but never called back. Nor did the Humbys make a formal complaint. Instead, one night they drove to Page's house and Beatrice took photographs of the Porsche and Range Rover on the drive as evidence of their continued standard of living.

Humby had also discussed a further home visit to Page this time with two former SO14 colleagues who were now at the MoD Police. The most senior of the pair was Sergeant Jason Molen. He had spent thirteen years at Buckingham Palace, where at various times he had been in charge of the control room and issuing weapons to other officers. He was also security chief when the Queen summer holidayed at Balmoral Castle.

Molen had avoided the Currency Club but was into property. Mahaffy had vouched for Page's Midas touch at a time when Molen felt the rental income from his buy-to-let property was lying 'dormant' in an Alliance & Leicester building society account earning just 7 per cent interest. By comparison, Page was offering 30 per cent over seven months on a £8000 investment in the Esher conversion property. Molen convinced himself that this level of return was possible because the property market was 'very buoyant'. He transferred the money to Laura's Clippers account at NatWest before signing any contract.

When the investment period was up, Molen started to get the run-around from Page. Only £1400 in cash had been paid, which was £1000 short of what he was promised. Molen, a part-time football referee, was left standing with just a whistle in his hand, when Page cancelled a meeting after a match to pay the remaining return. 'I've got problems at home,' he told Molen and made it up by sending him and his wife on a £2500 holiday to Israel in November 2005.

The BAT-arranged trip also represented a commission payment to Molen for introducing two other SO14 sergeants, Rob Pearce and Barry Crosby. Page had wanted to keep Molen sweet because he was an influential officer at SO14.[12]

However, by June 2006, Molen had had enough. By now aware of the DPS investigation into Page, he drove early one summer morning with Humby and Pearce to confront him at home.

When the door opened, Laura stood there, her boys playing noisily in the background. It was 7.30 am and she was trying to get them fed and ready for school

'Can we speak to Paul?' Molen asked.

'He's not in. He's away on business in Bristol,' she told the trio coldly.

Within seconds, though, the conversation heated up.

'Where's our money? Humby demanded. 'People have invested their life savings!'

'I've got to take the kids to school. Go and get a coffee and come back later,' Laura told them.

The three policemen went back to their car and watched her leave on the school run. Some fifteen minutes later, she returned with the youngest Harry, who was now almost two years old. The trio walked purposely again to the doorstep and rang the bell.

'If Paul doesn't ring tonight I'm going to the DPS,' Molen told Laura. She had no idea what this meant. 'Tell him Barry Crosby wants his money too. He can't be here because he's now retired to Spain but I'm looking after his interests,' Molen added.

Humby then chipped in. There was no love lost between him and Laura. 'I'm not going down the route of solicitors. I've got my own methods,' he told her.

'Are you threatening me?'

'Take it whichever way you want,' Humby replied.

'You all knew what you was letting yourselves in for. You all knew it was high risk. You're greedy. Can you now leave my house?'

The SO14 officers suddenly felt wary of looking oppressive. Especially as Molen believed Humby was secretly recording the heated and unequal encounter.[13]

When Page learned of the visit later that day he swapped a few texts with Molen. One, in particular, stood out. Page texted: 'It's all gone wrong. I'm just looking after my family. That's the end of it.'

Laura had her own problems with creditors coming to the house after the collapse of Wicked Wardrobe in the summer of 2006. The ladies boutique had lasted just over six months. It was a failure foretold having rented in the wrong location and bought high-end stock for a low-end market.

One fashion supplier knocked on her door in May wanting settlement of a £4000 debt. She invited him in and he explained how he'd tried unsuccessfully to call her but in the end spoke to what he thought was Laura's partner, who said she was merely an employee.

'Look. I'm really sorry. I ran up a lot of debt when I set up Wicked Wardrobe,' Laura explained. 'But don't worry. My husband's a trader and he will pay it off at the end of the week.'

The supplier bought the story. The Porsche and Range Rover on the drive gave it credibility, he convinced himself. But when the money never appeared, the matter was passed to the courts for resolution.

Maria Abraham, the sales agent of another supplier, was given a more revealing spiel when she came round in June after Laura had stopped taking her calls. Laura would only talk on the doorstep. Maria felt she was very nervous and unhappy.

'I'll be honest with you. My husband has more or less stopped working because of depression. I'm worried about him and about losing my house.'

Maria hadn't met Page but knew from Laura that he had put £60,000 into setting up the business.

'He's become more depressed and aggressive since his dad died and now his mum's terminally ill and in hospital. Give me ten days and you'll have your money. I promise.'

Again, the fancy cars on the drive encouraged Maria to believe that the family was good for a few thousand pounds. Again, the money was never paid and the matter passed to debt collectors.[14]

Laura was telling some truth to her creditors about her husband's mental state. He was depressed only she didn't know by how much. His drinking was getting worse and he was starting to take less pride in his appearance.

Often nowadays when the bell rang Page would hide in the house and whisper to his wife, 'You answer it and tell them to fuck off!' She would do his bidding but it was in defence of her family not of her dishevelled husband. When the caller had been seen off, Laura would find Page in some alcove and give him a mouthful.

'How dare you make me have to do that,' she'd yell at him. It was not the act of lying that annoyed her. It was that her once cocksure husband was now cutting a pathetic figure at home, incapable of taking care of business and looking after his family.

At Page's request the blinds were now almost always shut in the house. He had taken to sitting silently by the front window looking at the cul-de-sac.

'Who's that? What's his game?' he'd say to himself or Laura as she passed through the sitting room.

'Paul, you're paranoid!'

£ £ £

A letter containing catastrophic news for Mark and Sufia Copley dropped through their letterbox at Barn C on 7 July 2006. Lawyers acting for Mortgage Guarantee informed the couple they were repossessing all three barns. The legal letter went on to say that the Copleys had 'exercised unauthorised occupation' of Barn C and would have to leave immediately or face court eviction proceedings.

The notification threw the family into a panic not least because their two young children were settled in local schools and would shortly be homeless. Mark Copley immediately texted Humby explaining that agents for Mortgage Guarantee had padlocked the now repossessed barns. Humby in turn texted Page but got no reply. However, on the Jimmy's grapevine he heard that Page was telling others it was all part of his plan to raise cash and steady the ship.

Since March, Page had been promising Mortgage Guarantee that he would pay them £100,000. By 24 May 2006, the finance company tired of the excuses and demanded full repayment of the loan, which was now a little shy of one million pounds. The development was not even in a finished state to sell and Mortgage Guarantee felt the work that had been done 'fell well below building regulations'.

In the days leading up to Copley receiving the legal repossession notification, his colleague Jim Mahaffy had notified Mortgage Guarantee of an interim charging order on the barns to the value of £151,000 that his lawyers had obtained against the Pages.

For their part, the Copleys fought through lawyers to remain at Barn C. They explained to Mortgage Guarantee how £150,000 was paid to Page towards buying the barn, albeit in a very unorthodox way. The finance firm was unmoved and ordered them out by the end of the year but not before the Copleys put their own charge on the barns. The Humbys did the same for £131,000 but it was debatable, even in a boom market, whether after Mortgage Guarantee had taken its share there would be any equity left in the barns once they were finished and sold.

The three Jimmy's officers had also opened another front in their quest to get money back: they were now giving information to the Operation Aserio team from the Met's anti-corruption squad.[15]

£ £ £

In mid-March 2006, Steve Phillips stopped at the Riverside Inn for a chat with Bristol landlady Anne Carter. She was one of his customers but, on this occasion, he wasn't selling fruit and veg.

'I'm leaving my job, Anne, to work for my friend.'

'That's a big step, Steve. Who is he?'

'He's a Royal Protection officer in the Metropolitan Police

who's taken time off to run a property business. I've been working for him on the side getting investors from around here, which is what I wanted to talk to you about. Property development is a good way of making money, Anne. There's short- and long-term investments available.'

'It is appealing, Steve. But I'd only be interested in a short-term investment. I've got my own money and the money I owe on VAT to invest, but I'd need that back by August.'

'I'll speak to Paul Page – he's the boss of United Land and Property Developments, the company I'll be working for – and see what short-term opportunities there are and then get back to you.'

Despite all the problems of the last year, Philips was still very interested in Page's recent offer to work full time as his Bristol agent. There was talk of redundancies at the catering firm where he worked and Page was offering a salary of £2000 per month, use of a Porsche and the possibility of expansion. He'd also asked Phillips to look for a suitable shop in the Clifton area of Bristol where he and Laura were thinking of opening a kitchen-fitting business, another boutique or a luxury car-hire firm for him to manage.

As far as Phillips could see, Page had good contacts in all three sectors. New kitchens were being offered to Bristol investors in lieu of returns, although none had ever been fitted. Meanwhile, his wife had reported back, after visiting Wicked Wardrobe the previous year, that the clothes range was impressive. Of course, unknown to the couple, by the time of the job offer the boutique was bust and creditors were looking for Laura.

The Pages saw Bristol as an escape route from their London situation. What to Phillips looked like a chance to be part of a growing business in a housing bubble was, for Page, a flight from an escalating fraud.

He maintained the charade by asking Phillips to send his P45, a copy of his passport and his last wage slip for ULPD's accountant, who didn't exist.

Phillips already had a number of good reasons to question Page's business ethic and stay well clear of the job offer: investors close to him had not been paid their returns; Page's explanation that his accounts were frozen by an Inland Revenue investigation should have rung alarm bells, especially as cheques had bounced, loan repayments to his wife and cousin had stopped, his mum had not received money on her loan to the mysterious Premier League footballer and there was a spread-betting account where the balance went up and down. But Phillips appears to have ignored all this for the glitter of fool's gold.

A few weeks later, he was back at the Riverside Inn as a newly appointed ULPD employee.

'I can offer you a two-month investment opportunity, Anne. If you invest £20,000 in ULPD we will guarantee you a 30 per cent return. That's £6000 in eight weeks,' he told her enthusiastically.

Anne Carter needed little convincing. She signed the contract Phillips had prepared and gave him £20,000 in cash. On leaving the pub, Phillips spoke to Page who arranged to meet him halfway between London and Bristol. At the Junction 8 service station on the M4, Phillips handed over £19,000 of Carter's money. Page told him he could keep £1000 for himself as commission.

Days later, Phillips was back on the phone asking the publican if she knew anyone else who would invest. But Carter wasn't willing to introduce others to the scheme until she saw some readies.

'When I've got my £6000 and my investment back I will introduce you to other publicans I know, Steve. You can meet them in my pub and tell them all about it.'

Phillips reported this back to Page, who pulled up the £6000 return two weeks before it was due. Anne Carter was impressed and told Phillips she would reinvest the £20,000 in a similar scheme. She also recommended him to Marcus Williams, her stock taker and the son of another local publican who owned the Hauliers Arms. 'He's someone who can make some money for us,' she told Marcus.

On 12 May, he and his father, David Williams, met Phillips at the Riverside Inn and signed a contract to invest £30,000 for one month at 35 per cent. They were encouraged by the fact that Anne Carter had received such a healthy return on her initial investment and was now rolling it over with an extra £15,000 in cash, which she gave Phillips the same day.

Page drove to Bristol five days later to thank Williams and his son for their investment, which they were told was returnable at any time. However, no sooner did the £30,000 hit Phillips's HSBC account then it was transferred to the CMC account in his wife's name. Had David Williams known this he would not have agreed to put in a further £10,000 a few weeks later, which Page had claimed was vital for buying some land. This time, Williams agreed to transfer the money to the NatWest account of Page's father, Terry, who also put it all into a CMC account he too had opened for his son to use.

During these days between May and June, Page and Phillips hoovered up new investors that the Bristol publicans had innocently recommended. Phillips would warm them up with an excitable pitch then Page would arrive in his Porsche, a day or so later, smartly dressed with development plans under his arm to seal the deal at a pub or Tesco café. He would ask for cash where possible, saying all his was tied up in property at the moment. Alternatively, he asked for the funds to be transferred to a family member's bank account.[16]

211

Not everyone Phillips lined up took to Page. One publican listened to the speech and decided it was 'crap' and that Page was 'too much of a wide boy'.

There was also some explaining to do to those Bristol investors who had come into the scheme in 2005 and by the summer of 2006 were still waiting for returns. Page arranged to see some of them at Phillips's house in staggered half-hour meetings.

One was Andy Boucher, a work friend of Phillips. He'd had a quick and good return on an initial investment, which lured him to put in a further £16,000. Page was profusely apologetic for the delayed returns on this second investment and expanded on the bogus tax-probe excuse.

'The Revenue investigation is now over, Andy, and ULPD's bank account is about to be unfrozen so I can start distributing all the returns. It was all a load of nonsense really. They've fined me £400 for not keeping my books in order,' he told Boucher, who left feeling reassured but still £16,000 lighter.

Another concerned punter was local motor trader Adrian Marsh, a neighbour to Phillips's mum. Page had strung him along for months about his intention to buy Marsh's house. It was just a ploy to get at a pot of money Marsh and his wife had come into after recently selling a rental property. Page persuaded the couple to invest £20,000 for six weeks at 30 per cent. Marsh sent the money to Adam McGregor's bank account. He was aware that McGregor was another policeman but unaware that his £20,000 was transferred by Bald eagle to a CMC account.

When the returns never arrived, Marsh was also fobbed off with the false tax-investigation excuse. He put his house back on the market and, while waiting for the taxman to thaw the ULPD bank account, an apologetic Page offered him a free Caribbean holiday with a travel firm he said was 'in his pocket'.

It was enough to persuade the couple to make another short-term investment of £25,000. 'They invested £15,000 into my HSBC account and £10,000 into Adam McGregor's account on the direction of Paul Page,' Phillips recalled. 'Paul told me to put £11,900 of this into our CMC account and £3000 as wages and money owed to me.'[17]

With still no returns in sight or of the sound of Caribbean steel drums, Marsh and Phillips drove to Page's house unannounced in June. He invited them in and produced ULPD bank statements showing large cash flows and spun a tale of a substantial sum of money from Dubai that had caught the Inland Revenue's attention.

Marsh left thinking, 'It's not right but things do go wrong in business'. However, when the returns remained as elusive as Page, Marsh and Phillips made a second visit to his house. This time the man inside was in a very different mood and refused to let them in. Laura was crying at the front door and told them to come back later.

Phillips took Marsh to the barns site and then phoned Page at home. Laura answered and arranged to meet them at Lakeside shopping centre. She arrived with the children but without her husband. Laura gave Marsh a few hundred pounds in cash and left.

Weeks later Marsh paid a third visit to Page's house. This time he came with fellow motor trader Alan Sweet. Phillips had hooked Sweet with an offer of a 30 per cent return in two months on a £25,000 investment. 'I asked Phillips to give me some background in respect of Page and he told me he was a serving police officer employed on Royal Protection duty. He went on to say that Page set up [ULPD] three years prior and that most of his investors were police officers and solicitors. I was happy with this and agreed to invest … to purchase land or property in the Essex area,' said Sweet.

Laura answered the door when he and Marsh came knocking. Gone were her tears and sympathy. This Laura was in no mood for another investor's sob story.

'He's not here. He's in hospital,' she told them curtly.

Marsh was unimpressed and pushed the matter.

'You should have made an appointment rather than turn up on my doorstep unannounced,' she told him. 'And you look like Freddie Mercury, now fuck off,' she shouted at Sweet before slamming the door on them.

The two Bristol car dealers thought they would have better luck with McGregor, who lived nearby. The policeman joined them in their car around the corner from his house while they explained their concern that Page and Phillips had not been straight with them.

Marsh and McGregor have two rather different recollections of the conversation that followed. In his witness statement, Marsh suggested McGregor admitted it had all gone 'horribly wrong'. Marsh said he then asked what had happened to the £10,000 put into McGregor's bank account. The policeman, he said, denied any knowledge of the transaction.

According to the version McGregor gave to anti-corruption detectives from Operation Aserio, the £10,000 was withdrawn in cash and given to Page outside the bank. McGregor also said that, far from accepting the ULPD bubble had burst, he defended Page and told Marsh and Sweet that his friend would not defraud anyone.

McGregor had by this stage his own mounting problems with friends and family who he'd brought into Page's scheme. This included a Bristol couple who'd invested money set aside for their wedding and house move. McGregor would end up paying back most of their £10,000 from his own pocket.[18]

Meanwhile, antique dealer Ian Butlin came up with a clever way to recoup some of the £30,000 he'd invested when he tired of Page's excuses. 'I decided to tell [him] I had a fictitious investor who wanted to invest. I believe because of this Page got Steve to give me £3000 cash as a partial return on my investment. I was trying anything to get money back. I tried this again later but Page didn't give me any more money.'

Salesman Paul Bartlett tried the same ruse to recover the £10,000 he had withdrawn on his credit card to invest over two months for a 40 per cent return. The money was transferred to Anjam Khan's account. Bartlett planned to use the anticipated profit to help set up his own business. But after months of waiting he became suspicious and set up a meeting in a Bristol pub with Page and a friend posing as a potential investor. Page offered the new blood the same deal. He then turned to Bartlett and asked him if he would open a CMC account. 'Paul explained that it would be used to bet on the stock market and he would supply the funds. I declined the offer. He told me I would get my money back and that he had £1.8 million stashed away.'

Bartlett bore no malice towards Phillips for the loss of his money and the break-up of his marriage. He felt Page had used Phillips. However, publicans Anne Carter and David Williams, and some of those they introduced to the scheme, believed Phillips and Page had 'deceived' them and there was never an intention to repay their investment.

The balloon went up for the publicans when Jeff Pennell, an investor they had brought in, alerted them that ULPD had been dissolved on 30 May 2006. Pennell thought to check the Companies House register when he received no return on the £10,000

Phillips had persuaded him to invest in ULPD on 8 June. To his horror, he discovered that the property company was already bust, something Phillips also did not know.[19]

Companies House records showed that ULPD in fact was on the verge of being dissolved since June 2005 for failing to file proper accounts. Phillips, however, appears not to have done any of these checks when he started acting as an agent for Page and then an employee.

Bristol organized crime detective Mark Davey had made the same discovery about ULPD in the summer of 2006. He and his wife decided that they were not going to take Page to court to recover their £10,000 because they felt they couldn't afford legal fees and renovate their new house at the same time.

Instead, Davey wrote to Page asking for return of his money or a meeting to resolve the matter amicably. 'Over a period of months we have been promised through Steve that the money would be paid back in full with interest,' he wrote. 'This has not occurred and I have requested to meet you through Steve, who has been protective towards you and the difficulties that you have recently experienced … I would like to know, in writing, what has happened to our investment.'

Davey got no response from Page. The couple were aware they bore some responsibility for their predicament. 'In hindsight, my wife and I were naïve and foolish to make such an investment in the manner in which we did, without any written guarantees,' the detective later explained in a witness statement. 'Neither of us is inclined to take investment risks normally. We based our decisions largely on trust. It has put considerable strain on our marriage and our relationship with Steve and Nicky.'

By the late summer of 2006, relations between the Phillips and the Pages had completely broken down. Nicola was particularly worried about their future with so much discontent among Bristol investors. Her husband was more trusting of Page's plans for expansion in Bristol and had set up a business bank account for a yet to be formed company he called Aristo Car Hire.

Nicola started to go off the Essex couple after an incident during a June visit to Bristol. The Pages were staying at the Jarvis Grange hotel nearby. Both families had gone out for a meal but the Page boys were playing up so they returned early to the hotel. Phillips and Page stayed in the bar while Nicola and Laura went to the room with the boys. The women sat on the sofa while the boys ran riot around them. Nicola took her chance to ask Laura about the business. Her husband not been paid his wages for a few months, the loan repayments had stopped and she was concerned about having to face family and friends who had invested with Page.

'Laura, we are going to be OK? I mean about all the money that we have invested and that Steve has got for you?'

'Yeah, yeah, everything is fine. Don't worry,' Laura replied.

The four boys were making it impossible to continue the sensitive conversation so Nicola joined her husband in the hotel lobby. As the couple headed for their car, Nicola turned to Page and said, 'You'd better go and help Laura'.

By the time they got to their car, Page had rung and told the couple to come back. He was riled because Laura had told him that Nicola felt he was a bad influence on her husband. When the Phillips got to the hotel room, Page was in the middle of a furious row with his wife. 'The room had been trashed, even the baby's cot, and they were at each other's throats,' Nicola recalled. They left immediately.

Violent rows in front of the children were now a frequent part of family life. Laura was tired of taking the brunt of wives and others while her husband drank and deluded himself that he could gamble his way out of the situation rather than own up, which is privately what she had told him to do.

Days later Nicola called to say they were coming to London for their money. 'If you come up here I'll knock your fucking block off,' Laura told her and slammed the phone down.

Shortly before resigning from ULPD and closing the CMC account, on 24 July Steve Phillips wrote to Page:

> I have to advise you that things are getting totally out of hand here. Of the money collected from people in this area to invest with your firm (my wife included) not one has been repaid despite your promises.
>
> These investors are people who can ill afford a loss and the lack of return of this money is seriously affecting their lives both marital and financial. I would ask that some return be made at the earliest possible time. I and my family are now experiencing personal threats and threats against our property.

Chapter 15

Death threats, guns and gangsters

Page parked his Range Rover in front of BAT's offices in the quiet central London mews and waited for Fahim Baree and Anjam Khan to emerge. They had agreed to talk in private, away from more irate colleagues.

Baree was under heavy pressure to get back their money, which when combined with BAT boss Rahul Sharma's company investment stood at over one million pounds. Not everyone at the travel firm knew the full facts behind Baree's involvement with Page. Most knew he was his best mate, but not all were aware that while finance director of ULPD Baree had deposited investors' money in a CMC spread-betting account for the Royal Protection officer that was now £38,000 in debt.

Baree had tried for as long as he could to do what Page had asked of him and 'change the nappies' of loose-bowelled BAT colleagues by assuring them that all was well at ULPD. But the continued lack of returns and herd panic that followed had ended the popular delusion about Page's scheme and the time for wet wipes was well over when he arrived outside BAT's offices in early April 2006.

It didn't take long for the black Range Rover to be spotted by Dharmendhra Patel, one of the last BAT boys to invest. He rushed to confront the elusive Paul Page. When he got there another BAT investor, Matthew 'Mash' Smith, had joined in. Mash had invested £50,000, almost half of which Baree had put into his CMC account on Page's instructions.[1]

The conversation by the Range Rover was getting heated by the time Patel arrived.

'Where's our money?' demanded Khan, a £170,000 investor.

'When the barns are completed and I get money from other investments I will pay people off,' Page told the group.

'You've been saying that for fuckin' ages, what's the score, Paul?'

'The barns will be completed soon and sold by the end of May. Your money is safe.'

It was a very confident performance, thought Jit Mandalia, another BAT investor who had joined the discussion. It was also a pack of lies.

The barns were way off being completed and Mortgage Guarantee just weeks away from repossessing them. Page had promised the finance firm a £100,000 sign of good faith payment that would hardly make a dent in the almost one million pounds he owed them.

It wasn't that Page didn't have the money. Days earlier he'd secretly secured £133,000 from Baree's mother who had re-mortgaged the family home in east London. But the story of how this money was secured and then squandered casts Page and Baree in a shameful light.

Akhtari Baree was coming up to retirement as a social worker. She wanted to buy a place in Dubai to live near her family or at least as a holiday home. As a widow with grown-up children, she had no desire to get older in east London after a lifetime of dealing with its problems. Her Leytonstone two-up, two-down was mortgage free after the death of her husband nine years earlier. It had also been rising in value, especially since London won the right to host the 2012 Olympics.

Baree had been trying since January to help his mother remortgage her home. When he told Page of his mother's retirement plans, his best mate saw pound signs.

'It'll kick-start the barns project, which has ground to a halt. If I can get the barns to a finished state then mortgage them for £987,000, I can pay investors back,' Page told Baree.

'I'll do it for you, Paul. But, you know, I'm going to need this back, it's my mum's house we are talking about.'

Baree didn't tell his mum he was going to ask her for the remortgage money until after she had it in her account. The remortgage with Abbey National was arranged with help from brokers and ULPD investors Paresh Solanki and Bimal Lodhia, who by this stage had invested £130,000.

Baree wanted to get his BAT colleagues paid and off his back and redeem the £30,000 investment raised by remortgaging his own Leytonstone home in 2004. He still trusted Page not to have him over. But a simple check would have shown that by March 2006 there was little equity left in the barns to make the plan financially viable.

By Baree's own account, he already believed that Page owned the property outright but had borrowed £250,000 to renovate it. A check would have revealed the barns had actually been bought with a massive loan from Mortgage Guarantee and that St James's Palace officers had placed huge charges on the development, which would leave next to nothing for anyone else when satisfied.

Another suspicious aspect of this whole episode concerned the application form sent to Abbey National. It was wholly misleading, if not fraudulent. The building society was led to believe Mrs Baree lived at Paresh Solanki's house, earned more money than she did and that the loan would be used for a retirement home.

She signed the form without apparently checking it because naturally she trusted her son to look after her interests. He never took her to an independent mortgage adviser, who, if aware of the true facts, would in all likelihood not have advised that she gamble away her future on rescuing ULPD and the barns project.

So how did such a false mortgage application get made? Baree and Solanki admit that they filled out some of the detail. Solanki, however, says he did so without speaking to Mrs Baree and doesn't know how his home address appeared on her application form. Solanki believed that Lodhia had filled it out. But Lodhia denied any fraudulent or misleading conduct in connection with the application form.

For his part, Baree admits that 'the mortgage was taken out on the pretence of getting a holiday or retirement home for my mum' but denied any deception or collusion with Page and others.[2]

Wherever the truth lies, on 27 March 2006 Abbey National did loan Mrs Baree £150,000. That day her son sat his mother down and asked for most of it.

'I need it for a barns development project Paul and I am involved in. You will get it back with some interest in a few months,' he told her. 'Paul will take care of the loan repayments too.'

Mrs Baree still felt the bond of a surrogate mum towards Page and wanted to help. That day she transferred £140,000 to her son's Barclays account. The following day Baree met Page and Laura at a solicitor's office to notarize two letters, which all three had signed.

The first was an agreement that Page would pay Baree £544,000 by 30 May 2006. It said:

It is confirmed that Paul Page is fully responsible for the receipt and return of the below mentioned funds back to MF Baree. It is also confirmed that Laura Page has no lien or claim on said funds received through her bank account and that she was only acting on Mr Pages [sic] instructions to use her account as a vehicle for money movement.

The £544,000 represented the consolidated debt Page accepted that he owed to the BAT investors including Sharma. Baree said he agreed the strategy of consolidating the debt following 'pressure' from his boss. A separate agreement was drafted to cover his mum's remortgage money, his own investment and unpaid returns. The figure Page agreed was £200,000, which he said would come from the money earned from selling Barn C to the Copleys.

Like the £544,000 guarantee, it was all pie in the sky, a cynical device by Page to get his hands on more cash and keep Laura protected from the shit storm that he knew was gathering on the horizon.

With the two worthless agreements in place, on 28 March 2006 Page directed Baree on how to disperse the money now in his account. £33,000 was transferred to Laura's NatWest account. On the form Baree described the purpose as a 'personal loan'.

The second transfer of £80,000 went to the Bristol HSBC account of Steve and Nicola Phillips. Again, Baree put 'personal loan' on the form and followed it up with an email. It was sent to Nicola but addressed 'To whom it may concern', reflecting the fact that Baree had no relationship with his fellow lieutenant.

'I was aware of the name Steven [sic] Phillips as another person generating investments in relation to the barns project, though I never spoke to him. My £140,000 investment was solely for completion of the barns project and I told Paul this and that it wasn't to be used to pay off people,' said Baree.[3]

However, court documents show that Phillips, on instructions, had immediately transferred all the £80,000 to his wife's CMC account for Page to gamble.

A day later, on 29 March, Baree withdrew a further £20,000 from his mother's mortgage money and handed the cash to his best friend. Page rewarded him with the use of a VW Toureg courtesy of Gripper Cars. Baree also pimped his own ride with some of the money that his mum had put in his account for the barns project. Despite being heavily in debt, he spent £1500 on a set of alloy wheels.

Baree's conduct around the remortgaging of his mum's home and his gamble with her future raises serious questions about his credibility. Before the fraud trial he told me that he'd done the remortgage to bail out his best mate and get his own money back. 'Even up to that point I still trusted him,' he said. 'There were warning signs around. I didn't see it, I just fell into a big hole.'

But looking at what Baree must have known by March 2006, his claims of being a foolish, trusting dupe either show an appalling myopia or simply lack credibility. One major personal warning was the £38,000 debt incurred by Page in his friend's name. Page had given Baree a worthless note in November 2005 taking responsibility for the debt. Yet, four months later, with the debt still unpaid, Baree was willing to accept another two letters from Page assuming financial responsibility for a loan almost ten times bigger.

Baree maintains that Page shafted him. And he undoubtedly did. But maybe Baree was also in so deep and under pressure from others that he made some very questionable decisions to recover the position; decisions that show him to have been either reckless or stupid or on the very edge of criminality.

£ £ £

The convoy of cars came to a halt outside Page's house in a manner that made neighbours in the cul-de-sac twitch their curtains. It was a May evening in 2006, one month after Page had lied outside BAT that money was coming from the imminent sale of the barns.

Among the group of five irate investors was Anjam Khan. He had recently met the Duke of Edinburgh at a Buckingham Palace reception where he was representing the travel company.

Laura was already by the open door as Khan, his brother Saeed, Baree, Matthew 'Mash' Smith and his brother-in-law approached. Page was crouching down in the living room while his sons peered out of the windows.

Baree could see Laura was very angry at the heavy-handed presence and knew she would do whatever to defend her boys.

'Why don't you all just fuck off,' she shouted.

While the others demanded that Page come out, Baree called the one Royal Protection officer from Buckingham Palace who he knew could reach his best mate. Baree had met the officer the previous year and also arranged a £7000 holiday for him courtesy of Gripper Airways.

'Mick? It's Fahim Baree. Look, I'm outside Paul's house with some investors from my work. To be honest there's a bit of a ruck developing. Can you get down here and talk to Paul?'

Mick 'the Don' Hickman was also an investor. One police document, which Page confirms, estimated that the Don had put £100,000 into the scheme.

'Mick's on his way here,' Baree told the others who began backing away from the house.

The Kenyan-born Khan brothers were particularly annoyed because Page had recently duped them into handing over a further £19,000.

Saeed Khan, 43, had handed over £10,000 on 12 April after Page explained falsely that he needed cash for an employee of Mortgage Guarantee to release part of the equity from the barns. Baree had also given Page £10,000 apparently for the same purpose. It was yet another extraordinary example of the lengths some in the BAT circle were willing to go to in order to get back their money.[4] Anjam was not involved in paying a backhander or sweetener but had put in another £9000 in the hope the barns could be completed.

When Hickman arrived at the cul-de-sac he went straight to Baree. Page was having a screaming row inside the house with Laura and wouldn't come outside.

'I don't want to be here, I've only come here to break it up,' the Don said.

He then turned towards the other BAT boys.

'You all piss off! And don't come back. I'll speak to Paul,' he told them.

Baree endorsed the idea and told the others that Hickman could diffuse the situation, find out the truth and let them know the score. He was, after all, also a serving police officer.[5]

£ £ £

'Get Paul Page on the fucking phone!' Rahul Sharma ordered Anjam Khan in the BAT office a month later. As he dialled the home number, Sharma warned Khan and Baree, who was sitting next to him, 'If Paul doesn't sign this fucking letter you two are sacked'.

Page had already told Baree that he would sign whatever nonsense his boss put in front of him. Another letter for Sharma was just words not worth the paper they were written on, he thought.

However, for the BAT boss the letter he drafted meant an awful lot more. Sharma had been getting it in the neck from his wife, who wanted confirmation from Page that the more than £100,000 debt would be repaid by 17 July. He was also panicking because it was already June and BAT's auditors wanted to sign off the travel company's annual accounts for the last tax year. But before doing so they required confirmation that the debt was recoverable. Sharma was concerned that the auditors would discover he had used company money in a private investment with a property company that had now been dissolved.

Khan handed his boss the ringing phone.

'Hello?' It was Laura who answered.

'This is Rahul Sharma from BestatTravel. Is your husband there?'

'No, sorry. He's out.'

'Listen, you fucking bitch! Tell Paul he's to give my money back. Now!' Sharma exploded.

'Tell him yourself,' Laura responded sarcastically but taken aback by the anger in the voice of a man she had never met.

'I'm going to kill you and your children if I don't get my fucking money.'

'I'm taping this call by the way and…'

'I don't fucking care.'

Khan and Baree were shocked by what they were witnessing. Their boss was making what sounded like a death threat against a mother and her five young children.[6] When the call finished moments later, Baree summoned the courage to admonish his boss. 'Don't ever make a call like that to the Pages again,' he said sternly.

Days later, on Sharma's instructions a letter was drafted which the BAT boss and Page signed on 6 June. It confirmed that 'BAT has invested £160,000 into ULPD in September/October 2005 for the [barns project which] is estimated to be completed by 10 July 2006'. The letter went on to record that BAT had received £70,000 leaving a balance owed of £90,000 to be repaid by 17 July.

Sharma was still unhappy with the text and on the same day had Page sign a new letter with different figures. This time, BAT's total investment was said to be £260,000. Of that, £146,000 had been paid back leaving £104,000 [sic] to be repaid by 17 July.

Page said he signed the letters because he didn't want Baree sacked from his senior sales consultant job of six years. He also understood that BAT needed proof that the company funds had been invested in property. In one NatWest bank document, Sharma had recorded the purpose of the transfer of £100,000 to Page as 'cash for trading'. However, Sharma, supported by Baree, denied during the trial that there was any attempt to dupe BAT's auditors and the accountancy firm never reported one in the company's accounts.

£ £ £

Page had a fascination with guns ever since his paternal grandfather bought him replicas as a boy. He would produce intricate drawings of the weapons, which his grandfather displayed in their Leytonstone house.

As a Royal Protection officer Page favoured a modern automatic sidearm, the Glock. Weapons would normally be left behind the gates of Buckingham Palace when officers clocked off. But Baree remembers 'a variety of firearms' Page would show off on visits to his house. 'Paul would claim that some of the firearms were real and showed me them. They were apparently official police firearms. He also showed me replica firearms. Therefore I knew he had access to guns.'

Page's record as a certified SO14 firearms holder was not a good one. It wasn't that long ago that he had his Glock taken off him for allegedly threatening to shoot his brother-in-law. Since then, the stress in his life had increased significantly. Angry investors were regularly ringing up or coming to his house unannounced; Sharma had made a heat of-the-moment threat to kill his wife and children and there was talk that Khan was receiving threats from Essex gangsters.

But this wasn't the reason Page had started surfing the Internet looking to buy an unlicensed weapon. He was convinced he needed a gun because Bimal Lodhia, the financial adviser and investor, had also reported threats and a mysterious robbery, possibly involving unsavoury Turkish and Russian investors.

Page planned to arm up and confront the foreigners with the help of a carload of trusted police officers but the mission was aborted, he said, because no one had their names.

Once again, threats of violence and suggestions of organized crime involvement with Page's syndicate were hanging in the air.

£ £ £

In July 2006, Adam McGregor turned up at Page's house clasping his credit card statements. He was still under the illusion that Page had bought the barns outright. It was a popular illusion because most other investors hadn't bothered to check. McGregor continued to put in money because he believed that when the barns were completed and sold the syndicate would clean up in the housing bubble.

229

'I've given you money left, right and centre when you needed it, Paul, on the proviso that all would come good on the barns, and now I need this money,' he told Page.

'Everything will be alright. Don't get upset, mate. The barns will be mortgaged and you'll get your money.'

McGregor was also worried about the spread-betting side of the business.

'There's far too much money going into CMC, Paul. Why isn't it going to the barns to get them ready to be mortgaged so I and my family can get some of our money back?' he asked.

'I'm hedging on different accounts.'

It was a reply McGregor didn't really understand but nor did he think it was obvious nonsense. So he left empty handed unaware that more than £1 million had been gambled and lost.[7]

However, Page knew he was going to have to show some proof of funds soon for his lieutenant to remain a believer. If McGregor saw a pot of gold, he thought, word would spread quickly in the same way the illusion of incredible returns had since 2002.

Days later, on 15 July, Page met McGregor at a cashpoint by the local Tesco outside Chafford Hundred train station where commuters were already returning from their City jobs.

Page had called the meeting to prove the barns had finally been mortgaged and there was a huge lump of money released in his Abbey National account from which everyone would be paid out.

He put his card into the hole in the wall, punched in his pin and at 4.51 pm removed the receipt slip to show McGregor, who was waiting nearby. The receipt slip read:

AT TESCO CHAF HUN EXP
TRANSACTION REFERENCE: 009524

ACCOUNT 4138
BALANCE £878,004.15
YOU CAN WITHDRAW NIL

McGregor studied the receipt and in that moment said he felt 'totally reassured', as if the pressure of debt and shame had suddenly been lifted from his shoulders. The last line of the receipt was rendered invisible by the shining hope of the one above it.

Now convinced he had proof of a real pot of gold, on Page's orders McGregor faxed the receipt to also hopeful Steve Phillips in Bristol and to Craig Gunn, the boss of Arrow Car Hire in Cardiff, who was owed £20,000. Just to make sure the word spread Page also personally faxed both of them.

Phillips was at the time fending off angry investors. On 17 July, two days after getting the faxed proof of funds, the Bristol agent texted the licensee of the Hauliers Arms. 'I received a fax showing funds in account waiting to clear. Given Paul your details.'

Word of the pot of gold spread throughout the syndicate and on 20 July Page went to a Sainsbury's cashpoint to get a new receipt slip showing the same balance of £878,004.15.

Five days later, he returned to the Tesco cashpoint for a third receipt to fax other key investors baying for proof of funds.

The whole exercise was another massive deception of investors to get more money and buy more time. Page had learned by coincidence that you could get an immediate bank receipt from a cashpoint showing a large balance without actually depositing a cheque or having any funds. All you have to do is type in an amount of money that you are pretending to deposit and the machine produces a receipt slip suggesting a healthy balance.

At the time of the hole-in-the-wall scam Page's Abbey National account was £4.15 in credit.

£ £ £

The scam was only ever going to buy Page a short reprieve. Not least because a week before he tried it out on McGregor, fellow police officer Mark Copley had received a letter from Mortgage Guarantee telling him the barns were being repossessed.

Page was wasting no time seeking an exit strategy. 'We're going to fuck off, love, put as much distance between us and the UK. It's all gone wrong. I need to regroup,' he told Laura knowing how she longed for a new start.

Page contacted Golden Sands Migration, a firm specializing in relocating Brits to New Zealand for £4000. He also rang the New Zealand police to register his interest in transferring from the Met. At the same time the Internet was trawled for information on false identities.

The idea of doing a runner had been tried a few weeks earlier but ended with a pathetic *volte face* at the white cliffs of Dover. Page had rented a villa for £2000 in the south of France from someone he met while they were filling up their flash cars at an M25 service station.

Laura loved the idea of Cannes and packed her entire wardrobe into three suitcases. The boys were taken out of school and stuffed into the Range Rover, which quietly rolled out of Chafford Hundred with the possibility of never returning. Page thought if he had a break away from the incessant whining of angry investors his winning ways on the markets and virtual casino tables would re-emerge. It was a classic gambler's delusion.

The family stopped at TGI Friday's at Lakeside, where the couple had their wedding reception almost ten years earlier. Then they drove to Dover to catch the ferry to France. It was fish 'n' chips all round but there was no hotel with any vacancy that night to accommodate the family. Page began to waver about running away and headed back to Essex with the kids asleep in the back.

When they arrived home, Laura took her three suitcases upstairs but didn't unpack for weeks. It was only when Page discussed New Zealand in July that she started to mellow.

The desire to 'run for the hills' was common among other Ponzi schemers of this era when it all came on top. Men such as US hedge-fund manager Sam Israel, whose $450 million dollar fraud collapsed in 2005 when investors lost confidence and asked for their money back. Israel had phoney auditors to 'verify' his made-up financial returns and then faked his own suicide to avoid a twenty-year prison sentence by parking his car on a bridge and writing on the roof 'suicide is painless' before going on the run.

Israel had sustained losses, which he thought he would recover in the next quarter. But the losses continued and with them came the lies to investors. 'I thought, "I can make this back". I wasn't worried in the least. I was a good trader. I was a workaholic. Was it hard to lie in the beginning? No. Did it get harder? Yes. I lived with the beast every day,' he told a reporter from prison after turning himself in.

Asked how investors can stop getting conned, Israel offered this advice: 'Seek as much transparency as possible. If they do not understand exactly how a manager is making money, do not invest. If there is a secret process that cannot be explained, run.'

£ £ £

'Hello, is that Detective Gemma Bradford?'

'Yes. Who's this?' asked the Avon and Somerset officer.

'Hello, I'm Detective Sergeant Mark Beckett from the Metropolitan Police's Department of Professional Standards.'

'Hello.'

'I understand you are dealing with a complaint about a PC Paul Page,' said Beckett getting straight to the point.

'Well, I'm looking at alleged deception offences involving Paul Page and a Steve Phillips.'

It was early November 2006 and DC Bradford was investigating a recent complaint of financial deception from the Bristol publicans and others.[8] Beckett, an anti-corruption detective on Operation Aserio, had been tasked to tell her of the Met's interest in the case.

'I'm ringing to let you know that Page is a Met officer from Royalty Protection on a career break. He is part of a bigger investigation we're doing.'

Operation Aserio had been going now for six months. The officer in charge, Detective Inspector Michael Orchard, lobbied Avon and Somerset senior officers for his squad to take over their investigation. Orchard explained there was a 'wider picture' and his anti-corruption detectives were already at the stage of liaising with the Crown Prosecution Service.

The local force didn't want to relinquish control so an agreement was struck that the Bristol police wouldn't arrest anyone without first consulting DI Orchard. It was an interesting accommodation between the two police forces and one that smacked of damage limitation by the Met.

Operation Aserio was already in touch with a handful of angry St James's Palace officers, including some who'd transferred to the Ministry of Defence Police.

One of them, former police constable Lenny Thiel, had every reason to talk to Operation Aserio. But if loyalty to Page was an

Olympic sport, Thiel deserved a gold medal for giving his friend every opportunity to come good. By late 2006, however, he was done waiting.

Of all the people he screwed over, Lenny Thiel was the one Page most regretted. He described him as a 'big bruiser, a muscle man, a soldier in it for the long run'. But Page also saw Thiel as a follower whose friendship and trust he would ruthlessly nurture and then exploit when he needed money.

The pair would double date much to Laura's annoyance, who was often kicking her husband under the table during dinner wanting to go home. Despite her pimped Range Rover, Laura felt embarrassed when Thiel, a member of a classic car club, once turned up with his date in a lime-green Rolls-Royce.

It was the love of cars that first brought Page to Thiel's attention. He noticed the flash motors he drove to Buckingham Palace during the Currency Club years.

Both men had joined SO14 around the same time but Thiel's initial investments did not begin until the first half of 2005. He was sitting on a pile of readies while living with his mum after a divorce and had £70,000 savings and cash from his share of the matrimonial home.

Thiel was looking to buy his own house but could also see the value of an investment opportunity that didn't tie him up too long. He knew Page was on leave and had property interests and was spread betting. The lure of preferential police rates on the barns development was enough for him to put in £110,000, most of which he invested without visiting the site. Separately, he invested £25,000 for the mysterious Premier League footballer wanting a short-term bridging loan.

Thiel had brought into the syndicate his mother, sister and a police friend, who put in his retirement money. At first there were returns in brown envelopes filled with £50 notes, which Page handed out during his rounds of the palaces. But by the second half of the year these stopped and were replaced by excuses.

Page told Thiel that Special Branch had frozen the ULPD bank account over a business deal in Dubai.

'I need some dough for one week, Len. It'll keep the company afloat while I deal with the Dubai problem. I'll give you a 50 per cent return on it, mate,' Page pleaded.

Thiel was already committed to the tune of £150,000. But Page magically produced ULPD bank statements claiming a £500,000 balance and two large earlier transactions of £1.8 million. The six-figure sum alone must have blinded Thiel to those other parts of the statements that were curiously Tippexed out. Nor did he appear worried that Page suggested he owned a portfolio of properties, none of which were in his name.

'I'll sign over ownership of one of the barns through my solicitors. It's worth £600,000, Len,' a desperate Page added.

'No need, mate,' Thiel responded. 'I trust you. I'm not the type who takes advantage of a mate's short-term financial difficulties.'

Thiel was happy to help out but he did speak to a Special Branch contact who said the counter-terrorism unit would only be interested in freezing accounts where millions had passed through and not the £250,000 Page was claiming had come from Dubai.

'I've checked your story out, Paul, and it doesn't ring true,' Thiel told him at their next meeting.

'That's because it's a lie, me old mate. I am actually under investigation by the Inland Revenue. I just didn't want to say,' Page replied quickly.

Despite these flags, Thiel nevertheless went ahead and transferred another £80,000 to Laura's ULPD bank account in August. It was his retirement money after thirty years' service in the Met. Thiel was leaving in November to join the MoD Police.

Days before he transferred the money, MoD officials responsible for vetting candidates had come to Thiel's house. They wanted to go through his financial situation to ensure there was no susceptibility to blackmail. He thought he might need documentation to explain his six-figure investment in the syndicate so Page obliged with a back-dated loan agreement, which Thiel then signed.[9]

For most of 2006, Thiel waited for his money. That summer he was going on holiday to Cyprus and told Page by text that he expected 'a nice surprise' when he got back. 'Oh fuckin yeah! Sorry to be a dick but pls txt me a bank account. Had a recent fire u know wot I mean,' Page texted back, referring to his burning of ULPD documents in anticipation of a visit from Operation Aserio detectives.

A sun-tanned Thiel returned to the UK on 14 September and texted Page at 1 pm. 'Back from Cyprus in the early hours and checked my account. Well, I guess you are consistent. Fuk me, I did everything you ever asked me to do, and fukin promptly! My pension money nearly a year ago gets me the most. I just wanted to help! You knew what it was, 30 years' worth. My house money and every penny I ever saved! I still have to pay £25,000 to Henry [the police investor] and replace my mother's and sister's savings. That's £40,000 on top! That's me well and truly fuked! I still have no idea what you did with it or where it went. I don't have an option but to try and get it back!'

Page replied with more lies. 'Lenny I banked cheque for six figure sum. Wen it clears you will be taken care of as promised. Today is a shit day for me!' He then called to ask for another £30,000 for a too-good-to-miss deal while he was waiting for a £800,000 cheque to clear.

Amazingly, Thiel agreed to help again but could only pull up £800, which Page collected from the MoD facility. Another £1000 was transferred to the NatWest account of Page's father.

Of the £231,800 Lenny Thiel gave to Page some had gone to other investors in true Ponzi style, and some had gone towards spread betting. 'I truly believed I could generate money. [Lenny] didn't care as long as he thought he was helping me,' Page told me.

But Lenny did care and finally, in early October 2006, realized that his friend had wholly betrayed him. 'No dough and you strangely forget to phone. I think you must have fuked everybody whoever trusted you by now. Probably more than once. Easy money eh?'

'Not true!' Page texted back indignantly.

'I have calmed down since you shafted us the last time,' Thiel replied. 'What happened to you? You weren't always the sad, devious fucker you are now! All talk and excuses. I really thought you had sorted yourself out! Cost me another £1800 to find out I was wrong. Time for you to change your phone and hide now if I remember the format.'

Still falsely indignant, Page replied: 'U r out of order Lenny. I am not going anywhere. Will sort it today I hope.' Of course, the day came and went and Thiel was still waiting for his money.

Page sounded like a cockney Julius Caesar when Thiel told him he was taking legal action.

'And u now as well! I'm blowing the lid. Final straw. Paper

trail. My ass lets make it public. Talk through briefs. Lets go for it! Spoke to ur brief. Told him I'll see him in court. Sorry mate, no choice now.'

Thiel didn't respond and Page followed up on 6 October with his last text: 'It's going to kick off massive. Laura has flipped! I'm fucked!'

Chapter 16

Royal Protection: the Osmans

Tuesday, 14 November 2006: In a nondescript room somewhere in Scotland Yard, senior officers from three secretive police units began a Gold group meeting reserved for high-risk and highly sensitive matters that affect the force's reputation and national security. Present were anti-corruption detectives from the Directorate of Professional Standards (DPS), Royalty Protection and Specialist Operations.

Seven days earlier, the Intelligence Development Group (IDG), a secret intelligence-gathering cell known as the 'Dark Side', had received information about a threat to the life of Page and his family. The IDG had worked on the intelligence for two days and believed it to be true so a Gold meeting was convened to discuss how to deal with it.

An officer from the 'Dark Side', only referred to in the Gold meeting minutes as 'Simon', was the first to speak. He started with a brief overview of Page's financial history.

'At this point in time, information indicates PC Page is £3m in debt,' he told the group. It was the first time the scale of Page's losses had been estimated.

'A group of Asians have lent £750,000,' Simon went on to explain. 'This group have adopted legal methods and now intelligence suggests that PC Page will be kidnapped by [the] suspect.'

The kidnap plot was known to a number of those in the Asian group because the person behind it had been 'talking about it for some time,' said Simon.

The strong inference was that someone within the Asian group or close to them had tipped off the police directly or indirectly about the kidnap plot.

In his assessment of the threat, Simon referred to a 'hit-man' apparently contracted to carry out the kidnap. The minutes put it this way: 'Has the hit man got ability – yes (high risk).'

The suggestion appeared to be that the Met knew the identity of both the contract killer or kidnapper and the person who had contracted him. They believed the motive was the loss of money and presumably the hit-man had been asked to kidnap Page with a threat to harm or even kill him if he didn't pay up.

Overall, the risk to Page and his family was assessed as medium to high, which meant the Gold meeting had to consider invoking a very special procedure for such cases.

The procedure, known as an Osman warning, was a response by British police forces to a European Court of Human Rights ruling in October 1998.

The Osmans, a London family of Turkish-Cypriot origin, had brought a case against the Metropolitan Police and a north London school for their collective failure to protect them from a psychotic teacher. He had become 'obsessed' with their son, a former student. In 1988 the teacher shot dead Mr Osman and wounded his son. He then wounded a senior teacher and shot dead his son.

On his arrest, the psychotic teacher told the police, 'Why didn't you stop me before I did it? I gave you all the warning signs.' The school claimed it had alerted the Met to the key issues and concerns about the boy's possible kidnap, but the police denied this. The teacher pleaded guilty to manslaughter with diminished responsibility and was locked away in a secure mental hospital.[1]

As a result of the Osman case, since 1998 the police were liable to being sued if they failed to act on information suggesting a threat to someone's life. Acting on the information meant more than telling the intended victim of the threat but extended to keeping them safe and, wherever possible, neutralizing the threat. The police had a duty to tell someone of a threat to their life even if that person was secretly under investigation.

The DPS told the Gold meeting that they believed Page was aware of the threat to his life. However, Detective Chief Inspector Jill McTigue from the specialist operation unit that dealt with kidnaps was unwilling to accept the assertion. She was an astute woman who had risen through the ranks of a male-dominated force including a recent stint in the anti-corruption squad. So McTigue knew exactly how much weight to attach to their claim.

'We can't just presume that Page knows about the threat,' she told the Gold group. 'The Met should err on the side of caution and serve him with an Osman warning immediately, while my unit researches the kidnapper.'

McTigue was right. Page had no idea that someone in the BAT circle or close to it was plotting to have him kidnapped or possibly worse.

Simon was tasked with drawing up the Osman warning letter to be hand delivered to Page the next day. He was told it should be carefully worded as the Gold group was concerned how the whole situation would look for the Queen and Scotland Yard if it ever got out.

Detective Sergeant Jim Wingrave then addressed the meeting. He was the investigator on Operation Aserio whose report into Page's finances and welfare two years earlier had been almost entirely ignored by senior management at SO14.

Wingrave reminded everyone that when he submitted his report in January 2005, while there was no intelligence to suggest criminal activity, it was clear that Page was dealing with very large sums of cash, involved with other police officers in high-risk spread betting linked to property investments and had a 'gambling problem'.

Wingrave had initially identified six individuals involved with Page. Now, sixty-one possible investors were known to Operation Aserio and Page's personal debt, separate to his gambling losses, had quadrupled from £250,000 to just under £1 million.

'Our plan is to arrest PC Page in the New Year. We have identified some of his victims as fellow SO14 officers, such as PC Richard Humby, and others who have joined the Ministry of Defence Police from the Royalty Protection command,' Wingrave told the Gold meeting.

Once again, McTigue piped up with an incisive question directed at the most senior officer present from the DPS.

'What was done in January 2005?' she asked.

'The aim is to get this officer out,' Detective Superintendent Tony Evans replied, sidestepping her pointed question. A more fulsome answer might have been that nothing had been done to interrupt the fraud or protect investors from Page, and Page from himself. Instead, SO14 and the DPS had secretly agreed a strategy that Page would never come back to work from his period of extended leave.

The discussion among the Gold group then turned to a list of concerns. At the top of that list was 'MPS (Metropolitan Police Service) reputation'.

It was decided to implement some immediate welfare for Page. The stated reason recorded in the minutes was not a concern for his spiralling mental state, but 'to regain some ground from January 2005'. In other words, the Met realized it had failed Page and his victims and had to recover the position to appear less exposed if it became public.

Another area where the Met had badly messed up was over its failure to monitor ULPD. The company had been approved as Page's outside business interest exactly three years before the Gold group meeting. Approval is required at a very senior level in the Met and the policy is in place to prevent an officer bringing the force into disrepute.

Page's application to register ULPD was authorized by then Assistant Commissioner for Human Resources Bernard Hogan Howe, in November 2003. In a letter to Page, he wrote, 'I consider that this business interest is compatible with your membership of the Metropolitan Police Service (MPS)'.

The letter also reminded Page that he should only conduct ULPD business in his own time, never on police premises, not with police resources, never to give any indication that he was a police officer to promote the business, immediately report any significant change in circumstances and, finally, ensure that his business activities 'do not cause embarrassment to the Commissioner or become detrimental to the image and dignity of the MPS'.

In every respect, by the time of the Gold group meeting in November 2006 Page had breached all these conditions. However, the failure was by no means only his.

The Met, through SO14 and its Human Resources Directorate, was required under police procedure 33/02 to review Page's outside business interest every year before renewing it. However, this hadn't happened and the simplest of checks were not carried out. No one spoke to Page about ULPD or checked official records, which would have revealed it was a ghost company suspiciously trading without having filed any financial accounts.[2]

The consequences of this failure to review would surely have dawned on some of those now sitting around the table at the Gold group meeting at Scotland Yard. It meant that for three years Page had been able to use ULPD as a vehicle for his fraud and tell potential investors that it had the Metropolitan Police's seal of approval.

The revelation is a personal embarrassment to Bernard Hogan Howe, who is the current Met Commissioner.

Back at the Gold group, it was decided that Operation Aserio would have to go from being covert to an overt operation. Serving the Osman on Page the next day would be an opportunity to also tell him that his financial dealings were formally under criminal and disciplinary investigation.

At this point, those present at the meeting took an extraordinary decision, which on the face of it appeared to have little or no regard for the victims of Page's financial shenanigans and everything to do with saving the Queen and Scotland Yard further embarrassment.

It was decided to give Page the opportunity to resign, which would be accepted there and then if he agreed. The value of such a Machiavellian offer was that Page would no longer be a royal police officer if the scandal ever became public.

Operation Aserio knew by November 2006 that many officers across the Met's specialist units and other forces were involved with Page's hedge fund. The easiest way to assess the scale of the fraud and vulnerability of officers would be to get Page to name names in return for leniency at court. But that was not the plan.

The plan devised between SO14 and the DPS and underwritten by the Gold group was to get Page out of the police with as little fuss as possible.

The line that would from now on be spun was that this was a simple case of a rogue cop and not a scandal involving Royal Protection officers and Buckingham Palace.

£ £ £

12.30 pm, Wednesday, 15 November: In another non-descript meeting room, this time in Jubilee House, the south London home of the anti-corruption squad, detective inspector Michael Orchard was getting a briefing from his boss about the resignation offer and Osman warning to be given later that afternoon to Page at his Essex home.

Detective Superintendent Tony Evans was being very specific about the exact wording to be used when delivering the Osman warning.

Orchard discounted the idea of using the local police even though they could be at Hatton Close in no time. At 4 pm, he briefed Detective Sergeant Jim Howells before sending him across London at rush hour to Page's house.

'I've tried calling him but nobody is picking up the home phone,' said Orchard, the perfectly named detective for the business of plucking rotten apples. 'If Page is out when you get there but his wife is in you are to give her the Osman warning as the threat is also against her and the family,' he added.

Detective Sergeant Howells was told not to deviate from the carefully worded script and to update Orchard, who would pass on developments to a SO14 superintendent just appointed to take charge of looking after Page's welfare.

At close to 6 pm, Howells and two detective constables walked up the drive of Hatton Close. It was dark but they could see Laura, who was standing in the doorway with Harry on her hip and saying goodbye to a girlfriend whose child she'd been minding.

Laura clocked the three men walking towards her in suits and overcoats. 'Here we go again,' she thought to herself. 'Three more greedy bastards after their cheese.'

'Are you Mrs Laura Page?' Detective Sergeant Howells asked.

'Yeah, who are you?'

Laura's friend was now in her car and about to leave but stopped when she saw the men at the door.

'Are you alright?' she mouthed through the car window. Laura nodded and her friend drove off.

'Can we come in? It is very urgent,' Howells said as he and the two other detectives displayed their warrant cards. Laura was starting to worry that something had happened to her eldest son, Thomas.

'We are Metropolitan Police officers from the Professional Standards Command, Specialist Investigations. Is your husband in?'

'No. My husband's at a meeting in Slough. He is not contactable. I don't expect him home until much later tonight.'

'We need to talk privately, Mrs Page. Can we come in?'

Laura showed the detectives into her lounge and plonked herself on the sofa. Howells and another officer sat on either side of her. The boys were running around playing with toy guns. One of them had trained a laser on the third anti-corruption officer, an irony that was lost in the tense moment. The boys kept coming back into the room with all manner of pretexts, which was annoying for Howells, who was no expert in Osman warnings.

'Can we please have some privacy, Mrs Page?' the detective said. 'I have some very important information to tell you.'

247

'I can keep these outside, but not Harry. He's tired and needs his bath. You know what they are like. You can say it in front of him,' Laura explained putting her youngest on her knee.

Howells produced the typed Osman warning letter meant for Page and started reading from it. 'I am Detective Sergeant James Howells from the Metropolitan Police Professional Standards Command Specialist Investigations Unit based at Jubilee House. You are not under arrest. You are not under caution. You're free to leave if you wish. I'm here to inform you that I have information that indicates your wellbeing may be in danger. Police have received specific intelligence, which suggests that you and your wife or family are in danger. Threats have been made that you may be subjected to violence to recover debts that you apparently owe to persons. I believe that you too are aware of this fact and that the situation may have arisen as a result of your lifestyle and/or business activities.'

'I half expected this,' Laura interrupted.

'Why?' asked Howells.

'Paul owed some money to people in relation to his business. Well, to say he owed them money is not right. He invested their money and like all investments the value goes up as well as down. Paul has given them some of their money back but they want more.'

'Who are these people?'

'I don't know, you'll have to ask Paul.'

'Have you had any concerns or issues in relation to yours, Paul's or your family's safety?'

'We've had a few police call but they said they would be trying to get their money back through the civil courts.' Laura named Humby, Molen and Pearce.

Howells was not across the detail of the case so he continued reading from the note: 'I must advise you now that you should take appropriate measures to ensure your own safety but must warn you this does not entitle you to break the law. If you do then you will be liable to arrest and prosecution. Do you understand that?'

The other officer on the sofa noted that Laura agreed and got her to sign the letter at 6.38 pm.

'Do you need any help from the Met?' Howells asked.

'I'll wait for my husband to return,' she replied calmly.

'Don't open the door to strangers and call the police if you have any concerns,' he advised her. Before leaving the house, Howells handed over a sealed letter for Page.

Back in the car, Howells phoned Orchard and told him the Osman warning had been given to Laura in Page's absence, that she was calm and didn't require any police assistance.

Meanwhile, Laura rang her husband after opening the letter.

'Hello, love,' said Page, who was driving.

'I've just had a visit from three intelligence officers saying our lives are in danger, Paul.'

'What? I can't hear you very well. Call me on Anjam's phone, my battery's low.'

Page pulled Anjam Khan's BMW X5 into a nearby petrol station and waited. Khan was in the passenger seat and when Laura called he put her on the car speakers.

'I've just had a visit from three intelligence officers saying our lives are in danger, Paul.'

'That doesn't sound right, love.'

'One of them, Howells, left a letter for you with his number. It says you should call him.'

'Love, hang up and call 999 then ring me straight back,' Page told her. He believed that if the threat was genuine then his old force, Essex Police, would have been briefed and there would be an unmarked car parked outside his house.

Laura explained to the emergency operator about the strange visit to her house.

'They said threats had been made against our lives and we had to move out. My husband is a Met Police officer and he's on his way home. They said there was a serious threat against our lives. It was to do with the lifestyle we are living.'

She was put through to an inspector at Chelmsford police station. He was puzzled by the story, had no idea what an Osman warning was and checked to see if any death threats to the Pages had been logged on the Essex Police computer. There were none because the DPS had left it to SO14 to tell the local force about the threat to Page but they hadn't done so. The inspector took down Howells's number and a description of all three men.

'Lock your doors and don't panic. I will make some inquiries and call you back in thirty minutes,' he advised her.

Laura immediately informed her husband that Essex Police had no knowledge about the threats. This made Page even more agitated and wonder whether he was being set up for a hit by one of his police investors.

By now in a complete rage, he called Howells and let rip, with Khan still listening through the car speakers.

'Who the fuck are you? What you doing coming round my fucking house and frightening my wife and kids? I am going to fuck you up if you don't tell me who you are.'

'PC Page, calm down. Where are you? I'll tell you …'

'Fucking calm down, you cunt!' Page interrupted. 'Come round my fucking house and tell my wife some bollocks that our lives are in danger, fucking calm down. If it was real you wouldn't have left my wife and kids alone. There'd be a police car outside the house, you cunt.'

'Your wife didn't want us to stay until you returned …'

'If anything happens to my family it will be on your fucking head, I'm telling you now.'

'Paul. Please listen carefully. The Osman warning I gave your wife is no hoax. It is real and we have specific intelligence of a threat against you and your family to do with debts you owe.'

'What's the source of that intelligence?'

'I don't know. And even if I did I couldn't tell you.'

'I'm taking my family to a secure location, and then I'm going to get a team together and start rattling a few fucking doors.'

'You may be on a career break, Paul, but you are still a police officer. I'm warning you to act within the law at all times.'

'Fuck the law! I'm gonna sort this out and get to the source of it and bash the fuck out of them.'

Howells managed to calm down Page, who was starting to believe the DPS detective may be genuine by the time he arrived at Chafford Hundred.

'I'm taking my family to a hotel tonight.'

'I need to see you tomorrow, Paul. Where can we meet?'

'Come to my house at 11 am.'

Howells agreed and said he would also get a message to super-intendent Sean Walters at SO14 to call Page. He was the senior put in charge of Page's welfare.

'OK. I'll call you in fifteen minutes when I know what the score is with my wife.'

Page rushed inside the house. Laura told him the boys were fine and that Essex Police had just called to say Howells and his two colleagues were anti-corruption officers for the Met.

Just then Howells called and Page offered him a possible explanation for who was behind the threats.

'I think it's coming from a family problem when I had my gun

251

taken away at SO14. There are members of my wife's family who are jealous of our lifestyle. Last Sunday it all kicked off again at a car-boot sale.'

Howells listened and reiterated that he could give no insight into the intelligence, but warned him again to stay within the law.

Page put down the phone, grabbed a small black case and jumped into the car.

'They're going to get it,' he told Khan, who was shocked to see Page remove a silver Beretta handgun from the case. He had no idea it was an air-powered weapon as they drove around the Chafford Hundred estate looking for would-be assassins.

None were found and back home, at 9.10 pm Page took a call from Superintendent Walters.

'Hello, sir,' said Page.

'I'm ringing about the Osman warning the DPS have just given you. I know you had doubts they are genuine but you can take it from me they are DPS and you should take the threat seriously. The DPS are there to help you and your family.'

'Thanks, sir, but I don't trust 'em. I think I know where the threat is coming from. I'll deal with it my way.'

'You mustn't do anything that would worsen the situation. I am here to offer you welfare support. Have you got my mobile?'

'Yes. DS Howells gave it to me tonight.'

'Well, you can call me anytime. I will call you tomorrow.'

Page had decided against taking his family to a hotel. Instead, he told Laura to put all the boys in their bedroom and lock herself in. She put a broom under the door handle for extra protection.

Meanwhile, Page assembled an array of weapons he had in the house and garage. Two swords and a bulletproof vest with CS gas were positioned by the front door while Page stood guard all night with an imitation handgun and rifle.

£ £ £

Page had been on his way back from a successful meeting with another hapless investor when Laura had called with the news of the Osman warning.

Anjam Khan had driven Page to meet the new investor, Abishake Gill, a baggage handler at Heathrow Airport. Gill had initially gone to Bimal Lodhia for mortgage advice, but the financial adviser suggested he could increase his deposit for a house by investing in a get-rich-quick-scheme with a guaranteed 20–25 per cent quarterly return.

Gill didn't ask and wasn't given much detail of the scheme before handing Lodhia £20,000 in cash in October 2005. A year later he rowed with his financial adviser after receiving nothing of what had been promised. Lodhia told Gill for the first time that his money had been pooled with others and invested with a police officer called Paul Page.

Weeks before the Osman warning, Gill had contacted Page who said he knew nothing of the £20,000 investment. If Gill reinvested Page pledged to recover the £20,000 and make more money for the baggage handler.

Gill didn't know who to believe. Lodhia and Paresh Solanki advised him to demand some collateral before reinvesting. They knew Page was desperate for money and privately joked that the once cool cop would now walk down the high street in women's clothing for a pound note.

Page had no collateral to give Gill. He was the proverbial busted flush. But with the perverted logic that only a hopeless gambler or drug addict could find acceptable, he found the courage to ask Laura if she would loan him her wedding ring. This was the £1500 band of silver and diamonds that he'd bought her during their Venezuela holiday six years ago to replace the £29 Argos wedding ring.

'You've had everything else, my Louis [Vuitton] and all that. But you can't fucking have this,' she initially told him. The £700 Louis Vuitton bag he'd bought her from winnings on stocks and shares had been sold already on eBay. That left only one of the designer's purses, which Laura wouldn't let go. But when he persisted about the ring she relented, removed it from her finger and put the symbol of their love in her husband's pathetic outstretched hand.

Page went straight to Solanki's office on 28 October. Solanki was surprised to see him looking so unkempt when he usually turned up looking 'very slick' and driving a fancy car. On this occasion, Page was in a shell suit driving an old banger.

Solanki drew up an agreement between Page and Gill, which valued the ring at £9000. Gill then agreed to meet Page after work on 15 November at the Marriot Hotel near Heathrow to discuss a further investment.

Khan picked up Page from his home and waited in a nearby café while Page and Gill met. The baggage handler was shown property plans but of course Gill didn't know that by now the barns had been repossessed and ULPD was dissolved. Page, sporting a baseball cap and sweatshirt, confirmed he was a police officer and assured Gill that his scheme was pukka. Gill was offered commission on any other investors he could attract. The meeting ended with Gill agreeing to invest £14,000 in return for holding Laura's wedding ring as collateral.

£ £ £

11 am, Thursday, 16 November: Page showed anti-corruption detectives Orchard and Howells into the living room. The house was empty and his demeanour was calm and polite.

'I'd like to apologize for my behaviour last night on the phone,' he told Howells.

'That's quite alright. It must have come as a shock and you were understandably concerned for your family's safety.'

Apology accepted, Orchard turned to Page and said: 'We are here to tell you something very specific. That is all we will be allowed to tell you around that. Therefore please listen and we will go through it.'

That was Howell's cue to start reading the same Osman warning letter. At the end of it, Page confirmed he understood it and signed the form at 11.10 am. He calmly tried to downplay the threat as historic, in the same way that the night before he had suggested to Howells it could be family related.

Orchard told him that SO14 was responsible for his welfare and Page said he would also be speaking to his federation representative, Mick 'the Don' Hickman.

That was Howells's second cue to formally notify Page he was now going to serve him with official notification of an investigation into his finances. The news sent Page into a rage.

'Why wasn't I informed about this? Why wasn't I allowed to have my solicitor present?

Howells didn't reply but instead read from the Regulation 9 Notice:

It is alleged that whilst on a career break from the Metro-politan Police Service you have amassed a large financial debt, which is now subject to county court judgments. Further that you failed to notify the MPS of this. Your business interest and financial status is now subject to investigation. The actions described are in breach of Criminal Law, code of conduct 12, general conduct and code of conduct 6, disobeying a lawful order.

Howells then cautioned Page, who made no formal reply. But when the formalities were over, he spoke cautiously about what he thought had gone wrong since the Currency Club.

'I haven't done anything criminal. There used to be about twenty to forty officers who I invested money for on the stock market. I know about them. It was going well but when I hit some difficulties and the gravy train dried up all of a sudden they wanted their money back,' Page explained without admitting to any criminal act. 'I had no idea I had to tell you about the county court judgments. I want to come back to work, my application to return is being processed, and I'm willing to assist with your inquiry.'

'Do you want to tell us anything?' Howells asked.

'No. Look this isn't right.'

This was Howells's last cue to deliver the Machiavellian resignation offer that he and Orchard had discussed on the way over from south London.

'What do you really want out of all this, Paul?'

'What do you mean?' Page replied.

'Most of this will just disappear if you resign.'

On hearing this, a chill went through Page. At that moment he started to believe that something serious was going to happen to his family from somewhere in the police. He now knew he was in trouble, alone and his own people had turned on him and he could no longer seek help there.

'I will take whatever steps are necessary to protect my family,' Page responded. The reply appeared incongruous because he thought that the DPS meant the threat to his life would disappear if he resigned from the police.

The DPS officers made it clear that he could resign straight away because they had the authority to accept it. But Page declined and they left.

£ £ £

Within minutes of the DPS leaving his house, Page lit up a bonfire of the insanities of his cop hedge fund. He had already burnt some paperwork back in April when he was first tipped off that he was being looked at. He now wanted to get rid of other contracts that would betray those police colleagues who hadn't taken him to the civil court or put charges on his house and the barns. Most of these were Buckingham Palace boys, some of who had made their money and moved on.

'[I] burnt a lot when I got the touch from the DPS. The only thing I had left was the ledgers, which no one could make that much of. I could have said I made them up [if questioned about it],' Page told me.

During the bonfire he had to run back into the house and put on a riot helmet because among the household rubbish were a few aerosol canisters. Had the DPS set up an observation post overlooking the house, it would have been a comical and incriminating video to later show a jury. As it was, no one was watching or listening in.

It fell to Mubasher Hussain to secretly record a phone call Page made to him within days of the Osman warning. Hussain, who was brought in to the scheme by Paresh Solanki, had invested £133,500 by this stage. Page was half cut when he called and keen to leave as little as possible for the DPS to find.

'I've got fucking internal affairs looking at me. Have you been told?' Page enquired.

'No.'

'Right, you need to get hold of Paresh, tell him if they try and contact him he's gonna have to keep his mouth shut or otherwise they're gonna go through his records, my records and anyone else's with a fine tooth comb, yeah? … Now basically they are looking at ULPD where you and everyone else has put money in … So contact anybody that you know who did and explain to them we are close to getting out the money and I am not gonna have this fucked up by these wankers who are investigating me on that, right? And tell them if they get any contact they don't wanna say nothing.'

'Yeah.'

'I'm sure you don't want to be telling them that you've been taking money off me last year or the year before, because they are gonna fucking bubble cunts up to the taxman.'

'Yeah.'

'I've got some news for you with regards to some funds before Christmas, right?'

'Right.'

'… which I'm gonna discuss with you on a different number. This number I'm gonna get rid of it today. I'll speak to you later on this evening on the new number. Don't say nothing to [Abishake Gill] at all about it. Fuck him. Alright?'

'I'm just deleting all of his calls to be honest,' Hussain told Page.

'Yeah, just leave him. I'm dealing with him. He's alright.'

'What are [the DPS] looking into?'

'They are looking into ULPD and all the rest of it because I'm Old Bill. They're seeing if there's any fraud and all that pap. But Bee [Bimal Lodhia] needs to be capped and Paresh urgently.'

'Okay.'

'You need to keep a lid on it all, right, otherwise we are totally, totally fucked.'

'Okay.'

£ £ £

Four days after the Osman warning, Page was wracking his beer-addled brain for clues to who would want him kidnapped or even dead. 'I knew that the amount of people I was involved with in the police service, the different departments they were in, there was some heavy people, some serious people involved with the various forces,' he told me.

Another suspect was Rahul Sharma, who had actually made an ostensible death threat weeks earlier. Then there were the apparent threats to Lodhia from Russian and Turkish heavies.

Another possibility he considered was that the Osman had something to do with what Anjam Khan had recently told him: According to Page, Khan had invested £20,000 from some Essex gangsters via a mutual contact. Page collected the money and had used it to pay back some of what he owed Surinder Mudhar, without him knowing its provenance. This was the brown envelope delivered to St James's Palace the night Cherie Blair and one of the Princes were attending a function.

Meanwhile, the story goes that the gangsters had apparently tired of waiting for a return and left an intimidating message for Khan, who played it to Page and also informed Baree.

Sitting in his house, looking through the window for suspicious activity, Page discounted that Khan or anyone from the BAT circle could be behind the threats that led to the Osman warning.

But the DPS, on the other hand, had intelligence naming Anjam Khan as a possible 'suspect' talking about the kidnap plot. What remained unknown was how the DPS came to this view.[3]

Chapter 17

Royal hunt of the *Sun*

*T*uesday, *21 November*: As Page cracked open his first can of Stella of the day, Laura flicked him a withering stare then left to take the boys to school.

The Belgian lager is generally not regarded as a breakfast beer. It tends to ruin the day's best-laid plans. But since the Osman warning, Page's life had gone into free-fall. His mind was now completely frazzled by the inescapable pressure of what he'd done with over three million pounds of other people's money. There had been little sleep in the last five days. An hour here and there when the alcohol eventually took hold. Otherwise, Page was buzzing with fear and adrenalin. The Kalms herbal tablets were not taking the edge off his pain because he was necking so many.

He still believed salvation was around the corner with his next bets on the financial markets, or maybe Arsenal to beat Chelsea. He was also banking on Abishake Gill, the Heathrow baggage handler, to come through with some, any, funds. But Laura knew her husband's knack for making money had been slipping away with every gulp of lager.

She was going to have her hair done after dropping off the boys. A friend had called to say her hairdresser was making a home visit and did she want to come over. Page's aunt, who was looking after two-year-old Harry, gave Laura £10 for the hairdresser. 'Well, if I'm going to die, I don't want my hair to look a mess!' she told her gratefully.

Aunty Pat had every reason to turn her back on Page. She had lost the family house after it was sold to finance her nephew's gambling, and was now living in a small flat with an uncertain future and bad health.

However, when Page told her about the Osman she came straight over to help with the boys. His aunt was worried about what she saw. Her nephew was in a desperate state; sitting on the couch in a depression so deep she thought he would kill himself. 'He was so desperate that any money he could scrape together he was putting into trying to make more and thinking the next bet would be the one,' she recalled.

Page still believed any threat to life was coming from police officers in the syndicate, not gangsters; otherwise he would never have let Laura take the kids to school. He believed police investors could shoot or plant drugs on him but never his wife and kids. Only cunts did that. They were still coppers after all. His reasoning was informed by his own involvement in the plot to beat up the Jimmy's officer over the Hearts pyramid scheme

By late morning, Page was pissed and sitting by the window surveying the cul-de-sac. He spotted a man parked oddly in a side road across the way. There was nothing covert about the car's location. The man inside it was in his late twenties with short hair. It looked like he was constantly on the phone and looking at the house. But Page's special window blinds meant no one could see in.

Page suspected he might be under some sort of DPS surveillance. A nearby house would offer a perfect observation post, he thought, but surely the anti-corruption squad would not be this conspicuous, unless they were there for his safety.

Aunty Pat was at the back of the house playing with Harry oblivious to how wound up her nephew was becoming. He paced around the sitting room like a cage fighter waiting for the bell to ring. 'The cunt is not getting away with this,' he mumbled to himself.

Page had hidden a small black plastic case under the sofa in the living room. Inside was a silver imitation gas-powered Berretta handgun, which he discreetly retrieved and put into the pocket of his Tommy Hilfiger jacket worn over a bulletproof vest.

'There's someone outside. I'm going to have a gander,' he shouted to his aunt. Coolly putting on some wrap-around shades, Page picked up the keys to her Escort estate parked on the drive, left the house and locked the front door behind him.

As he turned to open the car, Page saw the man parked across the road partially emerge and level a long lens at him. It was all over in seconds. The man was now back in his car and sped away when he saw Page get into the Escort. The driver turned left into Gilbert Road, flying over the speed bumps outside the school where Page's children were sitting in class. He didn't know if he was being followed so he ran the next red light to check. Page went with him.

As the cars approached Sainsbury's, Page dialled 999 and left the phone on the passenger seat. On Pilgrim's Lane, the policeman was level and screamed at him: 'Get out the car! Police.' The driver gestured back as if to say, 'What? What?' He stopped briefly and Page rammed into him. But the driver slammed his car into reverse and sped off in the same direction they had just come. He didn't know where he was going but had decided to get to somewhere public, so he followed the signs for Lakeside Shopping Centre.

Page performed a J-turn and for a split second enjoyed how it must have looked. By now the other car was some 100 metres away. When Page caught up he thought the driver was on the phone and wondered if he was calling for back up. His own mobile was on the floor, which he managed to retrieve and redial 999.

'I'm heading for Lakeside shopping complex,' he shouted into the phone.

Both cars arrived at the next roundabout at great speed, with Page beeping furiously. Council gardeners on the roundabout island looked up as the chase passed them twice. The driver thought if he kept going round then Page would get bored and pull away. But he didn't. Like a cop show, Page pulled in front of the other car ramming into it. He jumped out holding the Berretta and rushed the driver, pulling him out of the car.

'Police! Fucking stand still, you cunt!' Page barked in that convincing cop way as he held the man down and looked inside the car for evidence of a weapon. There wasn't one just a Canon camera with a huge lens.

By this time traffic on the roundabout had come to a halt. Page dragged the man to his feet and frogmarched him to the island with the gun still to his head.

'Who the fuck are you?' he shouted. The man offered no resistance, just pleaded not to die.

'Is this a fucking brown envelope job to come sort me out?'

'Don't kill me! Don't kill me! I'm a photographer for the *Sun*.'

Scott Hornby had been sent by the tabloid to snatch a shot of Page after a tip-off from officers at Jimmy's about the collapsed syndicate.

Page started to ease the gun away and put the pieces together:

the camera and the fear in his eyes suggested twenty-eight-year-old Hornby was telling the truth.

Two of the gardeners who had been watching ringside decided to approach.

'Call the fucking police,' shouted Page.

'Well put the gun down,' said one of the gardeners.

Page, still holding the gun to Hornby's head, said, 'I'm old Bill'.

'Show us some ID.'

'I don't have any,' Page replied. He felt one of the gardeners was a have-a-go-hero about to attack him with a rake so he put the gun on the floor.

With the sound of police sirens approaching and Page still restraining the photographer, his eight-year free-fall from trusted, Royal Protection officer at Buckingham Palace to half-cut, gun-toting crazy was at an end.

'It was like one of those Hamlet moments when you are sitting in the back of the police car with cuffs on and the music is playing and you are thinking, "How much more shitty can my life get? A fucking *Sun* camera!"'

Laura, meanwhile, had returned home with her hair done to find the front door locked. Aunty Pat let her in through the back.

'Where's Paul?' She asked.

'I don't know. He's been drinking all morning and has taken my car. He's not insured. But he said he'd seen something.'

Laura called her husband. It rang for a while and then Page answered sheepishly from the back of the police car.

'Er, I've been arrested, love.'

'What for?'

'Putting a gun to a *Sun* photographer's head.'

When Page got to Grays police station, where his police career had started, the custody sergeant told him he had to take a breathalyser. But Page came up with a ruse. He said he had impacted wisdom teeth, which was true, and that they had affected his glands, which meant he couldn't swallow or blow properly, which was a lie. Page knew it would take a few hours to get a doctor to take blood by which time he could vigorously exercise to sweat the alcohol out of his system. The police accepted his explanation and called a doctor.

As he had been arrested for a serious firearms offence, Page was put into a paper jump suit while his clothes were bagged for forensic examination. He refused the plimsolls and stayed in his socks. He asked for regular cups of water for his sore throat, which he downed after press-ups and shadow boxing in his cell. By the time his blood was taken he was very tired.

Laura panicked when she realized that there were very convincing imitation weapons in the house, including a rifle that her husband had bought for £1000. A friend was persuaded to come and take the weapon away under her coat.

At 8.15 pm, Essex Police arrived to carry out a search of the house. Laura, Pat and the boys were all in the sitting room watching TV when the officers walked in. Page had given them the front-door key.

'What's this, James Bond?' Pat asked.

Laura was taken aback when one of the officers asked her directly, 'Where are the guns?'

'What guns?'

'Your husband has told us exactly where they are Mrs Page.'

'Has he?'

'So where are they?'

'Oh! That gun. I've taken it to a friend's house.'

'Why?'

'Because I told her to look after it.'

'Well you'd better get it back.'

Laura collected the imitation gun and handed it to the officer, who had already started searching the house. Every time they found something she heard an expression of excitement over the police radios. In the conservatory they found some black imitation guns and one magazine. But it was the garage that did for Page. Officers found his police issue equipment belt complete with CS gas canister, a prohibited weapon under the Firearms Act.

£ £ £

Page was not the only person sweating on 21 November. When the DPS was alerted to his arrest another Gold Group meeting was hurriedly convened at Scotland Yard. This time the press bureau was also present to deal with the article that the *Sun* was preparing for tomorrow's edition.

Detective Inspector Orchard gave the Gold group an update on his team's inquiries. He described ULPD as 'a pyramid-style scheme' and said his investigation was trying to identify the other police officers involved and whether they were creditors and potential victims of crime. Detective Superintendent McTigue reported back that her inquiries into 'the kidnap threat' were also ongoing.

Discussion then turned to media management. Two senior Met press officers explained that press 'lines' had been agreed between the Met and Essex Police about what would be given to the media about the Lakeside incident.

One of the press officers was told to speak to the *Sun* journalist putting the story together and find out how bad it was going to look for the Met. The press officer was also told to 'emphasize that Page is on a career break'. This was pure spin to put distance between Page, the Met and the Palace.

The problem for the Met was that Page was still a serving police officer who had been allowed to remain on special unpaid leave since February 2004 while warnings about his spiralling conduct and the need for welfare had been ignored.[1]

SO14 Commander Steve Grainger informed the meeting that until last week's Gold meeting 'there had been no contact with Page'. In other words, the media could discover that for two years Page had been able to spiral out of control, obtain millions by deception and endanger public life through his own gun-toting actions, and those of investors plotting his kidnap or worse.

The meeting was informed that '[Page] has been offered the opportunity to resign which he has declined'. This was not something the Met was rushing to tell the media. It was decided that legal advice was urgently needed on whether he could be disciplined if he was on a career break.

'And what are we doing about informing Her Majesty?' the meeting was asked.

'Did PC Page have access to the Royal Family? It's something the media might want to know,' a Met press officer added.

That horse had long bolted and the DPS was already getting an alarming picture of brown envelopes coming into Buckingham Palace. Nevertheless, it was decided that a press officer would brief the Queen's spokesperson. Commander Grainger of SO14 had already told her protection officer, senior members of the Royal Household and the Home Office. No doubt she was not amused.

Grainger was supposed to visit Page in his cell that evening, but SO14 Superintendent Sean Walters called instead to inform him that Purple One had been made aware of his antics.

'You've fucking stitched me up and I'm going to the press to spill the beans,' Page spat back.

'We are not on a secure line, PC Page. Going to the media would only make things worse for you,' Walters replied.

The next morning, the *Sun* front page gave a flick of their exclusive, which dominated page four. The headline screamed 'RAGING COP HOLDS GUN TO A *SUN* MAN'S HEAD' and the strapline read 'Royal PC drags snapper from car. Probe over £1m he took from pals'. There was a demonic-looking picture of Page that Scott Hornby had snatched before the chase.

Reporter Anthony France quoted the photographer as saying:

'I noticed a silver car following me. I did a few turns but it was still on my tail, so I headed for the M25. It was then that he overtook me, stopped in the road and rammed the front of my car. There was a loud smash as the two cars collided. I struggled to keep on the road. I drove for a short distance and he rammed me again. This time I lost control. It was then that he ran out of his car with a gun in his hand. He kicked my door, pulled it open and dragged me out, screaming and shouting: "Who the fuck are you?" I said: "I'm a *Sun* photographer." He held me on the ground with the gun to my head. After a few minutes, he marched me towards the roundabout with the gun at my head. When we got there some gardeners were tending the plot. I asked him to show ID but he refused. The gardeners asked him to prove he was an officer but he again refused.'

The article repeated the Met damage limitation that Page was on a career break and the DPS was investigating how his company went bust leaving 150 officer investors £1.3 million out of pocket.

£ £ £

Thursday, 23 November: Richard Humby had agreed to speak to the Operation Aserio team at Jubilee House in the morning. Before the tape machine was switched on they told him that only Page was under investigation. More interestingly, the DPS said their investigation might remain disciplinary so Humby should not stop his civil action to recover money. Clearly, this was a message he should relay back to other investors.

Humby made it clear he regarded himself as a victim who had been conned into investing over £150,000. He admitted receiving some cash returns, then added defensively, 'Cash isn't a dirty word provided it's properly dealt with'. The money to invest with Page, he said, had come from a buy-to-let business, which he had registered with the Met.

Humby said Page had 'pestered' him to take a free BAT holiday. He explained that he didn't know Fahim Baree, who had organized the 'sweetener trips', but Page told him his best friend had £500,000 in Dubai. Page, he claimed, also told him a Mortgage Guarantee figure was 'bribed' to release money on the barns.

But it was the discovery in July that the barns had been repossessed that led Humby to solicitors, while others were still thinking Page would turn up at the door with a large cheque. 'I'm not gonna name names [of other officer investors] now because it's up to them to do that if they come forward,' he told the DPS, who didn't push him.

However, Humby was willing to speculate that the total investment with Page was more that £2.5 million. Jimmy's officers had invested about £900,000, but he was less sure about those at BP, saying it could be £400,000. And as well as investors from the

269

MoD Police and the Special Escort Group, five Essex businessmen were allegedly owed £750,000 he said, plus £600,000 to those in Bristol.

Humby said he and other officers hadn't taken the legal route earlier because Page warned them off saying that way no one would get any money back. But now one firm represented him, and at least six others, in trying to recover over £700,000. He said they had gone down the legal route because they were cops 'in this mess together'. SO14 he described as 'a fairly tight knit sort of place to work … it's a little family'.

Detective Sergeant Tracey Hunt explained to Humby that Operation Aserio expected to be 'inundated' after the *Sun* article and at least fourteen people had already come forward. She stressed that Page's activities could be genuine because at this stage the DPS didn't 'really know the score' about the scope. Some investors had 'ignored' earlier approaches by her team until the Lakeside gun incident, she said. 'It sort of forced our hand … and I think with it being in the press a lot of people thought "I'm not alone" because I think a lot of people felt they were on their own and didn't want to look stupid.'

£ £ £

Saturday, 25 November. As soon as he was released on bail, Page's priority was to 'put a cap' on witnesses giving evidence against him.

Some investors who had read the *Sun* decided that their money was lost for ever. Others were now too scared of Page to know what to do. So when he rang to assure them that those who stayed away from the courts and the DPS would get paid out of the money coming in February, they listened politely.

Page rang Mubasher Hussain again to discuss the situation with Abishake Gill. The Heathrow baggage handler had recently pleaded with Page by phone not to shoot him.'

Hussain, as usual, was non-responsive but recorded the call, which he later gave to the police.

'Sorry I didn't get back to you yesterday but I've been busy obviously,' Page explained with understatement.

'So are things looking better?'

'Yeah, I mean they've charged me with some load of bollocks. I've got to go back to court next week and go not guilty, and then I should imagine it will get written off, mate. It's just that they've had to charge me 'cause they're worried about the fucking newspapers and all that. D'ya know what I mean?'

'Yeah.'

'… if they write it off straight away it's gonna look like "cop gets off", you know, "cops look after cops."'

'Yeah.'

'… which is what they are already doing now, yeah.'

'Yeah.'

'Now look. I'm gonna give you my new secure number.'

'Right, okay.'

'You know Bee [Bimal Lodhia] stole that forty grand?'

'Yeah.'

'I need to find out what he's done with it.'

'How do I find out?'

'I am suspecting that he bought a place in Thailand and that Paresh [Solanki] was privy to that information.'

'I'm not sure if it's that much, I'm not sure that Abi's trying to add in his interest payments as well … It's difficult for me 'cause I don't know Bee. But I trust Paresh and I don't think Paresh would be in anything like this. Paresh would tell me. Paresh went to school with one of my best friends, so that's why I can trust Paresh. He wouldn't be ripping me off.'

'Do you want to chat to Paresh because I've got to be careful 'cause I'm still on bail for these serious offences. They've charged me with possession of a firearm, a handgun, and fucking non-sense like that.'

'Yeah.'

'… it's all fucking pants. It'll get written off 'cause the coppers who come round my house and told me my life's in danger are my fucking witnesses, ain't they? At the end of the day they've charged me with impersonating a police officer, fucking idiots. I am a police officer. So do you hear what I'm saying? The charges are gonna fall off large, I'll get off with it total.'

'Yeah.'

'So I need you to speak to Paresh. There's no way I took Abi's money.'

'I know you haven't. Paresh knows you didn't take it, but we are trying to wonder what Bee's done with it ourselves … To be honest we don't know how many other people Bee might have done this to either.'

'It's very crucial that we find out and give half of it back to fucking Abi to shut him up.'

'Yeah, yeah.'

'…otherwise he's gonna go to the fucking cops and obviously they are gonna to drag me in it.'

'Have you told Abi you haven't taken it?'

'I've had to, mate.'

'Leave him to me, 'cause he's thinking everyone's shafting him.'

'Bee took the fucking dough, mate, and what has he done with it, the cheeky cunt?

'I know.'[2]

Two days later, Gill and Page met at the Burger King on the top floor of Lakeside shopping centre. He gave Page £14,000 in a brown envelope and returned Laura's wedding ring. The money was from the Lloyds joint savings account with his wife, which he had dipped into without her full knowledge. Over the next few months Gill put in another £5500 by bank transfer to Page's father, bringing his total investment to almost £40,000. On one transfer Gill instructed Lloyds to enter the reference 'Abi Last Chance'. Terry Page transferred the money to CMC on the instructions of his son, who gambled it all away.

£ £ £

Wednesday, 6 December: Commander Sue Akers had decided that Page would be suspended. He presented himself at Romford police station with his new police federation representative because Mick 'the Don' Hickman had declared 'a conflict of interest'.

When a senior officer duly suspended him, a 'suited and booted' Page was polite, according to a DPS report.

'Who is the officer in the case in relation to the Osman warning, guv?' he asked. 'Because I'm not happy at being told me and my family's lives are in danger and then nothing happens.'

Detective Sergeant Tracey Hunt from Operation Aserio stepped in to explain it was Superintendent Sean Walters of SO14 and Essex Police managing the matter. 'We are doing the investigation into your financial affairs and monitoring Essex Police's investigation of the incident with the *Sun* photographer,' she said.

'Can I contact friends at work? There are people who have spoken to you lot, and then contacted me,' Page told Hunt with delight.

'You are not to discuss the investigation or interfere with it as outlined in the letter you had from Essex Police,' said Hunt. 'We will inform payroll you are back at work but suspended on full pay.'[3]

Back at home, Inspector Tracey Bell from SO14 called to touch base with Laura about her husband's welfare following the

Osman warning.

'We are going to the press,' Laura told the SO14 officer.

'Your husband is a serving police officer and can't speak to the press.'

'He is but I'm not.'

'It could make matters worse for him if you do,' Bell responded.

A week later, Laura was told to call Superintendent Walters at SO14 as he had some important news. She dialled the number with some nervousness.

'Oh hello, Mrs Page. I just wanted to let you know the good news. You will be pleased to know the death threat has been lifted which was behind the Osman served on you and Paul last month.'

'Well, I am pleased,' said Laura, 'but I am also angry at being kept in the dark about who was behind it.'

'Mrs Page, I can't go into the intelligence behind the Osman warning. This is just a welfare call to let you know you needn't worry.'

'I don't believe there ever was a threat, if you want to know the truth. We've discussed it, Paul and I, and think it was just a way for them DPS officers to get a foot in my door to question me.'

'Mrs Page, I can't go into this, especially not on a police line.'

'Well, let me tell you I can go into it and the truth will come out in court.'

'There is a time and a place, and I agree that is court. Can I speak to Paul?'

'He's not here.'

'Could you tell him to call me, please? If he doesn't call I'm afraid I will have to send officers around. Thanks.'

It has never been disclosed on what basis the Met now felt they could tell the Pages there was no longer a threat to their lives or the possibility of kidnap.

£ £ £

Monday, 18 December: Laura was pushing Harry around her local Sainsbury's when she noticed a woman employee smiling strangely at her. At first, Laura thought it was a parent from the school. She smiled back, but as they got nearer, the women's demeanour changed.

'Do you think you are going to walk in here and smile at me? I'm Lionel Gore's girlfriend.'

'I can tell, you fat fucking bitch,' Laura replied. 'I'm going to report you to the manager.'

'That's alright because you'll have Old Bill coming round. They are right what they say about you. You are a hard-faced bitch.'

That very day, Lionel Gore, an engineer, was giving a witness statement to Operation Aserio about his £45,000 investment with Page. In it, Gore explained that his brother, Nigel, had worked with Page at Buckingham Palace and recommended the scheme to him. Although Page had suggested taking up references from 'high-ranking officers' before he invested, Gore said he trusted his brother's judgement. The £45,000 investment came from selling his house and moving in with his girlfriend, Jenny Palmer, the woman now confronting Laura at Sainsbury's.

Gore had received cash returns of £5500 but then it stopped. He started to worry when he was laid off and couldn't get hold of Page. His brother, who had moved to Hampshire Police, told him to call Mick Hickman at SO14. Gore recalled in his witness statement how 'the Don' said he would have advised against investing in the barns after receiving nothing back from a significant amount of his own money given to Page.

Page had tried to mollify Gore by agreeing to pay for the 'once in a lifetime holiday' to Florida, which the engineer was planning with his children. But days before the departure, Baree had to cancel the holiday because of non-payment. When Lionel returned from a caravan staycation, he instructed debt collectors. They informed him that ULPD was recently dissolved and Page had a large number of country court judgments.

Laura couldn't wait to get home and tell her husband about the Sainsbury's showdown.

At 12.10 pm Page phoned Detective Inspector Michael Orchard at Jubilee House. He explained calmly that his wife had just been abused. But Laura took the phone off him and relayed her version of the story, in particular the part where Operation Aserio detectives had apparently described her as 'a hard-faced bitch'.

Orchard refused to reveal to whom his team had spoken but assured Laura that they acted with professionalism at all times. He advised her to report the matter to Essex Police. Something Jenny Palmer had already done.

Page took back the phone and told Orchard that DPS detectives were also telling witnesses that he had 'seen more money than they ever will'. No longer calm, he added, 'Listen to me, you slimy cunt, tell people my wife's a hard-faced bitch and I'll …'

Laura terminated the call before her husband got them into even more trouble.[4]

£ £ £

Thursday, 21 December: With just days to go before Christmas, the Copleys finally lost their eviction battle and had to move out of Barn C.

The next day, BAT investor Jit Mandalia was celebrating his birthday at a restaurant with his family. The children were sitting at another table while Mandalia discussed with his wife the lost money from their joint account. After a few drinks, he decided to text Page.

'Have a great Xmas. It'll be your last as next year you and your wife will be behind bars and your kids taken into care, cunts.' Laura reported the text to Essex Police but not that she had rung Mandalia back and left similar Christmas greetings.

Laura's efforts to give her boys the best Christmas possible were frustrated by Page's delusion that he could still gamble his way out of trouble. On Boxing Day morning, he was sitting with the laptop gambling on the darts.

'I'm not staying in if you are going to do that all day. How much have you got in there?' Laura asked.

'About £11,000.'

'Well, just leave it there and come out with us. I'm taking the kids to the leisure park.'

'No, no, no,' he said waving her away. 'If I stay at this all day I can get it up to £22,000.'

Laura left with the boys but didn't enjoy the day out. She couldn't bring herself to ring home to discover how much he had lost. When she eventually returned there was nothing left.

The resentment had been growing over the Christmas period and finally exploded between them at a New Year's Eve party. A few glasses of champagne down, Laura thought she had caught Page looking at another woman. That she wasn't even attractive made her more enraged so she attacked him without warning.

Page had never hit Laura, but the ferocious and unwarranted assault made him lash out. She stormed out of the party with her nose bleeding profusely moments before the bells chimed for a new year. 'I was walking around Chafford Hundred with blood everywhere and no one stopped to ask me if I was OK.'

Chapter 18

Annus horribilis

During a speech marking her forty-year reign, the Queen described 1992 as a 'horrible year'. Her son Andrew had separated from Fergie, who was photographed topless with a Texan toe-sucking millionaire; her daughter Anne divorced; her step-daughter Diana separated from Charles then participated in a tell-all book; and Windsor Castle caught fire sparking a public row over why the taxpayer should pick up the repair bill in a recession when the landlady was so rich.

The *annus horribilis* of one of her more unhinged Royal Protection officers came fifteen years later in 2007. It marked a personal nadir for Paul Page that would further damage the reputations of Buckingham Palace and Scotland Yard as they tried to get a handle on the escalating scandal.

£ £ £

'This is the last-chance saloon, mate. I've got no one else to turn to. I've got no one … I need the five [grand]. Is there any chance it's gonna be done?'

A desperate Page was once again trying to raise any amount of cash to feed his degenerate gambling. It was early 2007 and he was still peddling the lie that a corrupt Mortgage Guarantee employee was willing to release £870,000 equity from the barns but needed a £30,000 bung because of the charges placed by officers from St James's Palace on the development.

Mubasher Hussain was once again taping the call, which would eventually be passed to the DPS. Hussain was playing Page but also desperate to recover the money he and Paresh Solanki had invested of their own and on behalf of others.

'We're trying our bloody best. But the thing is all these people will ask for owed money by us,' Hussain told Page.

'I need that money, Bash, and I know you need it.'

'The thing is, you're gonna guarantee us £300,000 that you owe me and Paresh is gonna come back to us first before these other people?'

'I'm guaranteeing you will be paid out first. Don't worry about the other monkeys, yeah? You worry about yourself and I'll deal with my people. I've got another half mill in the pipeline and that is crucial to me, mate. I must have that.'

'I'm going to other people and Paresh is working on somebody but everyone knows that our name's dirt. We've given you everything basically that we bloody own.'

'You can tell them it's gonna come through. I don't know what you want to do with the first lot of money, if you're going to keep it or pass it, that's not my business.'

'Yeah.'

'At least you can give people something if you want to take

your cheese last, which I suggest is what you do, if these people are giving you grief.'

'I'm trying to explain to them that you are giving the money to [the man at Mortgage Guarantee plc] to sort out the mortgage [on the barns].'

'Don't give 'em names for fuck's sake.'

'What happens if you don't get the five today?'

'I don't even thought of that to be honest with ya.'

'Have you tried Anjam and Fahim?'

'No. We're at war at the moment because they stitched me up with my people, blubbering and all the rest. And basically my people want paying before them.'

'Me and Paresh got loads of money off people, we fuck up and don't give them anything back we're fucked.'

'You ain't gonna fuck up. Look, this has been instigated purely by the cunts who have put charges on the barns or we'd have the money ages ago. Fahim or Anjam, fuck them. They'll have to wait now because they've put me in a position and I'm backed into a corner where I need someone to step forward and do a deal with me.'

'Can I ask Bee if he can raise anything?'

'Don't ask him 'cause he's just a trouble-making shit, mate. There's things on him I'll tell you about later, mate. He's fucked a lot of people.'

Days later, Page still hadn't found anyone mug enough to give him money. He decided to try Hussain again with a new lie that Laura had kicked him out of the house and he was now in a hotel £5000 short of closing the deal with his fictitious man at Mortgage Guarantee that would solve everyone's problems.

'I arranged to stay another night in that hotel. My missus has got the hump with me. I'm saying to [my man], 'sorry mate had something to do'. Well, yeah, sit in my hotel room and fucking cry. I need that five, mate, and I need it now.'

'You still need the whole five?'

'I can't get Jack shit. I'm sitting on twenty-five. I want to get this done and dusted now otherwise I'm fucked, mate, I'm fucked for another half a mill as well. If you can square this up like now then I will sort out what I've said to you, on the basis you don't tell anyone. You and Paresh keep it to yourself and I will string the others along for another month or whatever.'

'Thing is what happens if we don't get the five?'

'Fuck knows. He ain't gonna give me a cheque unless he's got his money and he's already getting suspicious, mate.'

'Yeah.'

'It's gonna go bandy 'cause what I'll have to do is re-finance legitimate and they're gonna take a massive chunk off of that, mate. Hence why I'm paying out this money. Everyone wants a piece of the fucking pie. It's always the way. Now I'm sitting here like a cunt. I need a result in the next twenty minutes.'

With no money coming through, Page tried to raise the stakes with Hussain on a follow-up call.

'At the end of the day you've gotta think of yourself,' he told the IT manager.

'Mmmm.'

'I'm thinking of myself now,' Page added.

'Yeah I am.'

'All right? Fuck everyone else.'

The pair then discussed what was going on with Anjam Khan. Hussain claimed that BAT boss Rahul Sharma had given an ulti-matum to Khan and Baree that they must join him in a court action against Page or face the sack. Hussain said Khan wanted to meet the Royal Protection officer for reassurance and to get Sharma off his back. But Page wasn't worried because he said he

281

had 'shit' on the BAT boss and loads of money had gone through the bank accounts of so many BAT employees.

£ £ £

'Is that Paul Page?'

'Yeah. Who wants to know?'

'It's DS James Howells from the DPS.'

'What do you want?'

'Is everything OK?'

'No. I've had a shitty day.'

'Why's that?'

'I ain't telling you nothing. I don't like you and I don't trust you.'

It was two in the afternoon on Friday, 2 March and Page had been all morning on the Stellas. There had also been a domestic row.

'Well, where are you then?' asked the anti-corruption officer.

'At home.'

'There's something I need to talk to you about.'

'If you want to talk to me come here but I'll only talk with my solicitor present.'

Howells took the solicitor's details. But the call was principally to establish Page's whereabouts before the DPS came to search his house.

The slim pretext for that search was a complaint from the wife of PC Surinder Mudhar alleging that Page had intimidated her. Manjit Mudhar claimed that she'd seen Page and another man in a car outside her house early that morning when she left for the school run. Her husband had recently made a statement to the DPS.

The complaint was evidentially weak but the DPS looked

determined to arrest Page and search his house that evening.

At 6.40 pm the search team and a group of Operation Aserio officers led by Detective Inspector Orchard arrived in the rain outside Page's house. Orchard and Detective Sergeant Mark Beckett were in front and Sergeant Howells behind them, with a pink folder under his arm.

'Who is it?' said Laura from behind the door when the bell rang.

'Police,' replied Orchard.

The door swung open. Laura, wearing a jumper dress and a look that would kill, launched into a tirade of abuse.

'Fuck off outta my 'ouse,' she shouted. 'Why do this in front of my kids?' who were behind her in the hall. Page had by now joined his wife from the kitchen.

He squared up to the physically matched Orchard. Beckett, who was a lot smaller with a bottlebrush moustache, was taken aback.

'You're just a bunch of fucking cunts,' Page told them. 'What's this all about?'

Orchard explained he wanted to talk about an allegation of witness intimidation without naming the complainant.

'Fuck off!' said Page, edging nearer to the inspector's face. 'If you are not here to arrest me then fuck off! Love, call Essex Police, I don't trust these slimy cunts.'

Howells had phoned Page's solicitor and left a message but the call back went unanswered as he was on the way to her client's house. Page believed his old Essex Police colleagues would protect him from any DPS tricks.

By now, Page was nose to nose with Orchard and Howells felt an imminent head butt coming his boss's way. The aggression gave the DPS all the grounds they needed.

Beckett arrested Page on the doorstep for witness intimidation and read him his rights. Orchard then made a move to come into the house, putting his foot in the door. But Laura, back from calling 999, closed it on him.

'You've just jammed my foot!' the detective winced.

'Good! I hope it hurts,' she replied.

Sirens could be heard in the distance. It was Essex Police. Orchard told one of his men to bring the video camera and start filming the ugly scene at the door, correctly fearing that Laura would make a complaint against him.

Page was calmed by the imminent arrival of his old Essex buddies and yielded to the inevitable that he would be taken into custody while the DPS searched his house. It was agreed he could change into some jogging bottoms before being taken away. When he returned several DPS officers were by now in the hall with Laura and the children. Page decided to leave the anti-corruption squad with a gesture of defiance.

'If you want to search something, why don't you search this?' he told the assembled crowd while pulling down his jogging bottoms and parting his cheeks. *Annus horribilis* indeed.

In that split second of exposure, Page realized he had gone too far. The upside-down look of disbelief on Laura's face was one thing; the expressions on the faces of his huddled children was another. There was just silence from the DPS as he pulled up his jogging bottoms.

Essex officers agreed to escort Page to the DPS car that would take him to Romford police station. He walked calmly and uncuffed out of the house with Beckett alongside him. But before he got inside the car he had some final abuse for Orchard and Howells.

'You cunting slimy bastards,' he shouted. 'Don't let those cunts into the house unless they have a warrant,' he told Laura.

On the journey to the police station, Page tried to explain why he had reacted so badly to the DPS knock.

'They gave me a warning my life was in danger. It's rubbish. It's a fit-up.'

'I can't discuss it,' the DPS detective replied.

'Are you Beckett?'

'Yes.'

Back at the house, the DPS cameraman was filming Laura at the front door. The left side of her face was inflamed due to a gum infection.

'No point pointing that in my face. See your colleague?' she said, looking at Orchard. 'He's tried to intimidate me. He put his foot in the door and tried to push me.'

Orchard told her he was going to start the search. Laura conceded. She didn't want any more of her business aired in public.

'Look how many there are of you. Can you come in so I can shut the door? Where are you going to start?'

Orchard pointed to the garage, where Page kept his tarantulas and goldfish. She opened the door.

'There you go, help yourself,' she said.

By now, Detective Sergeant Tracey Hunt was in the house to deal with Laura and introduced herself.

'Hunt by name, cunt by nature,' Laura spat back.

Her parents arrived minutes later to take away the older, distressed children. When they had gone, Laura apologized to Hunt during the search of her bedroom,

'And sorry for the state of the house. It's going to be repossessed any moment and I can't be bothered anymore. We've got nowhere to go. I've lost weight with worry for what is going to happen to my children.'

While the search continued, Laura bathed Harry, popped another painkiller and called a DPS search officer in the attic a 'ginger cunt' for putting his foot through her ceiling.

Strangely, the DPS did not film the search of the house, which made it difficult later to rebut Page's complaint that 'three ledgers' containing details of syndicate members and their perks were seized but not disclosed in the search log.[1]

The DPS had logged the seizure of Page's Rolodex. It contained the names of many police officers, not all involved in his syndicate. One of the latter group was a former member of the Met karate team, Steve Gwillen, who at the time of the search was a senior officer on the DPS's Intelligence Development Group.

Far more damaging to Page was a notebook the DPS found in which the drunk Royal Protection officer had indulged his love of doodling. One in particular gave an insight into his frame of mind. It showed a childlike drawing of a house with a chimney. Inside the house was a British pound symbol. And underneath were words, some of which had been scribbled out as if Page had viewed the note in a moment of sobriety and thought better. It said:

United Piss Your Savings Up The Wall
Invest With Us And I'll Kill You When
You Need Your Money Back

When the search finished at 9.10 pm, Laura called Romford police station to learn that her husband had been taken to hospital after complaining of heart pain.

The next afternoon, Page was fit to be interviewed. He gave a prepared statement to the allegation of witness intimidation. As there was no criminal investigation into his business affairs he reminded the DPS that he couldn't be accused of trying to stop someone giving evidence against him.

On his solicitor's advice and in the absence of the identity of the person he had allegedly intimidated, no further comment was given.

Soon after Page was released on Saturday, he went to meet the *Mirror's* veteran crime reporter Jeff Edwards. He believed the tabloid chequebook would get him urgent cash to save his house from being repossessed. Edwards, however, wasn't buying.

£ £ £

That week, British bank HSBC had just announced a big loss in the US subprime market after homeowners started to default on their mortgages. The US investment bank Bear Sterns also admitted that it was closing its subprime hedge fund and had written off $3.8 billion. Analysts were suddenly predicting that in 2007 over two million Americans would lose their homes and a fifth of all subprime mortgages issued in the last two years would default.

These early signs that the housing and credit bubbles were bursting appeared as a repossession notice was sent to the Pages for defaulting on their substantial home mortgage.

It was ironic that half of Page's last weekend in Hatton Close was spent in a cell. It was typical that he spent the other half getting drunk while Laura held the family together and tried to save the family home she had spent so much money doing up.

They'd had some happy memories there since 1998, mainly around the birth of the children. But the walls of Hatton Close also carried the scars of violent rows as flying ornaments chipped the expensive wallpaper. There was also plenty of botched DIY as Laura tried to paper over the cracks and holes from other barneys where Page would punch the wall or kick in the banister.

None of it mattered now. On Monday morning, 5 March 2007 the mortgage company told a pleading Laura that unless the money owed was paid straight away their repo men were coming at noon the next day.

Page refused to help his wife pack up the house, preferring the company of Stella in an armchair. The more he drank the more belligerent he became, at points forbidding his wife to pack any further.

'I'm not moving and if they come in here then I am going to fight them,' he told her.

Laura's best friend came over to help put everything in bin bags and to give a new home to the hamsters. By Tuesday morning Page hadn't moved from the armchair except to get more beer.

'I ain't fucking moving. They will have to move me,' he told Laura while opening another can of Stella as she came down the stairs.

'Grow up, Paul!' she replied and continued packing.

As midday approached, Page went to the kitchen and took the largest knife from the butcher's block.

'That's what they are going to get,' he told Laura.

In the end, she loaded the bags into the Range Rover, secured Harry in a toddler's seat and waited for Page to get in without so much as a rude word to the repo men.

Laura had borrowed money from her mum to put their belongings into storage. There was change for an overnight stay at a nearby hotel. She and the children went straight to the room where they all jumped into the double bed and fell asleep watching the television. Page stayed in the lobby bar getting blind drunk. He was so pissed by the end of his party for one that he had to crawl along the hotel landing to his room.

His attempt to get inside woke Laura, who watched the last vestiges of respect evaporate as he vomited everywhere.

'Get a grip, Paul,' she thought to herself. For the first time in their ten-year marriage she was questioning the relationship. Page, meanwhile, was passed out in his own sick.[2]

£ £ £

Three weeks later, on 27 March, Fahim Baree received notice from CMC that he now owed £41,346. He had held them off since his account was closed fifteen months ago with all manner of excuses without disclosing the truth about his mum's re-mortgage money and his own involvement with ULPD. With the spread-betting firm threatening its solicitors, Baree felt it was time he gave up Page.[3]

There was reassurance he was doing the right thing when Baree bumped into Page's Aunty Pat the same day that the CMC letter arrived. She was surprised he knew about the £150,000 re-mortgage of her parents' old Leytonstone house to help Page complete the barns. Pat told Baree it had been repossessed after Page stopped making the re-mortgage payments and she was now living in a small flat with her homeless nephew and his family.

Aunty Pat's story evoked painful memories for Baree. His mum could no longer retire because she had to take over repayment of her £150,000 re-mortgage after Page stopped paying.

Two days later on 29 March 2007, Baree made his first witness statement to the DPS against Page. He described some details of his involvement with ULPD and CMC, a £7000 holiday arranged for SO14 investor Mick 'the Don' Hickman, his mother's re-mortgage and the bribery claim involving Mortgage Guarantee. Baree admitted his own role in providing 'money to sweeten' the finance firm, but was never questioned about that.

Despite becoming a witness against Page, Baree was still in contact with his former best friend because he wanted him to explain to his mum how the £150,000 re-mortgage money was all lost.

Unaware that Baree had made a witness statement against him, at 7 pm on Friday, 30 March, Page texted: 'Will be at mums tonight mate as promised what time you meet me.' When there was no response, Page left a voicemail forty-five minutes later. 'What the fuck you doin? I need you to know about the info they found in my house about ULPD that's got your name all over it. I'm waiting for you. I'll have to come round to yours. Ring me back for Christ's sake.'

Baree tried to put off the meeting but Laura had already driven her husband to Mrs Baree's house because he was over the limit.

'Can't do another night mate, leave mum to me I'm here now don't worry I'll explain,' Page texted. This worried Baree, who started to walk the short distance to his mum's house. He could see Page outside wearing a baseball cap. As he approached, Baree could smell the booze on him.

'What are you doing here?' he asked.

'I've come to see your mum. What the fuck have you been doing? Why haven't you answered my calls?'

Page then removed his hand from behind his back, which was worrying Baree, and patted him down. Baree denied he was wearing a wire.

'Have you made a witness statement? The DPS are trying to stitch me up.' Page asked.

'I don't know where you got that information from,' said Baree, unconvincingly.

'If you've bubbled me, you're dead,' Page told him.

Baree made a bolt for the front door of his mum's house. With the *Sun* incident fresh in his mind, he wasn't going to take the risk even with an old school friend.

The pair scuffled at the front door causing Baree's older

brother, Fahid, to intervene. The commotion had interrupted a phone call Mrs Baree was having in her bedroom overlooking the street. She came downstairs barefoot. Pushing herself between her sons, she now saw Page looking very angry.

'Go inside, Fahim,' she said. He obeyed. 'What's wrong, Paul? What is happening?' Mrs Baree asked.

'Do you know what Fahim has done to me?'

'What are you talking about?'

'He's bubbled me.'

'What does that mean?'

'He's made a witness statement to the police. Let me go inside,' Page pleaded.

'No, Paul. You are angry, Fahim is angry. This is not the right time for you to be together. Stay here and talk to me.'

Page noticed that Mrs Baree was carrying a phone and asked why the light was on.

'I was talking to my niece,' she replied. He took her hand and inspected the phone. Satisfied there was no recording he folded his arms and said: 'Do you know £10 million is involved?'

'No. But I know you have problems.'

'Fahim is finished,' Page added. 'Let's go in,' he asked again.

'No, Paul. Listen, darling, whatever has happened we need to sort it out calmly,' she replied holding his hand and stroking his face.

At that point, a concerned neighbour asked Mrs Baree if she was OK. Page told him to go away. He wouldn't swear in front of his surrogate mum. 'It's a family matter,' he added.

Mrs Baree reassured her neighbour and then putting her hand on Page's chest, she said: 'Paul, I'll talk to you later, darling, calm down. I'm not sure what is happening.'

Baree's brother came out as his mother went inside. The two men moved to the street.

'I want Fahim to speak to my solicitor. If I am going to be in a prison cell I'll make sure he'll be in it with me. If my kids suffer so will his.'

'Look, the police are coming, you should go,' he was urged. Laura was also calling her husband to get in the car. Page returned, they argued and left.

The next morning officers were out looking to arrest Page for witness intimidation. A warning on the police computer read: 'Suspect is an ex [police] instructor and karate expert so officers please take care in dealing with him if located/arrested.'

£ £ £

Page knew that this second witness intimidation incident within one month meant he would probably not get bail, but would now have to spend a few months behind bars on remand until his trial in June for the gun incident with the *Sun* photographer.

He was still desperate for money and selling his story seemed like his best punt, despite the recent knock-back from the *Mirror*.

Investor Mubasher Hussain believed the disgraced Royal Protection officer had cut an exclusive deal for £300,000 with Fleet Street's famed chequebook. Anjam Khan thought it was £450,000. Such figures were wildly beyond what any tabloid would ever pay for any story. Page of course was talking it up to pacify certain hungry investors.

At the time he was trying to sell his story, there was a growing atmosphere of caution in the tabloid press following a successful Met operation into the *News of the World* for accessing the phone messages of Prince William and Prince Harry and their private secretary, Jamie Lowther-Pinkerton.

Operation Caryatid began after a series of exclusives in late

2005 by royal editor Clive Goodman caught the attention of the palace. Officials suspected voice messages left on the phones of the princes and their private secretaries had been accessed. Lowther-Pinkerton took his concerns to SO14 boss Lord Loughborough who brought in the anti-terrorist branch. Detectives set up surveillance on Goodman and Glen Mulcaire, a private detective on the tabloid's payroll.

The police would later suspect that the *News of the World* also had SO14 officers providing information for cash, including copies of the palace staff phonebook or Green Book kept in the control room, which the tabloid bought for £1000. This was on top of regular cash payments to two supposed SO14 officers given the payroll pseudonyms 'David Farish' and 'Ian Anderson'.[4]

Operation Caryatid eventually arrested Goodman and Mulcaire in August 2006. They pleaded guilty and were sent to jail in January 2007.

Weeks later, Page reached out to the tabloid through a former SO14 officer and Currency Club investor. Constable Andy Beck had done most of his service in SO14 or Diplomatic Protection. Beck had recently transferred from St James's Palace to the House of Commons when he agreed to introduce Page to a journalist contact at the *News of the World*.[5]

The meeting was set for Monday, 2 April 2007. Page was still wanted for the Baree incident. On his way to meet the reporter he took a call from Aunty Pat. 'The DPS have been here looking to arrest you for threats to kill,' she told him.

Page aborted the meeting with the tabloid and headed for his in-laws house where Laura and the children had gone to stay after a nasty row.

'Love, the police have been round to Pat's. They're after me. We need to fuck off quick,' he told her by phone on the way over.

Laura's parents were horrified that she was going to stand by him again. But Laura had resolved to tell the boys they were all going on an adventure knowing, like Page, that it may be a long time before they saw their father again.

Meanwhile, Page called his father to borrow some money. They agreed to meet in the toilet of Terry's local pub. It was Page's turn to receive an envelope of £3500 in cash. Unknown to his father, Page was savouring the idea of getting one over on the DPS and going on the run for a week. After picking up the family they went to Lakeside shopping centre. Page gave Laura some cash to buy what they needed for a week in Cornwall. She returned with toothbrushes, pyjamas, clothes for the boys, pay-as-you-go phones and some make-up.

The evening was spent at the Hilton in Brentwood, Essex, from where the family headed for Padstow, a Cornish fishing village made famous by TV chef Rick Stein's eateries. On arrival, they couldn't get into his posh restaurant so opted for fish and chips at Stein's takeaway.

'That'll be £7.50 each,' the man behind the fryer said.

'Fuckin' hell! For that money I'd expect Rick Stein serving it to me,' Page exclaimed.

The family spent a lovely week in a rented five-bedroom house in another part of Cornwall larking around on the beach, fishing and swimming. 'We lived it up,' Laura recalled.

When it was time to face the music, Page rang his aunt to borrow some more money. She agreed but told her nephew that they would have to find somewhere else to live from now on.

In a hotel breakfast room on the outskirts of London, Laura urged her husband to eat well before handing himself in to the DPS.

'I'll have toast,' he said stoically.

Just before 6 pm on 10 April, Page parked the Range Rover outside Dagenham police station. He said bye to his boys and kissed Laura then went inside where he was charged with threats to kill and witness intimidation of his former best friend.

'Love, they are not letting me out,' he told his wife from the police phone.

£ £ £

DPS detectives Mark Beckett and James Howells arrived at the Avon George Hotel overlooking the Clifton Suspension Bridge on 20 April 2007. They had come from London to take over the Bristol fraud investigation from Avon and Somerset Police. It had been decided high up within the DPS and without any consultation with prosecutors or the police watchdog that Page's Bristol agent, Steve Phillips, would from now on be treated as a witness not as a suspect.

At the hotel, local detective Gemma Bradford was waiting to hand over her investigation to the Operation Aserio detectives and introduce them to Phillips. Just three weeks earlier, Phillips had contacted Bradford offering information on Page. He presented himself as a victim of crime who had lost £60,000 and told her that he possessed files on fifteen investor victims in the Bristol area.

Bradford had already taken witness statements from several Bristol investors who suspected Phillips of involvement in the fraud. Adrian Marsh, for example, had just made a criminal complaint against Phillips, who he felt had held back information and payments. Phillips was about to be arrested by Avon and Somerset Police but the action was put on hold while the DPS lobbied to take over the case.

Soon after Beckett and Howells interviewed Phillips, who

denied acting fraudulently but under Page's instructions, his name was 'removed' from the crime sheet even though Marsh had never withdrawn his allegation that he was part of the deception. In fact, Marsh was expecting to see Phillips in the dock holding hands with Page. But the DPS had other ideas and was carefully building a 'rogue officer' case.

Page knew he had to get Phillips on side with his solicitor. In the days following the incident with Baree, he sent his Bristol agent texts saying it was in his interest to make a statement to his solicitor about 'all the money you took from your people'. The second text in early April, which Phillips also gave to the DPS, said: 'I have some good news regarding the idiots that are investigating me. Call me when you can mate. Also my contacts in the press would like a meet with you totally confidential.'

Meanwhile, Page was telling his other agent, Adam McGregor, who had introduced Phillips, to 'keep his trap shut'. The DPS had spoken to McGregor. But as with several other SO14 officers from Buckingham Palace, McGregor was still refusing to make a witness statement against Page.

£ £ £

The bubble burst for Page when the prison door slammed behind him. 'It was not when I had my house repossessed or when I was lying on the floor in my aunty's house, it was when the door shut in [Pentonville] prison and I realized I was not with my family anymore and I'm a police officer in prison.'

Six days later, on 17 April 2007, his 36th birthday, Page received cards from his boys which lifted his spirits because he was worried for Laura. She was being formally interviewed on his birthday about the alleged threats to kill Baree. She made no comment.

That night Page wrote back to his sons. He promised his eldest James that they would go over the park for a game of football on his return and told Samuel and Matthew to study and eat their dinners if they wanted a trip to the toy shop. Harry, his youngest, who he called his 'little diddy man', was also promised a toy for good behaviour.

Days later, after a prison visit from Laura, he penned her a letter. Page told his wife how much he missed her and how good she looked, which made him feel proud. He was cheery having received a food parcel: six packets of chicken pot noodles, a tin of bean sprouts, sweet corn and three tins of tuna, six packets of long-life milk, some milk powder, a packet of tomato Cup-a-Soup and a bottle of Heinz ketchup. He wrote:

It felt like Christmas. To appreciate such basic items felt strange, I will probably faint when I get the radio. I seem to have adapted to this very basic existence very well. I think I am using the intense training and eating regime to keep my mind busy because if I think about you and my boys for too long I know I will snap! I have become stronger both mentally and physically. I couldn't give a stuff about those bastards anymore and never want to see or hear from them ever again when this is all over … all the bitterness and attention wasted on those pathetic individuals has now left my system and I see now that I must concentrate solely on my family! Therefore when I get out we will sort out a business plan like I was working on before I left, this we will both agree on, and follow to the letter, if we do this I am convinced with you by my side we will rise up and be the success in our own right without hangers on.

A further letter on 24 April displayed confidence that he was going to be found not guilty over the *Sun* incident, which was coming to trial in June. 'I know how difficult things are for you. You know I love you and will always love you … they will not break us ever so chin up love,' he wrote echoing Lord Snowdon's last words to his suicidal lover.

'I know I can succeed doing something, also if things go right we will have money from newspapers plus a large claim on the Metropolitan Police. My story in prison coupled with all that other stuff will be dynamite so I've been told. See you tomorrow and remember I am your husband, I am a strong man and will survive with you at my side.'

Laura had been battling on the outside to find a home for her boys and money to feed them after Page's police pay was stopped as soon as he was remanded to prison. In the past, she had pawned items such as her £15,000 Rolex, which raised £3000, and given it to Page for gambling. This time, any money she got was going towards renting a small flat in Chafford Hundred.

She resolved to pawn the jewellery gifted to her from the period in their married life when Page was making huge sums gambling with just his own money. A gold bracelet with diamond chips, £1000 earrings, her £1300 engagement rings and £1500 wedding ring. The last item raised just £225 but Laura would never see it again because months later when she went to redeem the wedding ring it had been sold.

Her father had agreed to help out with the deposit on the flat. But he made her wait, which she felt was his way of reminding her of the error of her easy come, easy go attitude to money.

The flat was unfurnished. However, Laura had seen an item on the news about legal claims against banks that overcharged customers on overdrafts, transfers and other fees. She recovered her bank statements and calculated an overpayment of £13,000. After a lot of pestering, the bank settled with her for £10,500. When the cheque arrived it was straight down to Argos to furnish the flat.

Laura had also been to see local Labour MP Andrew Mackinlay, a tenacious parliamentarian who wrote to the Met Commissioner Ian Blair asking him to review the stopping of Page's pay. However much the Met wanted to play 'hard ball' with one of their officers, the MP wrote, the family shouldn't have to suffer. The DPS wrote back saying Page's pay had been restored and backdated.

On 28 April, Laura got a letter from Page telling her not to lose any more weight. As well as some drawings for the boys he included a sketch of a tattoo he wanted his wife to have just above her bottom, but only by a female tattooist. Page wrote that he too was going to get the same one on his arm like they had talked about years ago.

'I really miss you, love. I hate being locked up 23 hours a day and told what to do. I wish I was at home with you and the boys, even if Pat was snoring her head off that would be heaven right now.'

While on remand, the first witness intimidation matter was dropped. Mrs Mudhar had refused to give a witness statement rendering an already weak case even weaker.

Days later, in early May, weeks before his trial over the *Sun* incident, Page was released on bail. At the insistence of the DPS he was given an electronic tag around his ankle and put under a curfew. Page had to present himself daily to his local police station, not go inside the M25 area unless it was to see his lawyers, and must surrender his passport.

'They've trussed me up like a Christmas turkey,' he told Laura.

'I think the DPS think I'm a flight risk. They've probably found that New Zealand emigration form stuff on my computer and the Internet searches I did for new identities.'

On at least one occasion, Serco, the private company monitoring the tag, were called to the new flat thinking Page may have tried to abscond. It was some metal compound in his favourite cereal packet that had triggered the alarm.

£ £ £

The trial for the assault on the *Sun* photographer, Scott Hornby, at Basildon Crown Court was supposed to last only ten days but ended up taking four weeks. Page was facing five charges: possession of a firearm with intent to cause fear; possession of a Section 5 firearm (CS spray); false imprisonment; dangerous driving; and impersonating a police officer, a charge he was very guilty of since joining SO14.

The prosecution had successfully applied to the trial judge for reporting restrictions. Page thought there would still be a lot of media interest. On the first day, photographers were outside the adjacent Magistrates Court. Page laughed when he told his barrister, John Cooper, how he had outwitted the stupid snappers who'd gone to the wrong court.

'Not quite, Mr Page,' said Cooper. 'They aren't here for you, they're here because Jade Goody is up for a driving offence.' Playing second fiddle to an ex-reality TV contestant turned tabloid fodder was not what Page wanted to hear.

It also annoyed him that there were a series of secret hearings between the judge, the DPS and the prosecutor. So-called Public Interest Immunity hearings are ways for the state to discuss sensitive material with the judge concerning informants, intelligence material, phone taps and bugs, and matters of national security, which they don't want to disclose to the defendant.

In the end, the DPS never disclosed to Page's legal team the intelligence material naming Anjam Khan as a suspect behind the kidnap plot.[6] The minutes of the Gold Group meetings were also kept secret. It was never established whether this was done with the agreement of the trial judge or whether the DPS simply never disclosed the material to the Crown Prosecution Service in the first place.

Such material was important to Page's defence as his barrister aimed to show that his client's actions on 21 November 2006 were a reasonable reaction to the Osman warning he had received days earlier in a less than orthodox manner.

The barrister suggested that the DPS had left the family scared and feeling unprotected. It was also suggested that the Osman warning was a pretext to get into the house and inquire about Page's business activities. The prosecution countered that further protection was offered to the Pages but they had declined and made out that Laura was now lying to help her husband.

Page and his wife also gave a flavour from the witness box of the brown envelope culture at SO14. Laura told the court: 'I've met quite a few police officers and given them cash and I know quite a few of them had home improvements and holidays that have never been brought up ... we've been homeless for four months with five children. These people have still got their homes.'

On 27 July, the jury returned a not guilty verdict. Page clapped his hands and, like all hopeless gamblers, thought his luck was changing.

'I'm on a roll, love!' he exclaimed.

The verdict stunned the DPS. The next day Paul and Laura Page were informed by letter that they should attend Grays police station. On 1 August, the couple were arrested and interviewed under caution for deception and money laundering.

Laura made no comment and was released on police bail. Page gave a prepared statement rather than answer DPS questions. He was concerned about the poor disclosure and complained that files taken from his home during the 2 March search were deliberately 'lost' because 'it may be embarrassing to the Metropolitan Police and the Royal Household'.

Addressing the fraud allegations, he said:

I did not at any time mislead investors or prospective investors. All persons were fully briefed and understood that they were taking part in a spread betting syndicate. However, I also explained that should the spread betting be less successful than anticipated there was a safety net of equity on completion of the barns development. In any event this equity was not realized due to charges being placed upon it by panicked investors and this led to the property being repossessed … I prepared a brochure as a specimen in anticipation of future business I intended to conduct. The reason the guarantee [that investors' money would be repaid] was on the contract was because I was advised to include it by a number of police officer investors who wanted to use it to show their wives and for it to appear to their wives that there was less risk than there actually was. All investors understood that I could not make such a guarantee. As a result of this venture I've lost everything, including my home. I wish to express my regrets regarding the losses that have been suffered by investors but to stress that they were fully aware of the risks. And I believe this allegation has come about as a result of bad feeling from persons wishing to blame me rather than accept responsibility for their own actions.

Elsewhere, a much bigger Ponzi-type scam was starting to unravel and, like Page, those responsible for it were looking for other people to blame.

Rumours were swirling around the City that big European banks were about to take a massive hit. The rumours were confirmed eight days after Page gave the DPS his prepared statement.

On 9 August, the European Central Bank announced that 49 banks were to receive 94 billion euros in cash, three times the normal level of demands. The cause was defaults on subprime mortgages, and the reason for the increase in defaults was that the adjustable rate mortgages had risen from their low teaser rate to a higher one and households couldn't repay.

In other words, banks had deceived many low-income customers into buying a house without explaining properly that the interest rates on the mortgage could go up and their house could be repossessed when they couldn't pay. But before the wave of repossessions and homelessness took hold, the banks often sold these high-risk subprime mortgages to investors looking for high returns in a low-interest-rate economy. Ratings agencies too close to the banks and brokers facilitated the mirage by giving false reassurance to investors that these toxic, mortgage-backed derivatives were safe or low risk.

That month, US president George W. Bush gave a cynical speech on the overly optimistic assumptions about the housing market and irresponsible lending, forgetting his own administration's role in both. Bush said it was not the government's role to bail out those who had bought houses they could never afford. It would, however, soon become the role of governments to use taxpayers' money to bail out the banks that had orchestrated this Ponzi-style deception on international investors and the less well-off.

On 13 September 2007, Robert Peston, the BBC's business editor, broke the news that Northern Rock, the fifth biggest UK lender, had asked the Bank of England for an emergency loan. The following day saw a full-scale run on the bank as customers queued round corners to withdraw their savings. Northern Wreck, as it came to be known, held almost 19 per cent of UK mortgages.

Four days after Peston's scoop, the government stepped in to guarantee all remaining Northern Rock deposits. The share price of international banks started to dive and they stopped lending and started hoarding money to prepare for the hit they were about to take.

Still thinking he was 'on a roll' after his acquittal, Page tried to reactivate his CMC spread-betting account in late September. His call was put through to Gina Plowman, a client relations manager. Page was unaware she was also the one dealing with Baree over his £41,000 debt and under court order had provided the DPS with details of six other CMC accounts connected to Page.

Laura was livid when her husband told her that CMC would not reopen an account because of the outstanding money owed by Baree. It didn't help that the person imparting the bad news was a woman. Laura had no love lost for Baree, who had given CMC the letter from Page accepting responsibility for the debt.

'Basically, I don't know if my husband explained the situation to you,' she told Plowman by phone. 'But [Baree] asked my husband to sign that letter because had my husband not signed it [Baree's] wife was going to basically tell him to leave because she didn't know he had such a big debt … So my husband signed that basically, I told him not to and he did it for a friend,' Laura explained.

Plowman agreed it was Baree's responsibility to monitor whoever used his account but said politely that CMC was not interested in doing any more business with her husband.

£ £ £

On 24 October, the couple returned to Grays police station to answer bail on the fraud case. The DPS had nothing new of consequence to put to either of them. Laura again gave no comment, while in another interview room her husband explained that he too was being tight lipped because the DPS investigation had been 'corrupt from the very start'.

Page then left the police station for a meeting in London with the Insolvency Service about the collapse of ULPD. In this interview he was completely different: respectful, expansive, confessional and contrite, although at times self-serving. It would be the first time that Page gave more than a flash of the defence he was going to run if the matter ever got to court.

The official soothed Page's concern that the DPS would use the interview to build their criminal case against him. 'They are able to use the information to guide them in their own investigation,' he told Page as the tape recorder whirled, 'but they are not allowed to use anything you say here to then follow up with criminal proceedings.'

'I have a slight issue with that, but what I'll do is attempt to answer any of your questions that you put to me honestly and fully,' Page replied. He then started the remarkable interview with a startling admission.

'I have not and never did follow, if you want to call it, proper business procedures,' he told his inquisitor. 'Would it be beneficial to you if I sort of started off with how, you know, United Land & Property Developments came about or do you want me to just answer questions directly?' The official gave way.

Well, if I start with, back in the late 1990s, obviously for the purposes for the tape I'm a police officer currently suspended. Back in the late 1990s, I was serving, when I'm still attached to the Royalty Protection Department based at Buckingham Palace. At the time, during the period of 1998 through to 2001, I believe, I became involved in share dealing to quite a major scale. I believe in that period of, just a short period of about eighteen months, I turned over about £3 million of shares value wise in different deals. That was perfectly legitimate. What became apparent to other officers was my wealth. This interested a large amount of other officers. It was no secret I dealt in shares because it was always on the telly in the canteen. I was always on the phone speaking to my share advisor, stockbroker and obviously people began to be interested and wanted to know how to make money.

I made money, lost money, but I made substantial amounts. I then created a private club called the Currency Club, which was purely for police officers. Basically, I pooled resources of a number of officers, Royal Protection Department, if I was going to mention figures, maybe £150,000 accumulated from over ten officers. I was basically trading currency through various spread-bet accounts. This was all tax-free. I ran the whole operation from one screen and I would decide what was bet on and what wasn't. Profits were withdrawn in cash, I would count it, put it in envelopes, take the money to work. It was then distributed via other officers to different royal palaces. It started to become very

306

big very quickly. People were earning, you know, a quarter of their wages each month and I, you know, I drew this to the attention of senior officers and there were quite numerous times I was just asked to tone it down, not have it on police radios. Stuff like that. We basically got a bit worried that, you know, I was working at the royal palace and things were being mentioned on the radio whilst bodyguards were with the Queen, you know, basically what happened things got a bit naughty.

I could see it growing. Other people were helping me. It was like a tier system. I was at the front. There would be some more people who deal but as you can appreciate, police services are like a bonded unit. People will not invest their money unless they know what's going on, who the person is running it and yes, I ran that for quite a while and it grew and it grew until, you know, there was in excess of 130 to 150 officers involved.

The position came when I sat down with other officers and had to work out a way of – I couldn't be at work controlling as much money as I was – I mean, we were handing out £30,000 to £40,000 a month; police cars were driving all different parts of London or I'd drop off money to places at work. If I said to you this money probably wasn't declared, I'm not going into the realms of naming loads and loads of officers and ruining their careers. I ran everything. It was down to me. I don't know who declared what, yes? So I'm not accusing anyone of tax dodging or nothing like that. What I did was I created a system and I ran it the best I could and then we progressed to how ULPD came about.

I wanted to get out of the money markets because it was physically demanding. It was wrecking my home life. I was working twenty-four hours a day sometimes. I was working the New York markets, the English markets, the Japanese markets, the Hang Seng, the Chinese markets in gold and currency and indexes and it started to take its toll of me. I did branch out and other officers were tasked with watching certain markets at certain time periods. I actually paid officers to work for me on post. I would have to outsource my job to someone else who was on annual leave or whatever and they would be paid in cash and work it. On the books it would just show a straight swap.

Anyway, so attention started to be drawn to what was going on. I mean, I was driving a brand new Mercedes car, all legitimate. As I said, it was wearing me down but obviously people did not want me to give up whatever because it was, you know, large amounts of money, and it was a case of well, what do I do? I need to get out of the job but I can't walk off and say, 'Well, I'm running the spread-betting book'. Obviously there was sports gambling involved in it as well, football, as well as other areas. And I sat down and had a meeting with other people and they said, 'Well, why don't you create a company'. I always wanted to do something in the property arena and I think this idea that I would gradually move out of the spread betting, you know, currency trading and we would all move into the property sector and I would buy, which I did. My idea was, you know, I'll create a property company and I'll use that as a vehicle and will gradually come out of the spread betting into the property sector.

Page then explained how he went to Mortgage Guarantee, a firm for those with poor credit. He put in a portion of the syndicate's money as a deposit, he claimed, but couldn't remember how much.

Because don't forget, at that time I was controlling millions, yes, and once we opened this company we pushed it on to quarterly payments to get the pressure off me having to accumulate thirty to forty thousand pounds every month. So at least I had three months to do it. What I wanted to do was I wanted to get away from that fast-track sort of life and go into, I won't use the word legitimate because everything I've done, as far as I'm concerned, has been legitimate, although things have happened and I'm sorry for what's happened but, in my eyes, everything I've done has been legitimate.

Page explained how trust was a big factor in his scheme. He receipted people whose money he took but never asked for receipts for the cash returns paid out. The reason? In the event the taxman suddenly turned up, Page didn't want paperwork around for his legitimate business.

I had the main job of dealing with the finances and, you know, all the running of twenty, maybe thirty, spread-bet accounts all over the place, all over the country and my main role was to keep things rolling over. I mean, I don't know if you know it but there's very wealthy people involved with me and there's professional footballers from the different clubs and a gentleman called Sharma, I mean his business is worth £100 million. And I'll say it for the purposes of the tape. It grew to people outside the police service including members of the Royal Household. My idea was I wanted to legitimize myself in a less stressful environment … It got too much for me. We started taking heavy losses. I'm not going to blame any individual. It was my, I had a think, it's all my fault, right?

£ £ £

The next day, Operation Aserio detectives interviewed Page's father at Plaistow police station. The DPS officer said:

> We're conducting an investigation into fraud and money laundering in relation to a company called ULPD run by your son. It is suspected that Paul Page obtained money under false pretences and that money was passed through various accounts in order to disguise it. Our inquiries have revealed that some of these monies were paid into a NatWest account in your name. Cash was then moved from this account into a spread-bet account called CMC, which it is believed, was set up by you. Can you give an innocent explanation as to what you knew about the monies going through your bank account and the CMC spread bet account?

On legal advice, sixty-one-year-old Terry Page declined to comment and was arrested on suspicion of money laundering. Operation Aserio was right to be asking these questions but had so far limited its circle of interest to Page's family.

The next to receive a visit was Laura's mother. At 8.50 am on 4 December, Detective Constable Gary Tucker gave the same preamble with a slight variation:

> Our inquiries have revealed that some of these monies were paid into two of your accounts, an Alliance & Leicester and NatWest account in your name. Cash was then moved from these accounts into a spread-bet account called CMC, which it is suspected was set up by you. It is also suspected that these monies were also used to pay other third parties, including your daughter, Laura Page, and that cheques were

issued on your account to investors, which bounced. As a result I am arresting you on suspicion money laundering.

Marie Keenan was stunned: 'All I did was let him use my bank account. That was all I did wrong. I didn't think anything of it when he asked me to set up the CMC account,' she said.

The DPS searched the house. In her bedroom, on the top shelf of her wardrobe next to memorabilia about the Royal Family, banking documents were discovered and seized. She was then taken to Grays police station for interview, but gave a prepared statement instead in which she said Page was essentially an honest boy.

He was infuriated to discover his seventy-five-year-old mother-in-law had been lifted. At noon Page arrived at the police station on a mission to get her out. 'Can I speak to the duty sergeant?'

'And your name is?' asked the civilian at the desk.

'Paul Page. Tell him I'm a suspended Met police officer. I used to work here when I was at Essex.'

Minutes later the sergeant appeared and ushered Page into a consultation room. Page explained he was concerned for Marie Keenan's welfare but clearly wanted to send a message to the DPS.

According to the sergeant's pocket-book note, over the next twenty minutes Page explained about his 'spread betting syndicate that included numerous police officers, including royal and close protection officers'. He told the sergeant for the first time that 'police vehicles had been used to convey betting money to police officers at relevant stations'.

Page accused the DPS 'monkeys' of sending him to Pentonville prison so that he would either 'get done' or 'crack' and roll over. The sergeant's note recorded the following complaint:

Mr Page stated that 20–30 royal protection officers would

311

need to be arrested as they had done the same thing as Keenan and if they weren't arrested it would show the Met Police DPS are out to get him … Mr Page stated he hadn't given names of officers involved because he was loyal to them [but] he had told the truth to Andrew Mackinlay MP.

The DPS was immediately alerted. Three days later, on 7 December 2007, they arrested Adam McGregor at home. He had been promoted to sergeant by now and was working at Paddington police station but commuting from Bristol, where he lived with his girlfriend and young son.

'I'm DS Mark Beckett and this is DS Tracey Hunt from the Directorate of Professional Standards. Are you Adam Spencer McGregor?'

'Yes.'

'Can we come in, Adam?'

'Sure.' Adam showed them into his lounge.

'We are conducting an investigation into fraud and money laundering in relation to a company called United Land and Property Development run by Paul Page. It is suspected that Page obtained money from investors under false pretences and the money was passed through various accounts in order to disguise it. Our inquiries have revealed that some of the monies were paid into a NatWest account in your name. The cash was then moved from this account to a spread-bet account called CMC which it is believed was set up by you. Can you give an innocent explanation as to what you knew about the monies going through your bank account and the CMC spread-betting account?'

Adam gulped. 'I feel really stupid. I put a lot of my own money into Paul's scheme. I've lost a lot and can prove it. I'm maxed on my credit cards.'

'What about the £25,000 Steve Phillips gave you for property development? That went into your bank account and then into the CMC account?'

'I'm not disputing that's the case. I introduced Steve to the scheme, but I don't recall the details of that transaction right now,' replied Adam.

'Well, as a result of what you've said, I believe you might be involved in offences of deception and money laundering so I am arresting you.'

The DPS officers seized McGregor's computer and took him to a local police station for a formal interview that lasted almost three hours. In that time, he told the anti-corruption officers about the Currency Club years, how he recruited his family and friends into the scheme and other policemen, some over a round of golf, some at Balmoral.

McGregor explained he had to sell his Essex house to pay off £100,000 debts to banks, credit cards and to those who he had recruited.

'I'm gonna sit here now and say it once and once only, how stupid I feel about the whole scenario and how, you know, how it looks from the outside looking in, but you must appreciate that it wasn't like that at the time, it was very viable, a perfectly good business opportunity.'

McGregor denied any dishonesty. 'If I'm deceiving people, what sort of scam artist gives people back money that they've got off them?' he said.

His defence to the allegations was in part one of idiocy, avarice and misplaced trust. Page had offered him a secured contract on his investments but McGregor said he declined because he trusted the guy. Even when Page turned up desperate for petrol money in 2006 it still didn't register that the scheme was bankrupt and his money lost. And after it was clear the wheels had come off he said he didn't put a charge on the barns or Page's house because 'there was a big queue'.

Beckett tried to make him feel better. 'At least you didn't pay for him to have his clamp taken off!'

'What's that all about?'

'Oh! Don't,' said Beckett, sounding like comedian Frankie Howerd, although he more resembled the comic actor David Jason.

'See. I knew you'd laugh at some point,' replied McGregor, realizing the tone of the interview had changed. 'You must have had a good office lunch on that one!'

For months, Beckett and Hunt had been trying without success to get McGregor to give information about Page. His arrest undoubtedly upped the stakes for McGregor but he gave no explanation for why he was now being so open with the DPS.

He did, however, give some strange justification as to why he had kept money that was transferred into his account by those investing in the barns or transferred it to CMC.

The DPS detectives told McGregor that the losses on his CMC account were in excess of £400,000. Bald eagle accepted that by trusting Page with his CMC password he was liable for any debts.

But he argued that he regarded any money Page put into his account as payment of the investment money and the returns he was owed. As such, the cash McGregor transferred to CMC was 'his money' to gamble with or allow Page to gamble with if he wanted to.

Bald eagle accepted that he knew some of the money coming from Page or elsewhere into his account *was* for the barns renovation and not spread betting. McGregor argued that he was justified in sending to CMC the £25,000 Phillips initially invested for property because he believed there was 'a big pot' of maybe £3 million in the barns as collateral to pay back the Bristol agent and others.

When the DPS officers told him that the barns had been bought on a mortgage, McGregor said he felt sick. He thought it had been bought outright with investors' money. McGregor did not just deny acting dishonestly, but denied receiving any commission for introducing investors whether in cash, cars or free labour to do up his bathroom and kitchen.

Phillips, he said, was another introducer in the Bristol area who also had a CMC account. McGregor was now also willing to name other players from SO14 and the MoD Police. This included Mahaffy, Copley, Hickman and Pearce but he couldn't remember the names of some sergeants in the palace who were also ULPD investors.

McGregor also named Rahul Sharma but did not mention that he was on duty in a police car when he escorted the BAT boss's money back to London. Nor did he find time to mention sitting on the Throne of England.

The DPS discussed McGregor's long interview and sent a report to prosecutors who decided he would not be charged. Detective Inspector Orchard recorded in a police book that the lawyers didn't believe McGregor had actually operated the CMC account or was aware of the deception. Orchard also recorded that Operation Aserio, from then on, regarded McGregor as a 'victim'. It was also decided he would face no police discipline.

Going into 2008, all three of Page's agents were now witnesses in the rogue-cop fraud case.

£ £ £

Anjam Khan approached Page with trepidation. He climbed the grass verge dragging heavily on his cigarette. It was a dark Saturday afternoon on 17 December 2007. Page was wearing a baseball cap and military-style jacket. He had grown a beard and looked unkempt.

Khan could only guess what Page now knew. The disgraced policeman wanted to meet in the field by his old house in Chafford Hundred. But Khan was nervous about any isolated, open space without CCTV. What did Page know, he kept wondering. Was he going to get beaten up or have a bullet put in his head?

Mubasher Hussain had set up the meeting. Khan agreed because of the renewed pressure from family, friends and others to get their money back. His father had just been diagnosed with cancer and Khan was finding it difficult to look many people in the eye anymore.

The grass verge where Page was standing overlooked Sainsbury's at Lakeside. Khan dragged nervously on his cigarette as he reached the top. The smell of alcohol on Page's breath was immediately apparent as he let Page pat him down.

'Are you recording me?' Khan asked as he reached towards Page's stomach. Page stepped back and lifted up his clothes to reveal a lean, bare, wireless midriff.

'It's Fahim's fault I was away for six weeks in Pentonville. I've lost six weeks with my kids. You don't know what it was like inside, but I got away with it. The jury believed me, and now the police can't touch me. They fuck me about, I've got so much shit on them they won't know what's hit 'em.'

Page kept ranting while Khan sparked up another cigarette. Page told him he was going to make £450,000 from the *Mirror*.

Khan didn't know what to believe. He could sense Page was getting angry again.

'Have you made a statement like Fahim?'

Khan at first denied it. Then he said: 'I was forced to give a statement. You and Fahim put me in this situation. You dragged me into it.'

In fact all three Khan brothers had become witnesses against Page in the fraud case. Khan had also recently made a witness statement supporting Baree over the threat to kill incident outside his mother's house six months earlier. Page and his wife were now charged with this.

'We can't talk anymore,' said Page, realizing that he could get into trouble for interfering with a witness.

But Khan then appears to have suggested a way out. He offered to withdraw his evidence supporting Baree in the threats to kill case if Page paid him the money he was owed. Page made no reply and left. He immediately reported Khan's offer to his lawyer who then contacted the DPS. Page also told Hussain that he had taped the meeting on the hill and gone to the police.

The next day Khan rang Page.

'What's this Bash is saying about you going to the police?'

'I've got you on tape,' Page replied.

'I don't care about any tape, you can shove it up your fucking arse.'

The call degenerated into a ferocious slanging match. When all the 'cunts' under the sun had been thrown at each other, the handsets went down. Khan then contacted Beckett at the DPS. The officer simply gave him and Hussain a warning about any further contact with Page and left it at that.

Despite the concern over the kidnap plot, and now the offer to undermine Page's prosecution for money, Khan was still put forward as a reliable prosecution witness.[7]

Chapter 19

God save the Prince

On 2 September 2008, Michael Orchard, the detective inspector in charge of Operation Aserio, received a thick envelope. It wasn't stuffed with cash but it was from Page – his defence to nine charges of fraudulent trading, intimidation and threats to kill.

Page and his wife had been charged in late January. In general financial terms, he was accused of trading (as ULPD) with intent to defraud creditors and then launder, with her, the proceeds of that fraud by transferring creditors' money through bank accounts.

The decision to jointly charge Laura outraged Page, especially when others, some of them police officers, also had allowed their bank account to be used for onward transfer to spread-betting accounts but were now prosecution witnesses against the couple.

As for the threats to kill, the case was evidentially weak, especially against Laura, and suggested a lack of even-handedness by the DPS, when one considered what they apparently suspected of Anjam Khan. He was now a prosecution witness who still hadn't been interviewed about the alleged kidnap plot against Page and his family.

This side of the prosecution case looked decidedly like a tactic to heap pressure on Page to plead guilty and avoid a trial in return for his wife going free. But Page was doing nothing of the sort.

The Met had sacked him on a fast-track discipline board for fraud days before he was charged with the criminal offences on 27 January. His lawyers complained this was done in contravention of police discipline rules and 'in order that the ensuing publicity [of the fraud trial] would relate to an ex-policeman not a serving officer'.

Anyone reading Page's defence case statement, which landed on Orchard's desk seven months later, would have known that bad publicity was something the Met and the Queen were no longer able to avoid. Page was not going quietly. He wanted blood on the carpets at Buckingham Palace and snot on the walls of the court. And as Orchard turned each page of lurid allegations, he knew it would personally be a dirty fight.

But it was not just the Met's anti-corruption squad that was in his line of fire. Page was also doing his best, and funniest, to undermine the carefully crafted image of SO14 as an elite unit. He mentioned the nicknames, allegations of drug dealing, trading in hard-core pornography and a general culture of drinking, sleeping on the job, gambling, piss-taking and fast buck-making among palace cops.

The most sensational claims, however, were reserved for a high-profile member of the Royal Family.

Orchard précised the defence statement and sent his report to senior managers at the Met and the Palace. A new Gold group had been convened to risk assess the potential fall-out. Of immediate concern were Page's allegations about the Queen's second eldest son, Prince Andrew, the Duke of York.

The defence statement said this of the royal:

It was not just the Royalty Protection officers who abused their position, members of the Royal Household also frequently did. The biggest culprit was Prince Andrew. [He] would often have lady friends come to visit him, including frequent visits by Ghislaine Maxwell, daughter of the disgraced late Robert Maxwell. Very rarely would they have to sign in the 'gate book' when entering the Palace grounds, in direct contravention of accepted protocol. In addition royalty officers would be told on occasion to drive these 'lady friends' home when that was a clear dereliction of their duties. When on occasions [officers] challenged Prince Andrew and/or his guests [he] was verbally abusive. Any complaints made to the department were not properly dealt with.

Prince Andrew was in his seventh year as the UK's Special Representative for International Trade and Investment when Orchard's précis landed on the desks of senior Scotland Yard officers.

Never a darling of the British media, the Prince, dubbed 'Air Miles Andy', was already facing criticisms, which he denied, of cashing in on his trade ambassador role.

Page's allegations about the Prince's personal life chimed with old tabloid stories about his eye for pretty women after separating from Sarah Ferguson in 1992 and divorcing her four years later. 'Randy Andy', 'the Duke of Pork' and 'Andy's Candy' were just some of the headlines that followed him around the globe.

The new allegations from a former Royal Protection officer carried more embarrassment for the Palace in that Prince Andrew's alleged entertaining was at his mum's house, behind her back and didn't look good for a father of two young princesses, Beatrice, eighteen, and twenty-year-old Eugenie.

'Bottom line, rules were breached to cater for his entertainment,' Page told his legal team. He regaled them with allegations of girls from a club near Chelsea Harbour being taxied into the palace at night and personally escorted out by the Prince, or examples of Andrew's alleged rudeness to SO14 officers, one of whom considered offering out the royal for a bit of Queensberry rules.

On another occasion, this time when the Queen was away, it was claimed that the internal CCTV picked up a suspected intruder on her corridor. Page and others was sent to investigate because they couldn't identify the person. He claimed it was Andrew in t-shirt and jeans who launched into a tirade of abuse along the lines of, 'This is my fucking house. I can go where I want. Now fuck orf!'

On 4 September, the Crown Prosecution Service wrote back to Page's lawyer saying they regarded 'a great deal of [the defence statement] as totally irrelevant' and that shortly a judge would be asked to strike out huge parts of it.

On hearing about this Page went ballistic. 'Abuse of police resources was rife in all manners, including members of the royal family,' he told his legal team. 'That's part of my case and the jury need to know it all.'

Overlooked in all of his anger was the fact that the prosecution was not saying, and never did, that Page's claims about palace culture were false, just that they were irrelevant to defending the charges he faced.

£ £ £

The second aspect of Page's defence statement that was troubling for the Met Gold group was his attack on SO14. For the first time a former Royal Protection officer from Buckingham

Palace was going to reveal the inner workings of what many in the public thought was an elite unit of fit, effective, highly trained and motivated officers protecting the Royal Family. Instead, Page was intent on describing his former colleagues as 'a bunch of weirdoes' that were ineffective against the new terrorist threat.

'The Royal Protection department was in a world of its own,' Page explained to his legal team. 'This drunk got past one of my lot because he was on the phone, probably to me,' he joked. 'Prince Charles was outraged when he learned and wanted to have military protection to replace us. The internal investigation pulled the CCTV and those in charge were bollocked.'

An example he gave of the ill-disciplined culture among SO14 officers was the use of nicknames, which gave the impression of a Sunday league football team of hung-over, middle-aged dads, not a Praetorian guard. Among the best ones Page offered up, complete with explanations, were:

The Don – Federation representative and well respected.
Monkey Boy – was built like a gorilla.
Fagin – unhealthy interest in the Royal Family.
Elvis – was a part-time Elvis impersonator.
Doug the Slug – overweight and lazy.
Eddie the hen – always moaning and spitting feathers.
Barry Norman – as he watched films all day.
Mr Angry – he had a short fuse.
Elton John – looked like the singer.
Two heads – had a split personality.
MAPS – stood for 'my armpits stink'.

The defence document was designed to cause as much embarrassment to SO14 and make the Met think twice about going for

Page. It portrayed SO14 as a posting for lazy officers, those who wanted to be out of harm's way, others who were frustrated with the legal system or who wanted 'downtime' to study for promotion or pursue outside business interests on duty. These were hardly the qualities necessary for tackling a determined suicide bomber.

'[There was] an agreed understanding that what happened at Royalty stayed at Royalty,' the document claimed. And what happened was sleeping on post, a ring-round system to wake up snoozers when the boss did an inspection, photos on the throne, arriving for duty whilst hung-over and handling weapons while still under the influence.

One of the allegations Orchard highlighted in his memo to SO14 management concerned Princess Diana's former personal protection officer. Page had alleged that he was ordered to pass Ken Wharfe, even though the inspector had been drinking.

The defence statement said: '[Page] was tasked by a senior officer to undertake an officer safety test on [Wharfe]. [He] had missed his scheduled test so [Page] was told, unorthodoxly, to control this test in the underground car park of the department's base. The defendant expressed his concerns to a senior officer but was ordered in no uncertain terms to pass the officer so he could continue with his protection duties.'

At the time this is said to have happened, Wharfe was bodyguarding the Queen's cousin, the Duke of Kent, at Jimmy's. He was also secretly preparing a book about his years as Diana's bodyguard, which was published days after retiring in the summer of 2002.

Now a security consultant who regularly comments on policing and the Palace, Wharfe said he was unaware of his mention in the defence statement. Fitness training did sometimes take place in an underground car park, Wharfe confirmed, but uniformed officers from SO14 (1) like Page didn't train personal protection officers from SO14 (2), he said.

> This guy wouldn't have anything to do with me. I don't know what he is going on about. Seriously, I'm laughing but this is absolute bollocks. I've never heard anything so ridiculous. You speak to anyone from our department working in protection; the whole point of turning up for physical training exercise half cut never happened. I've been very critical of my department whilst serving, and subsequently, but one thing I would say is from a professional standpoint – the inability through alcohol to perform work is something I've never ever seen in my life so I don't know why he has an axe to grind against me. When I left in 2002 my profile was pretty high for reasons you know. It would appear to me he has caught into this and thought, 'I'll throw some shit at Ken Wharfe'. My record of service was exemplary and I was physically fit up until I left, and still am. Whilst I find it amusing, for Page to say that makes me slightly uneasy.

The Met Gold group shared this unease the more they considered Page's defence statement. The following claim was especially relevant to his response to the financial charges. 'The prevailing attitude within the Royalty Protection Department was that it was a licence to print money for officers. Thousands of pounds could be earned on overtime for doing very little.' Worse still, the examples Page gave were 'selling steroids and hard-core pornography from within the locker rooms [of Buckingham Palace]'.

It wouldn't take much to envisage this material in the hands of a tabloid headline writer.

£ £ £

The mudslinging aside, Page still needed to answer head on in his defence statement the fraud and money laundering case against him. He chose to do so by blaming a casino culture of reckless gambling inside SO14 at the expense of royal security. The way the Hearts scheme at St James's Palace had been dealt with was given as an example of the recklessness and double standards at work in Royalty Protection.

In terms of his own Buckingham Palace hedge fund, Page admitted he 'foolishly' put officers on commissions and handed out gifts and bonuses for bringing in others. Soon, he said, he found himself at the top of 'a pyramid scheme'. He also admitted abusing his police position with others to facilitate the scheme while on duty.

Up until the formation of ULPD in 2003, Page claimed 'senior officers at Buckingham Palace had been turning a blind eye'. He admitted making 'substantial losses' on various spread-betting accounts but denied acting fraudulently. He said some of the witnesses now aligned against him were unreliable or lying about their true involvement in the pyramid scheme and the money they had invested or got back.

Having given an indication of his defence, Page's lawyers requested disclosure of more than 10,000 documents amassed by Operation Aserio. One question they wanted answered was when and what did other government agencies and watchdogs, such as Her Majesty's Revenue & Customs and the Financial Services Authority, know about his hedge fund?

And what did twelve banks and building societies – NatWest, HSBC, Alliance & Leicester, Lloyds TSB, Halifax HBOS, Nationwide, AA Savings, Abbey, Barclays, Woolwich, Virgin One, National Savings, Scarborough and MBNA – do about the huge volume of money being transferred between account holders?

While waiting for answers, Page offered me this insight into how he really felt heading towards trial:

> I am quite happy to stand up and argue the toss in court. But what I am also arguing the toss with is this is a corrupt investigation. The DPS aren't the beacon of excellence that is claimed. They decide who they are going to arrest and who they are going to let go. Integrity is negotiable in their eyes because they are the protectors of the Met. If they want to hush a story up it is clear they will go to any lengths to do it.
>
> If I am guilty of something, fair enough, give it to an outside force to deal with. What they are doing is pinning it all on me. If there is an offence it's a wider offence. There's more people implicated. If you go along the lines of money laundering then anyone who has had any part of monies going backward and forward is guilty of money laundering. That has all been airbrushed over. Basically the statements they've taken off people have been directed, as much as they can, against me, myself and I. Their line is: 'He was a rogue officer.' Let's face it; they don't want ten, fifteen, twenty people in the dock, all officers. It will be horrendous.

Then there was this self-defensive and frugal admission:

> I should have took my head out of the clouds a lot earlier and I should have realized that this road I was embarking

on was only going to end in one avenue and that was disaster. And in my defence I can say the intention was never to deceive anyone it was to make money for myself, first and foremost, but then for everyone else. But that confidence and that drive went too far. It just went too far and reality went out of the window. We all got sucked into it, not just me. Armed police escorts, people being let into garden parties and God knows what. When you step back and realize what's gone on, you realize it's something that I regret, I regret doing. I'm not proud of what I've done but at the other side of the coin I don't see why I should be treated – because I'm now a potential damaging item to the Met – that I should be fitted up in the way that I have been and that evidence should be tweaked and massaged in order to make it fit the box in order to push a conviction against me for something I believe I am not guilty of. It's not criminal. It's neglect but it's not criminal. And if it is criminal then there should be another hundred people in the dock with me that the police know about and have evidence against. But we know that will never happen.[1]

£ £ £

While prosecutors in the UK were considering Page's defence statement, the greatest modern exponent of the Ponzi scheme, Bernie Madoff, was confessing to the US authorities about how he stole billions of other people's money on Wall Street and in London.

Madoff confessed but refused to cooperate with his prosecutors. Many of his immediate family were involved in the firm, but Madoff, who was about to turn seventy, said it was all his own doing. He told the court, 'When I began my Ponzi scheme I believed it would end shortly and I would be able to extricate myself and my clients from the scheme … I always knew this day would come.'

Other than the scale of the fraud, there were many behavioural and structural similarities between Madoff and Page.

The Wall Street kingpin had the trust of people, especially among the Jewish community, and he was able to make investors believe they were part of an exclusive club whose success depended on secrecy. His business grew not just because people liked and trusted Bernie but because he paid brokers and feeder funds healthy commissions to send investors his way. And the more the investors were willing to part with, the more commission the broker received. Secrecy was a condition of getting into the Madoff club and he promised high returns but expected his investors to ask few questions, just invest in his ability to make money.

Madoff and Page targeted different types of initial investor but with the same aim, to use their credibility to lure in others. Madoff hooked key US and European investment banks, European royals and members of the House of Lords. He was credible because of his former position as chairman of Nasdaq, the New York stock exchange trading securities. In the same way, Page's police-officer status lent him credibility among fellow royal policeman and civilians, and he used his SO14 posting and warrant card to lure wealthy business people.

Social psychologist Robert Cialdini identified six things people use to gain trust. Among them are returning favours, commitment, consistency, being an authority figure and being liked. They can all be faked, he observed.

Madoff and Page created illusions that being part of their hedge fund meant being part of an elite group of savvy investors that set them apart from the mugs and muppets. Madoff would deliberately turn people away to maintain this illusion. Like Page, he wasn't registered to dispense investment advice, and would lure investors with a promise to subsidize losing months from his own winnings.

Returns of 10–12 per cent year on year were simply too good to be true. Madoff claimed losses in only three months in seven years of trading. Those who reported suspicions of fraud to the US regulator were ignored until it was too late. One whistle-blower had raised the alarm as early as 2000. But the regulator did not listen; quite possibly because, like the Met's anti-corruption squad, it is too close to what it regulates and didn't want to prick the bubble.

The US regulator eventually opened an investigation into Madoff in 2006 but concluded a year later that there was no evidence of a Ponzi scheme. Journalist Erin Arvedlund, who investigated his career, wrote that investors and regulators ignored red flags because laziness and greed overwhelmed good judgement, because Madoff was trusted, safe and conservative and had been referenced by family and friends. Others, she said, knew Madoff was cheating but went along with it because he was a successful cheat.[2]

However, when confidence in the banks started to shake in late 2007, Madoff's investors began to panic and wanted their money back. He couldn't cover the bill even with the millions he had squirrelled away. Finally the regulator stepped up and in.[3]

£ £ £

On 14 September 2008, news that US investment bank Lehman Brothers was bankrupt sent a financial shockwave around the world and triggered the worst financial crisis in seventy years. In the days that followed, global stock markets collapsed and wiped $600 billion off share prices.

Generally speaking, the banks, auditors and regulators had created a massive illusion that they were well capitalized. In other words, the banks were claiming they had a cushion of deposits to absorb any losses from their fuelling of the credit and housing bubbles. This had been done through the sale of toxic derivatives made up of high-risk debt that was fraudulently sold to small investors and pension funds as low or no risk.

Suddenly, the world woke up to the fact that bankers had been operating a giant Ponzi-type mis-selling of these toxic investment schemes, especially in the mortgage market, known as collaterized debt obligations (CDO) and credit default swaps (CDS).

The bankers and hedge funds had earned huge fees and bonuses from deceiving almost everyone in the chain. Mortgage owners had been suckered in with teaser interest rates, and investors looking for higher returns bought CDOs unaware of the high risk because credit agencies had conspired to downgrade it.

Whole countries were now at risk of bankruptcy and, in the case of Iceland, it did go bust, owing ten times what it earned. A massive deregulation of the financial sector had led to an insane credit boom in Iceland where newly privatized banks borrowed ten times the gross domestic product and encouraged people to invest in derivatives that were now all worthless.

On 15 October, Page was watching a television news item featuring Iceland's prime minster, days after Laura had been made bankrupt. 'He should be in the dock holding my hand,' Page quipped to his wife.

Meanwhile, UK Prime Minister Gordon Brown had just announced a massive bank bailout plan worth over £500 billion to put things on a 'sounder footing'. It involved injecting money, guaranteeing bank bonds and effectively nationalizing some banks. Despite their reckless and greedy management, some bank executives walked away with huge pensions, pay-offs, but not a hint of prison.

The nearest any of those responsible for the financial collapse came to a court was when they were questioned by parliamentarians. In October, Alan Greenspan, former chairman of the US Federal Reserve, appeared before Congress. The man who had fuelled the credit bubble and championed unfettered free-market capitalism, in the belief that banks and markets would self-correct and not allow themselves to implode, now admitted this was 'a mistake'.

The eighty-two-year-old millionaire consultant banker told the Committee on Oversight and Government Reform: 'Those of us who have looked to the self-interest of lending institutions to protect shareholders' equity, myself included, are in a state of shocked disbelief.'

Asked if it was ideology that made him regulate mortgage derivatives and bank lending ineffectively, Greenspan admitted there was 'a flaw' in the model he and others had promoted. The flaw was that greed had trumped self-preservation in the financial sector.

It was around this time that I discussed with Page his model for gambling on the financial markets. SO14 officers and civilians had been dazzled by Page's apparent ability to make money from buying and selling currencies and commodities. He had once schooled an awestruck Richard Humby about the 'system' he used to hedge his bets.

'What was your system?' I asked.

'I just made it up,' Page replied.

£ £ £

Geoffrey Rivlin QC is a no-nonsense judge who runs his court like a benign dictator. He is a stickler for detail and protocol, polite but not accustomed to being challenged.

As the most senior judge at Southwark Crown Court, Rivlin was always going to be the presiding judge for Regina v. Paul and Laura Page. Southwark is where most of the capital's fraud and police misconduct cases are tried. It sits on the south bank of the Thames in between London Bridge and Tower Bridge and opposite the City skyscrapers and the Tower of London on the north bank of the river.

On 21 October 2008, all parties in the case met at court to discuss management of the trial, which was due to start in six months. Page was unable to be there but the content of his defence statement was the main topic of debate.

'A great many allegations are made by Mr Page in relation to his workplace and what's going on there. As far as the Crown are concerned, a great deal is totally irrelevant,' said Richard Mandel, the junior prosecution barrister. Page, he said, should have to flesh out the allegations in his defence statement and identify individuals in SO14 who were responsible for the colourful misconduct being alleged.

Rivlin agreed and summonsed both sides to his chambers. According to a well-placed source, the judge was 'panicking' over the defence statement, in particular the references to the Royal Family. He believed that the case could spiral out of control from a straight fraud into a media circus unless experienced barristers, so-called Queen's Counsel, held the reigns. Rivlin ordered that each side should have a QC and a junior barrister paid for by the taxpayer.

Laura couldn't wait to get home to tell her husband what had happened in court.

'Guess what? We've all been given QCs for the trial.'

'That's great love, it means they are taking us seriously,' Page replied.

'But that's not the best bit. Just before the hearing started the prosecution barrister approached my barrister and told him they would make a deal. If you pleaded guilty they would drop the charges against me.'

After discussing the offer with their legal teams, it was decided that they would carry on. Although the case against Laura was weak, it was still a gamble to go to trial. But Page had one last roll of the dice left in him and persuaded his wife to come along for the ride.

The Met and Palace's worst fears came true when, in the first weeks of December 2008, news leaked of the contents of Page's beefed-up defence statement. My article in *The Times* also exposed the attempt to prevent Page from putting forward in his defence details about the Palace culture.

Page's MP, Andrew Mackinlay, was quoted saying: 'The Royal Family and Household are not above the law; neither are the inner workings of the Metropolitan Police. Nobody would entertain such an application if it were Joe Bloggs. My constituent is entitled to present his case in full.'[4]

A second article followed days later highlighting a lasting image from Page's defence statement. It referred to his claim that Prince Andrew would make his personal protection officers fetch the golf balls he hit around Buckingham Palace garden when they should have been guarding him. The story was picked up by the next edition of the satirical TV quiz *Have I Got News for You*.

Judge Rivlin was not amused by the coverage and appeared to

accept the prosecution suspicion that Page was behind the leak. At the hearing on 15 December to deal with media coverage, newly appointed senior prosecutor Douglas Day QC drew the judge's attention to Anjam Khan's witness statement in which he said Page had claimed he would sell his story for £450,000. The figure seemed heavily inflated to anyone with an inkling of how journalism works. Consider this. The *Daily Telegraph* paid around £100,000 for the CD Rom containing all MPs' expenses, the political scandal of the decade.

Rivlin was also worried at the volume of senior SO14 officers, members of the Royal Household and DPS that Page's legal team was planning to summons to give evidence. Page would have called the Queen if he could, but she is exempt from giving evidence.

His team planned to call the head of SO14, Lord Loughborough, who the Queen had just honoured for services to policing. The citation in the Queen's New Year's Honours List said Lord Loughborough had the Met commissioner's 'total confidence' to protect the royals and 'lead his staff effectively'.

On 4 February 2009, Judge Rivlin gave his ruling on future publicity surrounding the case. He was particularly peeved that newspapers had ignored his request to remove from the Internet the published articles. Rivlin ordered no more publicity about the defence statement or the case in general until the trial started on 15 April.

> It is the view of the prosecution that some parts of this [defence] statement amount to clear attempts by Mr Page to deflect the case away from himself by putting attention on others – allegations which he knows are likely to attract significant media attention … I am now quite satisfied that

334

the prosecutions concerns are justified, and that the stance that has been taken or is likely to be taken by the media is such as to make the action I propose to take today all the more urgent and necessary … my only concern is the risk of interference with the administration of justice and that this trial should not be adversely effected by publicity of any kind. It is not my concern to place any gag on anyone.

Chapter 20

God save the Queen

Laura couldn't shake her bad mood on the eve of the trial. She was angry with her husband but also at the DPS for dragging her into the dock and away from her sons. 'All for what?' she thought. 'Something I could walk away from if Paul went guilty and took one for the Queen.'

Laura was still committed to their earlier agreement to stick two fingers up at the Crown's offer and roll the dice one last time. 'When the morning comes,' she told herself, 'I'll put on my head and be the hard-faced bitch they all expect me to be.'

For now, though, there was still an evening ahead of fears for the future. Her five boys: what would happen if both their parents went to prison?

Then there was the thought of facing her twin sister in court. 'She's going to be saying nasty things about me, Paul. I don't want to retaliate. She's my flesh and blood.'

'Don't worry, love. I'll be next to you holding your hand,' he told her with a can of Stella in the other.

'All I do is fucking worry about these,' she shot back, pointing at the boys. 'And you won't be holding my hand all the time. Remember what my barrister said about when we're not in court? You'll be off in your conference room and me in mine.'

Before sitting down for some Stella time, Page had been preparing for the trial in his own way. During the day he worked out in a shed in the car park that he'd turned into a gym, much to Laura's amusement. 'I'm working on having the tightest arse so no fucker can get inside,' he joked with her.

There was not going to be much time during the trial to spend with his boys and Page was well aware his oldest son, James, now almost fourteen, needed the most love. Through the highs and mostly lows of the last decade, his once innocent eyes had seen bad things, not least the violent rows between his parents, and once again he was fearful of losing his dad to prison.

James knew enough to know what happens to cops on the inside. Page was desperate to reassure his son that, after Pentonville, he knew he could handle the prison system. To make sure, though, he had been trying to get back to his karate-fighting weight of fifteen stone.

Page's other form of trial preparation was reading legal books. The prosecution disclosure had not been as forthcoming as it should be, he thought. There were documents in the Operation Aserio files that he believed were being held back, especially about the Osman warning.

Page had made an important promise to himself, which would have far-reaching consequences for the conduct of the trial. If the level of disclosure didn't change in the first few days he was going to be 'a right cunt' with the judge.

By the evening, his bullish frame of mind was still in evidence when he took my call.

'I've been waiting for it to start for so long,' he said.

Page had a secret plan in the event his legal team felt the trial was going badly for the couple. He would 'go guilty' to get Laura off. He knew he was guilty of some things, but not all of it. Ever the gambler, Page felt there was a 'trade' to be done with the prosecution: his silence on SO14 and Prince Andrew for Laura's freedom.

'The most I'll get is a two spot,' he told me. In fact, the maximum was seven years at the discretion of a controlling judge he was planning to further piss off.

As we talked, Page suddenly became remorseful when he considered the type of policeman he had been during the mobile classroom days before joining Buckingham Palace.

Bad memories of a mentally ill man he had mistreated were bothering him. The man was praying on his knees in the middle of the road. Page had persuaded him on the way back to the police station that he'd get released quicker if he did an impression of the comedian Bruce Forsyth in front of the custody sergeant. There was much hilarity in the custody area when the prisoner did his best Brucie.

Tonight, however, on the eve of his trial and possible incarceration, the laughter was replaced by concern for whatever became of the prisoner. 'Maybe he was classified as a bigger loon and getting electric shock treatment,' Page wondered out loud.

£ £ £

'To all manner of persons who have anything to do before the Queen's justices at the crown court draw nigh and give your attendance. God save the Queen,' announced the usher as Judge Rivlin walked in and Court One rose to its feet on 15 April 2009.

The south London jury chosen for the trial was a multi-cultural affair. Rivlin told them in his soft but authoritative voice that the fraud case they were about to hear wasn't going to be easy but was 'an important one' from a public point of view and would require their attention for the next three months.

No sooner sworn in, the twelve men and women of the jury were asked to leave the courtroom while the judge heard legal arguments about whether prosecution witnesses could be cross-examined about their police discipline and criminal records. The defence also wanted to specifically question SO14 officers involved with Page about their on-duty antics that were so graphically laid out in his defence statement.

Rivlin accepted that officers could lose their jobs if the allegations of ill-discipline were proved under cross-examination. Put another way, if an SO14 officer would risk his career by sitting on the Queen's Throne then it was conceivable he would also engage in high-risk spread betting while on duty.

With a now alert media watching for signs of an Establishment cover-up, the judge agreed that, although a 'borderline' decision, the defence could cross-examine SO14 officers about the culture operating at the time of Page's hedge fund.

After a short break, Day opened the prosecution case to the jury at 11.35 am. Page, he told them, had 'devised and implemented a fraudulent scheme' and his wife was 'well aware, or at the very least suspected [her husband] was indulging in fraudulent activity' when she 'laundered much of the money through bank accounts in her name' to finance his gambling and their 'lifestyle'.

Page had wanted Laura to show her disapproval to the jury while Day was talking, but she refused. She was livid that her husband had made such a show of her but still managed to keep a poker face.

Day told the jury the central question facing them was whether people had invested in property or spread betting. He explained in great detail how three hubs of investors were separately conned into putting up money for property largely on the strength of Page's 'ability to inspire confidence' using a 'bogus' company and 'unrealistically high' returns of anything from 70 per cent to 120 per cent.

Fifty-five minutes later the opening was over and court adjourned.

'You are going to have a field day!' Day quietly told the press bench as he walked past on his way out.

£ £ £

'I thought I was more attractive than that,' Page remarked to his wife on the morning rush-hour train into London two days later when the trial resumed. He was looking at his picture in the newspaper. Laura had no time to stroke her husband's ego, even though it was his thirty-eighth birthday. She was too fixated on what her twin was going to say from the witness box.

Laura's parents were not coming to court. They didn't want to take sides and were worn down by the split between their daughters. The DPS was no longer pursuing Laura's mum but in the run-up to the trial she tried to be a peacekeeper between the warring twins. They would pass messages through her and on one occasion the DPS had to warn Laura to back off because Lisa felt intimidated.

She hated the way Laura had treated her after lending the couple £35,000 from her divorce settlement. When Lisa needed it back to start a new life with her new man there were excuses. When £30,000 finally came back, Laura told her, 'You're lucky you got that, if it was down to Paul you'd have got nothing'. Her mother made up the rest by secretly taking a bank loan.

That morning, Lisa strode purposely into the court wearing all black. She scanned the courtroom for her twin on the way to the witness box, a small table and chair straight ahead and to the right of the judge. The defendants were allowed to sit together outside the dock behind their legal teams on the other side of the court nearest the jury. Laura had to crane her neck as Lisa walked in. Their eyes locked fleetingly but neither woman betrayed any emotion.

Day capitalized on the drama of sister turning on sister when he asked Lisa to explain the fall-out. She described how Page had duped her into becoming secretary for ULPD and the concerns she had as a single mum that it would affect her working tax credits. Her parents had 'pressured' her to loan the defendants money, she told the jury.

It was an accomplished performance. The defence had little to go on but what they had was met with defiant responses. Not once did Lisa look at her sister, including when she left the witness box seventy-five minutes later with a smile for her waiting boyfriend.

Next up was Adam McGregor. The two defence barristers hoped to score major points with a tag team approach to cross-examining 'Bald eagle' on his finances and antics at Buckingham Palace.

Day, however, had already deliberately undermined his witness during the opening speech two days earlier.

Unsurprisingly, when the DPS investigation into the fraud got under way, Mr McGregor was arrested on suspicion of complicity in the fraud and interviewed under caution. He gave a convoluted explanation for his conduct: he regarded money paid into his bank account as his own; spread betting was separate from property development and was just a means of hedging; lenders were fully protected by a large portfolio owned by Mr Page. It is unlikely that these notions were products of Mr McGregor's own mind. Mr Page had managed to dupe Mr McGregor into questionable conduct, which could have got Mr McGregor into serious trouble. In the event, Mr McGregor was not charged with any offence.

His comments to the jury had left the impression that Day half believed McGregor should also be in the dock for twice taking investment money ostensibly for property and putting it into a spread-betting account for Page.[1]

McGregor had been promoted to sergeant in 2006 and was now working at Westminster police station. He glared at the defendants on his way to the witness box.

Day's template for getting evidence from his witnesses was to allow them to explain how they got involved with Page, who they had brought into the scheme and how excuses for non-payment began and affected their lives.

McGregor warmed to the task. He told the jury he was still paying back investors. Of his own circumstances, he said:

> I trusted Paul and to my detriment I didn't for a second think that he was lying. I thought at some point he would be true to his word … I lost my house. I had a nice big four-bedroom house, which I was forced to sell because I had so many debts. It was a choice of selling my house or going bankrupt.

He admitted there was a blurring between property and spread betting when it came to his own investments. 'As long as I got that money back at a later date that was all I was concerned about … I didn't ask for documentation because I trusted him … I've had money from Page, I'm not going to say I didn't.'

The more important point was what he had done with other people's money. Under cross-examination by Rupert Pardoe, Laura's barrister, the jury was told that McGregor had earned up to £3000 per month working at Buckingham Palace and £4000 if he was sent to Balmoral.

However, between May 2003 and May 2006, £310,000, almost a decade's worth of police income, had gone through his bank account for spread betting from investors who thought they were investing in property.

McGregor admitted he was 'very naïve and very stupid' to have done this, but Page was 'very charismatic' although he accepted that 'greed' had also played its part. He said he never refused a request by Page to transfer money, didn't bother to keep records and was aware that other bank accounts, possibly controlled by policemen, were being used in this way. He admitted that he had withdrawn investors' cash to give to other investors or to pay for their holidays.

'So in overview, at Paul Page's instructions you received and put out more than £300,000 to spread-betting organizations?'

'Yes.'

'On Paul Page's instructions you withdrew cash sums to give to those who contributed to the investment scheme?'

'Yes.'

'You made specific representations to investors?'

'I approached colleagues, friends and family members.'

'You made it clear you thought it was a good thing?'

'Absolutely.'

'No records were kept of money coming in or out of your account?'

'Other than my bank accounts.'

'You say you've done all this because you utterly trusted Paul Page?'

'Yes, absolutely.'

'You say all prospect of criminal and discipline [proceedings] came to an end, you got a clean slate [in 2008]?'

'Yes.'

'At the end of this the outcome for you was you were promoted to sergeant.'

It was then the turn of Page's barrister, John Cooper, to cross-examine McGregor about high jinks at the palace. First blood was an admission that the witness had provided an armed police escort into London for Anjam Kahn carrying £35,000 of syndicate money. The jury tittered when McGregor tried to explain that this wasn't an inappropriate use of police resources because the escort was only for a few minutes and he was on a refreshment break.

McGregor accepted the proposition that his job at SO14 was to keep the Royal Family safe and secure. But out of the blue, as if he knew it was coming, he admitted having fallen asleep on post in the middle of the night with the radiator on. He agreed that there was a ring-round system to alert officers when the sergeant was doing the rounds.

These were easy scores. The prize would be getting McGregor to admit he had sat on the Queen's throne. Cooper had come up with the wheeze of cross-examining while holding what looked like a photograph in his hand.

McGregor happily agreed it would be unacceptable for a SO14 officer to sit on the throne with one's feet and thumbs up in a comical pose, but said he couldn't recall anything like that happening during his five years at BP.

However, moments later, with a little nudging from Cooper, McGregor suddenly coughed that he may well have sat on the throne, but not in a comical way and certainly without causing any criminal damage to the seat of power.

'There are hundreds of rooms in Buckingham Palace always empty ... I may have sat on the throne,' he told the gobsmacked jury.

'That would certainly be inappropriate and disrespectful?' Cooper probed.

'This maybe at 2 am,' McGregor replied.

'The time matters?' Cooper enquired, giving one of his theatrical semi-turns to the jury.

'It's not an ideal scenario. I don't recall doing it. I'm not going to sit here and say I've not done it.'

'Photos?' asked Cooper with the piece of card in his hand.

'I don't recall.'

'Could you have done?'

'Possibly ... I'm not going to say I may not have done that because I might have done that in the past.'

'Why do it?'

'Perhaps to say you've done that, maybe to your grandchildren.'[2]

£ £ £

The throne admission made all the newspapers and was the talk of SO14 officers waiting to be cross-examined. They were minded into court by a representative of the Royal Protection Squad.

First on was Constable Mark Copley. He was still at St James's Palace. Asked by Day if he or his wife would have invested £155,000 in spread betting, Copley said: 'I'm not a gambling person and my wife doesn't gamble on religious grounds. So no, we wouldn't gamble.'

The repossession of the barns by Mortgage Guarantee had a devastating effect on his family, he told the jury, especially as 'all our life savings were with Page as well'.

Cooper laid a trap, which Copley fell into like a green officer not used to giving evidence in court. It concerned the letter the witness had written to Page in 2005 after Copley's building society had raised concerns over the highly unorthodox financial arrangement to buy one of the barns. Copley had claimed to his bank that his £155,000 investment with Page was a deposit on the barn. A further £160,000 had to be borrowed from the bank to complete the purchase. But the 'deposit' had not been paid to a solicitor or ULPD and the bank suspected money laundering.

From the witness box, Copley assured the jury there was never a concern in anyone's mind that the barn purchase might involve the laundering of dirty money. But when Cooper produced the letter, it must have dawned on the police officer that the evidence he had just given was at odds with what he wrote in 2005.

Copley looked uneasy as he read the letter. It took him an embarrassingly long time to admit that he had written it with his wife's knowledge. The hiatus was understandable when considering this troubling sentence: 'I think [the building society] suspect that we are using dirty money as part of the cost of the barn and the "extra" £45,000 is dirty and you are laundering it into the deal.'

Not only did the letter contradict Copley's court evidence it also showed that he had been willing to dupe the building society by offering to provide them with 'changed or backdated' documents and had stressed that the two Royal Protection officers needed to 'tell the same story' if it was Page's intention to put £45,000 from elsewhere through the barns purchase.

Copley's conduct was never subsequently investigated by the

DPS. But it must have raised questions in the jury's mind about whether the line between spread betting and property investment was really as sharply defined as Copley was suggesting.

Constable Surinder Mudhar had left Jimmy's and was now at Buckingham Palace when he gave evidence. He too had invested in the barns without going there first and knew Page had bought the property with a large mortgage.

Mudhar said he was 'confused' about the money he had given and received during his investment period. He admitted it was possible that he took a cut for transferring stranger's money through his bank account, including from a former BP officer who was in Australia doing a diving course at the time.

When asked by Cooper, Mudhar couldn't remember the reasons he gave his two banks for borrowing money to invest with Page.

'I told them I wanted the money. I can't remember, I may have said properties. I may have said something else.'

'Did you tell the truth?' Cooper asked.

'I can't remember.'

'The money from Halifax was given to Baree. Did you lie to them as well?'

'I do not know.'

Cooper then confronted Mudhar about allowing a stranger to deliver him cash at St James's Palace when Cherie Blair and Prince Harry were at a function.

'Is delivering £20,000 in cash official business of the police?'

'It's not to do with the police. It's someone I was expecting … he was parked up … he goes in through the gate, he couldn't go too far.'

In general terms, the Jimmy's officers that followed also told the same story and gave the same defence for why they had failed to carry out simple checks before investing in property. They all 'trusted' Page, who was a 'good salesman'.

One difficulty was the unrealistically high returns Page was offering. In Mudhar's case, an implausible 90 per cent. But several officers suggested the UK housing bubble made it all seem feasible.

James Mahaffy, for example, who kept his cash returns in a tin at home, accepted that 40 per cent and 80 per cent returns on his money was 'fantastic' but not unrealistic enough to wonder whether it was too good to be true.

Jason Molen, by now a firearms officer with the Civil Nuclear Authority, took a holiday to Israel as a commission for introducing other SO14 officers to the great property scheme. He told the jury he was getting at most 7 per cent interest on his building society savings, so the offer of a 50 per cent annual return was too good to miss. He said property was 'very buoyant' at the time he invested and he believed Page that there was no risk.

Police witness Duane Williams told the jury, 'The investments made sense to me at that time when house prices were going up and people were making money on property'. The returns were not unbelievable, he said, because in 2005 the TV schedules were full of programmes like *Under the Hammer*, *Location, Location, Location* and *Moving Abroad*, and the media was pushing up house prices. 'Everyone was saying invest in your property and it will go up, a £10,000 investment and your house will rise in value by £30,000.'

Amusing as it was from the press bench to imagine TV presenters Sarah Beeny, Phil Spencer, Kirsty Allsopp and Kevin McCloud in the dock holding Page's hand, these defences by Royal Protection officer witnesses properly illustrated the popular delusion and madness of crowds that had befallen the wider British public.

The courtroom received a welcome boost when the Humbys gave evidence; especially the airing of the secret tape-recording of Constable Richard Humby's conversation with Page in April 2006. Humby had already told the jury that he knew nothing about spread betting and believed he was investing in property and shares. Apparently there was no reason to doubt Page's integrity because he was a gun-carrying police officer who protected the Royal Family. However, Humby told the jury that although careful with money, he took off his hat to Page for conning him with his 'silky tongued' personality.

As someone who dabbled in the buy-to-let market, Humby believed Page's promised returns from property investments were achievable and not too good to be true. 'But now we are in a mid-recession,' he reminded the jury, 'when capitalism and profit are dirty words.'

Undoubtedly, the secret recording the jury was about to hear was bad for Page. But Humby was worried how he too would come across. It showed him trying to cut a private deal to get his money back and then there were passages like this:

> If you give me 10 per cent I'm not going to slag you off or think you're a cunt, because that's 6 per cent more than I'd get in the bank. I mean you've put a few grey hairs on my head, Paul! [Laughs] You know my marriage is fucking sort of on the rocks, well that's an exaggeration, but things have been a little difficult. You know it's not good when your wife thinks you're a cunt. So I'm asking, Paul, for complete and utter clarity with me.

Humby explained to the jury that he was playing a part to get back the £135,000 he and his wife had invested. Page had already alleged in a briefing to his legal team that the reason Humby's wife thought he was 'a cunt' was because he had invested some of her divorce money behind her back in the spread-betting side of the syndicate. Humby denied this in cross-examination and so did his wife.

Beatrice Humby walked into court in a black trouser suit looking like Jackie Onassis. Tanned with back-combed big black hair, glasses and green nail polish, she explained in well-spoken tones her distress and anger at Page's fraud. She said her husband, who was watching her evidence from the public gallery, had kept her informed all the way.

Richard Humby had earlier told the DPS that when they turned up unannounced and spoke to Laura, his wife's tears were put on to evoke sympathy and get some of their money back. However, Beatrice told the jury her tears were genuine and started to give the most intimate description of her state of ill health at the time of the encounter with Laura.

'I'm telling you it was not put on. I lost a stone in weight, I wasn't sleeping at night, I had developed haemorrhoids and was bleeding on the toilet,' she told the court as her husband buried his head in his hands. 'I suffered an awful lot. Do not add insult to my injury.'

Most of the SO14 witnesses denied Page's claims about widespread abuse of palace privileges, gate-crashing royal garden parties and a drinking culture in royalty protection. But a picture had emerged of widespread and reckless gambling on duty fuelled by a credit and housing bubble and a merry-go-round of brown envelopes.

Under cross-examination, Lenny Thiel, the man Page had used like a personal cashpoint, admitted there was a regular system of 'brown envelopes at the palace'. It made him 'uncomfortable' but he would meet Page in the car park and take his envelope of cash because he [Thiel] dealt with a lot of Asian people who insisted on it.[3]

Cooper memorably described the so-called elite Royal Protection Squad as 'more Hotpoint than West Point'. The revelations of an Arthur Daley culture at SO14 coincided with a timely front-page splash in the *News of the World*.

The tabloid revealed how two undercover reporters posing as Middle Eastern businessman had paid £1000 to a royal chauffeur at Buckingham Palace for access to the Queen's fleet of cars. Without security passes, the reporters walked through the Royal Mews entrance of BP past the SO14 guard to the garage where they were left alone with enough time to plant a bomb.

£ £ £

Three weeks into the trial and Page had had enough of the drip, drip disclosure from the DPS files of documents that he believed were important to his defence. A prosecution source explained that the Met was 'blocking' disclosure of certain documents about the first DPS investigation in 2004–5 and the intelligence behind the Osman warning.

On 5 May, Cooper was forced to tell the judge that his client had stopping engaging with his legal team until the disclosure issue was sorted out. Rivlin thought it was 'an unthinkable situation' that the trial could be derailed because Page was threatening to sack his legal team. Cooper said his client urgently needed to see a doctor because he was clearly under stress and may need medication.

In fact, Page was 'playing the stress card' to get the trial postponed until all police documents had been disclosed. If Rivlin didn't play ball and order the disclosure, he was prepared to run around the court with his pants on his head, he told me. And if necessary, he would sack his legal team and represent himself.

Page was gambling that Rivlin would then grant an adjournment for him to prepare his case and receive the necessary disclosed documents.

> It's all about time and money, the trial process. And I'm going to say to the judge, 'Give me my disclosure, don't discriminate and I'll be a good boy. If you don't I'll be a right cunt and cost you a lot of money.' My disclosure is a big part of my defence and if I'm to blame they are fucking to blame as well and the establishment shouldn't be allowed to cover it up … I've got my game plan and I'm going to stick to it. I don't give a fuck what anyone says and I'm going to fuck with the system. Like I've always said if they want to bring me to court give me the evidence now and then we've got a fair trial. If they don't want to play by the rules then I won't. Because I know how to play the mental card and I know how to play the fucking represent myself card.

At the doctor's that afternoon, Page was asked whether he felt depressed or suicidal.

'On the contrary,' he replied. 'There are people I want to kill. Do you want me to give you their names?'

'Let's leave it there,' the doctor said nervously. Sensing he had been taken seriously, Page revealed he was joking but left with a prescription for anti-depressants.

An additional tension in his life was the return of Laura's insane jealousy during the trial. She too felt murderous intent on seeing her husband spending time in the court consultation room with an attractive young solicitor. It caused a major rift between the legal teams when Laura made Page agree never again to be in the same room with the leggy lawyer and swear he fancied no one in court. Cooper told the couple this was unworkable because, for insurance reasons, he needed the solicitor present to take notes when he discussed the case with his client. He wanted their wishes in writing and told Page that if he was found guilty it would be his wife's fault.

'If I'm found guilty because I don't want any more grief off my wife then so be it!' Page joked. But he was livid with Laura for making him out to be a sex pest when it was her jealousy.

Just as Page was preparing to play the stress card and sack his legal team, he received news that his seventy-three-year-old mother was dying. Page was allowed to leave the court to be at her side in hospital. The next day, he sacked Cooper and the others. Page told me he was annoyed that his barrister wouldn't put certain matters to police witnesses, such as any involvement in freemasonry and the Prince Andrew allegations. 'At least if I end up in a cell I'll know I gave it my best shot.' Page also joked that he wanted a chance to make 'one last sales pitch' to the jury by the end of which they would be buying shares in ULPD.

Cooper couldn't stress enough how important it was that the next crucial witnesses, the BAT boys and Baree, were professionally cross-examined. But Page was unmoved. He was about to tell Rivlin that he was too mentally unwell to start representing himself straight away when his mother died midweek on 13 May.

The judge granted an adjournment but only until after the funeral on Monday and let Page know that if he still insisted on representing himself he would not be allowed to ask questions outside the rules of the court.

The weekend before Jean Page's funeral was also Harry's fifth birthday. He was too young to understand the pain his father was going through. 'Will Nan bring me back a present from heaven?' Harry asked his mum.

Page was spending long spells locked in his bedroom. Laura did all she could to comfort him but Page had just learned a very difficult truth about his mother, which made him reassess his childhood.

The Leytonstone boy had grown up thinking his paternal grandparents had brought him up because his parents weren't financially stable enough to give him a good start. The truth, his Aunty Pat told him, was a lot different.

The 27-year-old Terry Page married Jean in 1971, two months after their son was born. But it soon became apparent that Terry couldn't cope with his wife's past. It drove him to drink and violence. Not against her. He loved Jean greatly, who was ten years older and from a traditional Irish family. What Terry Page couldn't handle was that his wife had been abused and made pregnant by a relative.

When they married, Jean had a nine-year-old daughter who the family passed off as her sister. Like much abuse in these times, it was unspoken and swept under the carpet, but not by Terry Page. Jealousy and rage consumed him to the point he would regularly attack the alleged abuser, he told me. Every time he was before a judge, Terry would apologize and promise to behave. The courts were sympathetic, he said, but told him they would have to start sending him to prison if there was a next time, which of course there was. Terry was jailed several times and had a long battle with alcohol. 'I never knew what she saw in me,' he said.

At the crematorium on 18 May, Laura and Terry sat on either side of Page with reassuring hands on his back. The priest recalled how Jean would giggle at funerals and had said shortly before her death that her grandchildren brought her joy and laughter.

Page said his final goodbye to his mother as her favourite song, 'Killing Me Softly', filled the chapel.

£ £ £

The trial restarted the following day. Judge Rivlin had no intention of falling into Page's trap. He took the unusual step of making senior officers from Operation Aserio swear under oath that they were not deliberately withholding material that would damage their case or paint them in an embarrassing light.

The jury were not aware of the battle over disclosure. Public confidence in the Met was already nose-diving over its cover-up following the very recent death of an innocent man during the G20 summit. Newspaper vendor Ian Tomlinson collapsed and died minutes after a riot officer pushed and hit him on his way home to his hostel for down-and-outs.

Tomlinson had become caught up in an anti-capitalism demonstration in the City over the failure to prosecute banks and bankers for the global Ponzi-type scam they had operated. There was further outrage that the banking industry was sticking two fingers up at its victims by continuing an obscene bonus culture in the middle of a worldwide recession where millions were now unemployed and homeless.

The Met claimed Tomlinson had died of other causes until phone-video footage emerged of the riot officer assaulting him moments before he collapsed at the Royal Exchange.

There was a strong smell of Met cover-up at the Page trial too. One set of withheld documents concerned the November 2006 intelligence behind the Osman warning. The documents were only disclosed to Page's legal team shortly before the cross-examination of Anjam Khan.

It appears that the prosecution barristers had won an important dispute with the DPS that Page should know it was Khan who they suspected of being behind the kidnap threat to him and his family. Until then Page was convinced it was investor cops from St James's Palace.

Judge Rivlin agreed with the prosecution barristers that the Osman intelligence file, that the Met was so keen to protect from public scrutiny, should be disclosed. The file contained not just the intelligence about Khan but a set of the damaging police minutes of the November 2006 Gold meetings in the days running up to and immediately after the *Sun* incident.

The prosecution barristers were aware that disclosure of all this sensitive material had the potential to damage the DPS and Khan, their witness who had never been formally interviewed about the Osman intelligence.

The problem was this: did the decision not to interview Khan mean that the DPS hadn't taken the intelligence seriously? And if they hadn't taken it seriously then why was the intelligence used to justify such a serious step as giving Page and his family an Osman warning?

Over two years had passed since November 2006 when the DPS first received the intelligence about Khan. The prosecution barristers could see that unless he was interviewed before taking the witness stand it would look like the Osman warning had been an extraordinary pretext to get rid of Page, but one that ended up causing serious consequences for public safety, as the incident with the *Sun* photographer showed. It could also be made to look like the DPS had been dry cleaning their witness to help build a rogue-cop case against Page.

So just two weeks before the trial started, on 31 March a junior DPS detective was sent to interview Khan under caution. The travel agent made a witness statement denying any involvement in the kidnap plot.

It remains unexplained why none of the Osman intelligence file had been disclosed during Page's earlier trial for the assault on the *Sun* photographer in 2007.

Back at the fraud trial, Page had been persuaded to reinstate his legal team for the next round of BAT witnesses. Cooper was relishing the chance to cross-examine Khan. The barrister took the BAT sales manager through the night he and Page were driving when Laura called with news that DPS officers had delivered an Osman warning. Khan dramatically described how Page was threatening to beat up whoever was behind the threats. He said he too would have been concerned upon receiving such a warning.

Cooper took the opportunity to ask Khan whether he ever thought of telling the man sitting next to him, 'Actually it's me who is threatening your family'.

'That's the most absurd thing I've ever heard,' Khan retorted.

'You've told the jury lie upon lie upon lie since you got in the witness box,' Cooper said.

Earlier, Khan had confirmed McGregor's police escort but he denied telling Page that his boss was looking for quick money from spread betting after BAT took a financial hit following the 2004 tsunami. He said Sharma had invested to help his employees recover their money.

Of his own £115,000 investment, Khan said it was purely for property and expressed surprise that Fahim Baree had transferred some of his initial stake to a spread-betting account. However, he admitted transferring other investors' money to the bank accounts of strangers.

Khan, of course, was also a witness against Page in the threat to kill Baree allegation. Cooper took him through their dramatic meeting on the grassy verge in November 2007 and the offer to withdraw his witness statement in return for his money back. Khan denied that the offer constituted an attempt to 'blackmail' Page.

The cross-examination left the BAT witness looking exposed. His estate-agent brother also didn't fair too well in Cooper's hands. Saeed Khan strongly denied he was one of those involved in the plot to harm Page and his family. However, he admitted putting up £10,000 for Page to bribe an employee of Mortgage Guarantee to release funds from the barns. Saaed Khan described the money as a 'drink' or 'backhander.'

It fell to BAT boss Rahul Sharma to recover the position for the prosecution. He strode confidently into court in an open-neck shirt, stripy trousers and carrying a Chanel bag. But his evidence was anything but fragrant and even left the judge per-plexed and apparently unhappy.

Sharma accepted he had mentioned to Khan and possibly Page something about a £100,000 company cash-flow shortfall following the tsunami. After investing the same amount with Page, Sharma described having a brief wobble. 'I didn't really know what we were getting [into],' he told the court, so he asked for his money back. However, he reinvested the £100,000 because he said Page was offering a 20 per cent monthly return and worked for the Queen. Sharma said he never stopped to think how Page could pay such quick returns, but he was clear it was not from spread betting.

All was fine with the investment, he said, until the other queen in his life, his wife, discovered what he'd done. She was not amused about his use of company funds and the lack of security.

Sharma said he too became concerned that BAT's auditors would discover he had used company money in a private property investment. His wife wanted the money back and Sharma admitted that the jobs of Khan and Baree were on the line.

Before Cooper started his cross-examination, Rivlin made an interesting observation to the barristers about Sharma's evidence thus far. 'It must be obvious to everyone this witness is being somewhat vague about certain matters,' he said with Sharma and the jury out of court.

When cross-examination started, Cooper showed the BAT boss a NatWest document for the £100,000 investment in which he had recorded the purpose of the transfer as 'cash for trading'. Sharma claimed it meant trading in the barns not spread betting. He went on the attack and accused Page of running a Madoff-style Ponzi scheme.

When Pardoe took over the questioning, Sharma had already conceded that in the heat of the moment he had once made 'a death threat' to the Page family over the phone. When Laura's barrister asked him about the abusive call, Sharma conceded that he may have called her 'a fucking bitch' and said he was going to 'kill' her and the children. He apologized to the Pages but in the same breath, before leaving the witness box, asked for his money back.

£ £ £

Just before Fahim Baree was due to give his evidence, Laura had a vicious but illuminating row with her husband. The judge and jury were not there to hear it but the press, prosecution and defence barristers could hardly block it out.

It was just before the late May Bank Holiday weekend and Page had come to court in a tracksuit. He was expecting to spend the next few days locked up for refusing to comply with the judge's recent decision that he report twice daily to the police.

Laura sometimes goaded her husband into pissing off Rivlin, but on this occasion it dawned on her that if Page was banged up she would have no money for the kids as only he could sign their benefits cheque.

'I'm only fucking here because of you!' she shouted at Page. He could hardly argue with that but wasn't in the mood to back down either.

'Well, you fucking drove the Range Rovers.'

'Shut your fucking mauff!' Laura barked back.

'You knew what was going on,' Page told her dismissively.

In the end, he put on a suit, made no stand against Rivlin and was at liberty over the Bank Holiday with benefit money to spend.

£ £ £

Baree came to court in a grey suit and white open-neck shirt. Day took him gently through his childhood friendship with Page. Baree then explained how he was cool towards his best friend's property scheme until he saw him driving flash cars.

Baree had piled in with £30,000 without a contract and opened a CMC account for Page who he believed was spread betting as 'a side-line hobby'. He later opened a second spread-betting account with IG Index but distanced himself from any gambling. 'If I ever involved myself in any way with spread betting it would be on Mr Page's instructions,' he said. He also reminded the jury that he had been left with a £41,000 debt on the CMC account.

There followed a series of admissions: allowing his name to be used on ULPD sales documents, bringing in investors, acting as a conduit to pass on quarterly payments and allowing his bank account for transfers to strangers.

However, there came a point, Baree recalled, when he was under 'pressure' from Sharma and BAT colleagues to recover their money. His boss was beginning to 'panic', he said. But Baree denied any knowledge of a kidnap plot or being involved in threats.[4]

Throughout the ULPD fraud, Page had held off investors with the excuse that money invested through Baree in Dubai's booming property market had been temporarily frozen on its way back into the UK because of the war on terror.

Before the trial, Page's lawyers had asked for Baree's bank statements to be disclosed. They were looking for the £370,000 that Page had falsely claimed he had given his best friend to invest in Dubai, where Baree had family.

The lawyers' analysis of the account during the ULPD period found no evidence of such a huge amount of money going to Dubai. But they were looking forward to cross-examining Baree about an apparent black hole of around £100,000 that they thought they had discovered. The investors' money it seemed went through his bank account but hadn't been transferred to another investor or to CMC.

The star prosecution witness admitted to the jury that Page had paid for a family holiday to Dubai in the summer of 2005. However, he steadfastly denied investing any money from Page there.

When he was asked to explain the £100,000 black hole, Baree was unable to tell the jury where it had gone but he did confirm that the DPS had never questioned him as a suspect in fraud or money laundering.

By far the most dramatic part of Baree's evidence, however, came when he was made to explain the decision to remortgage his mother's house for £150,000. He said he did it because Page needed money to complete the barns, even though most of the money, £80,000, was transferred to Steve Phillips and from there to CMC.

Baree broke down in tears. But after regaining his composure and taking a sip of water, he said of Page: 'This is a person very close to my family that helped me bury my father …' He broke down again, before adding, '… He knew that home didn't have a mortgage. Page is just a liar. I'm sorry.'

Sadly for Cooper, Baree was the last witness he cross-examined in the trial. On 9 June, the barrister breezed into court and told the judge: 'My Lord, Mr Page met us this morning and has told us adamantly, despite us attempting to dissuade him, that he wishes to dispense with our services. I've reminded him about my Lord's letter and the potential very detrimental effect on his wife's case.'

Rivlin sighed. 'This is not the first time we've been here. Is there anything I can do to help?'

This time Page was going through with it. He told the judge he felt fit and competent to represent himself. In fact he had been drinking the night before and by Laura's reckoning was still pissed on the morning train into court, making a show of her by loudly bad-mouthing a woman passenger.

Day knew the decision almost certainly meant the end of Page's chances of getting off. However, there was concern that the former Royal Protection officer was now truly a wild card with no knowing where his style of cross-examination would go.

Baree was recalled to give more evidence, this time with his former best friend asking the questions. There was a buzz in court akin to the moments before the opening bell in a well-matched title fight.

But first, the judge was asked to decide whether Baree should be given a caution against self-incrimination. The unusual matter arose because his mother had given evidence directly contradicting her son about the application he, Paresh Solanki and Bimal Lodhia had organized to remortgage her house.

Mrs Baree denied that her son had taken her to a mortgage broker with her passport. This left the question hanging how were false details entered on the application form given to Abbey National.

In the end, the judge decided not to caution Baree. Page was unleashed to lob his first question at his former best friend, who sat with his legs apart like a man watching a lap dance.

'My Lord allowed me to ask you to come back, Barretts, to answer questions,' Page explained, deliberately using Baree's childhood nickname.

'Who?' bristled the witness. 'I'd like you to address me as Mr Baree.'

Rivlin intervened in the testosterone fest and told Baree it was difficult but he must answer Page's questions truthfully. Baree was visibly annoyed at being asked about his mother's remortgage and laughed at what he called Page's 'stupid questions'. However, he admitted telling Lodhia that there were debts he needed to clear with the remortgage money. When Page pressed further, Baree gave an extraordinary answer, that on the face of it looked like an admission of fraud. 'The mortgage,' he said, 'was taken out on the pretence of getting a holiday or retirement home for my mum, as you know.'

Page was already feeling the emotion when Baree added, 'My mum trusted me and trusted you'. At that point Page started to well up. 'I am not going to call her back,' he replied tearfully. 'I can't face her.'

There was a silence in court, which Page broke when he informed the judge, 'That's enough, I'm finished!'

Rivlin suggested a break to discuss the legal ramifications of what had just happened in court but without the witness or jury present. With Baree gone, Page started crying again. 'I want him out of here. I don't want him here anymore,' he told the judge.

Rivlin said it was open to Page to report Baree to the police for mortgage fraud but he regarded the matter as 'a drop in the ocean' especially as most of the remortgage money had gone to CMC.

Baree was recalled but only to face questions from Pardoe, who felt he should have been cautioned before giving further evidence. The surly star prosecution witness now suggested his mother may have been sitting in the car outside the mortgage broker's office, but he couldn't recall if anyone came out to verify her passport picture. 'You are lying on your feet,' Pardoe told him.

Bimal Lodhia's evidence was little help to Baree because the prosecution dramatically announced before he took the stand that they had dropped him as their witness. Douglas Day QC had told the judge and his opposite numbers on the defence bench that matters had recently come to light, which meant the prosecution no longer regarded Lodhia as a witness of truth.

It emerged that Lodhia had been made bankrupt in 2007. But when the prosecution barristers examined his bank statements and credit card history, they discovered it no longer married with the witness statement Lodhia had earlier given the DPS.

The prosecution had also disclosed that some of its witnesses had minor criminal offences. This included Lodhia, who had a shoplifting conviction as a youth.

Judge Rivilin took the unusual step of cautioning him against self-incrimination before Lodhia began his evidence. The mortgage broker denied acting fraudulently over the remortgage of Mrs Baree's house or stealing money from relatives and clients on the pretext of investing with Page.

However, his bank statements showed substantial monies were given over to Lodhia but near to £100,000 wasn't passed on to Page. He claimed his car had been robbed and all financial records were lost that could prove his innocence. He denied he had kept any investors' money.[5]

The jury was also treated to an elaborate story of how gangsters had become involved in Page's syndicate. Lodhia claimed a property developer client had borrowed money from some Turks and Russians to invest short term in Page's scheme. When they received no returns, they sent heavies to Lodhia's office and threatened him but the mortgage adviser didn't tell the police because he didn't want to get involved.

Witness Paresh Solanki didn't help either when he said he no longer associated with Lodhia. Solanki only admitted filling out the initial approval in principle form. He said he did so without speaking to Mrs Baree. He expressed horror that his home address had been falsely used on her application form. He said he believed Lodhia had filled out the rest of it.

£ £ £

There were more tears and hard to accept explanations when Bristol couple Steve and Nicola Phillips gave evidence. He explained to the jury how he had driven around the West Country in a Porsche bringing in investors, taking cash commissions from money going through his HSBC account and the CMC one opened in his wife's name.

Steve Phillips later undermined the prosecution case when he told the jury that he only ever acted on the instructions of Page and Adam McGregor. He said he didn't question their word because they were police officers and in McGregor's case a friend too. The fruit and veg salesman was taken by surprise when it was pointed out in court that Avon and Somerset Police regarded him as a suspect in the fraud. As far as he was aware, he said, the DPS saw him as an innocent victim.

That wasn't the view of Bristol investor Adrian Marsh. He told the jury that Phillips had lied to him and that he had expected to see him in the dock.

Pardoe made a good job testing Nicola Phillips's claim that she had no idea the CMC account she'd opened involved spread betting. Through many tears, she denied opening the CMC welcome letter, which contained multiple references to spread betting.

'Is what you said about CMC true?' Pardoe asked.

'I think I am ignorant, yes,' she replied.

'Do you read your own bank statements?'

'Yes.'

Pardoe took her to one where next to transfers of £11,000 and £20,000 were references to 'CMC Spreadbet Plc'. 'In one week you had caused to be transferred to CMC Spreadbet £36,000.'

'Because Paul asked me to,' she replied crying and holding a tissue to her nose. 'It was an account on the Internet, but I didn't understand what it was.'

£ £ £

Police officers are supposed to be used to giving evidence in court. But most of the line of DPS detectives who took the stand to defend the integrity of Operation Aserio looked like an inexperienced and overly defensive bunch with little mastery of the detail. 'Woolly' was how one prosecution source described their performance.

Page scored an early point with the jury when he showed the DPS had decided not to refer their investigation to the police watchdog until just before the trial. The Independent Police Complaints Commission (IPCC) had been set up in April 2004 as a result of the Stephen Lawrence case, and although a creature of the DPS there were some civilian commissioners who could give it a semblance of independence from the police.

Detective James Wingrave, who conducted the first financial investigation from November 2004 to March 2005, could not explain why there was no IPCC supervision of the DPS operation. His boss, Detective Inspector Michael Orchard, who had led Operation Aserio since its start in April 2006, admitted the non-referral was a mistake. Unconvincingly, Orchard explained that the DPS thought it was unnecessary because the events had all happened off duty, when Page was on a career break and had 'little dealings with the police'. However, he tried to reassure the jury by saying that 'a lot of senior [DPS] officers were aware of the investigation throughout because of the nature of it'.

Page's problem was that in exposing Met shenanigans and failures, he was also at risk of building his own gallows. 'If I was stopped earlier I wouldn't be in the trouble I am now,' he told the jury. He was going to 'take what's coming' but not without showing that Aserio was 'bent'.

Wingrave did not agree. He accepted that the DPS had received a suspicious transaction report about Page as early as 1999 but shifted blame to SO14. The DPS officer said he was 'surprised' that senior management at SO14, who he had briefed in 2005, hadn't acted on his recommendation to consider Page's welfare. 'We were concerned that a man with a gun guarding the Royal Family, with gambling debts, could be a risk to the Royal Family and other people,' Wingrave said.

The evidence that Operation Aserio wasn't fair was staring the jury in the face, Page told them. 'I feel the back row's a bit empty,' he said before asking Orchard to explain why his agents were not holding hands with him in the dock.

The inspector gave reasons that were difficult to conform with the evidence the jury had heard over the last two months. He said: '[Baree's] account was, with others, that he was a pawn in Mr Page's dealings without realizing the bigger picture.' McGregor was another 'pawn in Page's affairs' Orchard told the jury. Similarly, Phillips came forward and it was apparent he had lost money too. Orchard reasoned from an overly narrow and illogical position that the Bristol agent could not have been a party to any crime because he wouldn't have got his family members involved.[6]

Turning to the threats to kill charge, Page asked why no one else was facing a similar offence. Orchard's reply was remarkable. He said as the senior investigating officer he had only found out during the trial that Anjam Khan was a suspect behind the Osman warning he had personally delivered to Page in 2006.

The judge viewed much of these admissions as off the point. He was willing to allow Page some latitude in calling senior police officers. But when he wanted to call SO14 boss, Lord Loughborough, the judge refused. Instead, his former second in command was put forward.

Retired Chief Superintendent Peter Prentice was once the Queen's bodyguard. He had left SO14 in 2005 soon after receiving the briefing on Page from Wingrave.

Like a fighter pacing his corner and waiting for the bell, Page was itching to get at Prentice and ask all manner of impertinent questions. But when it came to it, like an institutionalised police officer, he still called him 'sir'.

Page opened with the claim that the management culture at SO14 was to cover up for problem officers without involving the DPS. Prentice said on his watch the anti-corruption squad had been called in on up to ten occasions. Page asked if any of these involved an officer with a drink problem who was nicknamed 'Shaky'. Prentice said no. What about an officer taking steroids who had his firearms ticket removed? Prentice recalled the case but not that the officer had also told his girlfriend while on night duty about his urge to put a gun in his mouth and pull the trigger.

Page next turned to the Wingrave briefing. Prentice put the blame squarely back on the DPS. He said the briefing was not overly detailed but recalled recording later in a note references to 'large amounts of cash' going through Page's account but 'no criminal or improper activities' revealed.

Prentice said the DPS did not mention the possible risk of a gambling-addicted SO14 officer in hock to bookies, and therefore vulnerable to a corrupt approach from criminals.

'DS Wingrave was surprised you didn't do anything.'

'He's got a right to his own opinion,' Prentice replied. He said his chief concern was whether Page should be armed on his return from extended leave and be in a post that could 'bring embarrassment to the Met'.

'I was told to move my operation away from the palace to avoid embarrassment,' Page explained. Prentice said he was unaware of the Currency Club or that Page had well exceeded his leave period.

The last line of cross-examination produced a remarkable

exchange between the former constable and his boss.

'Have you ever covered up anything at SO14?' Page asked.

'Such as what?' Prentice enquired.

'The forging of firearms tickets?' Page was referring to claims that some officers at SO14 had apparently forged their certificate to carry a weapon and when discovered by management it was covered up to avoid scandal.

'I can't remember,' Prentice replied.

'I know of two who were moved.'

'I had 400 officers over six to seven years.'

£ £ £

The prosecution case ended when Prentice left the witness box. Clearly there was evidence against Page; some of it came from his own mouth.

But Laura's team believed none of the evidence from prosecution witnesses had proved her guilt and told the judge he should therefore acquit. Pardoe also argued that earlier comments made by Rivlin amounted to a formal undertaking to let Laura walk. The judge reluctantly agreed and on 29 June she was acquitted.

That evening, Page told me: 'I don't give a fuck anymore, Laura's off.' She had been terrified of going to prison. Now she could dedicate herself to home life, which had suffered greatly during the trial. The family's benefits had been stopped and the electricity company had put them on a meter for non-payment of bills. Laura was once again having to tap up her mother.

More importantly, James had been excluded from school and was playing up at home. Page realized he needed to spend more time with his eldest son as the couple had openly discussed in front of all the boys that it would be a miracle if Dad got off.

Page was only going to call one witness in his defence: himself.

He had worked out his 'final sales pitch' to the jury but the following day jettisoned a structured speech in favour of a freestyle machine-gun delivery that gripped the jury for two hours. It was like watching an amateur underwater escapologist trying to wriggle free against the clock. Entertaining, sad and ultimately hopeless.

Throughout the trial, the jury had picked up hints that Page had something to say about Prince Andrew. Twelve minutes into his flow about the rule-breaking culture at SO14 he mentioned the Royal Family. 'It was not just the police who misused their position, members of the Royal Family also did,' he told intrigued jurors. Without naming which prince, Page described how 'instructions were given to let women in at certain hours of night without being put in the book'.

Like a jack-in-the-box in a black cape, Douglas Day QC sprung up and said to the judge: 'I'm not sure this has got any relevance.'

'It's about senior breaches of security and being told by senior members of the Royal Family to do it,' Page replied.

Rivlin agreed with Day but Page didn't care anymore about courtroom etiquette.

'If you are told to break the rules, we broke them and that happened on frequent occasions,' he told the jury.

Later on, when Page was again head to head with Rivlin, he raised the spectre of Prince Andrew. 'I'm fighting for my own corner now, the gloves are off. I'm going to make substantial allegations against Prince Andrew that I've seen with my own eyes and if I have to drag [other officers] here to prove it I will … it will go down like a bomb,' he told the judge.

When Rivlin slapped him down, Page took off his belt and tie and told the judge in which case he better send him down for contempt of court. The judge suggested a tea break instead.[7]

Page returned to bait Day that the prosecutor and DPS had only got a 'snapshot' of what had gone on in the Currency Club. There were other investors and bank accounts. 'You only got the tip of the iceberg', he said. Day seized on the comment to ask if Page was hiding money in an offshore bank account.

'Me personally? Not a bean. I've got nothing … If I had [other accounts] I would have given it to other people. I don't want to be in this situation … I want to get it over and done with,' Page explained.

Day told Page he'd sought out new victims to feed his 'gambling addiction'. This was the first time the prosecution had suggested a motive. 'In my eyes,' Page replied, 'at no stage was I addicted to gambling. But the [DPS] did decide that and said I needed to be stopped but did anyone stop me? No they didn't, Mr Day … I've done wrong and I've disgraced my unit but I didn't intentionally [do it].'

Page said only a few close colleagues, he named McGregor, knew the truth about his betting record but other investors never asked. 'There was so much money swilling around people were drunk with money. They didn't want to ask.' Day pointed out that if Page thought he was doing nothing wrong why was he burning syndicate documents. 'I was dealing in cash, I was paranoid that the taxman would come in and investigate. I thought I had done something wrong in not paying tax and giving people cash,' he replied.

This was Day's cue to draw attention to a particular doodle that had escaped the bonfire. The jury was directed to their bundle of court documents and Day started reading: 'United Piss Your Savings Up The Wall. Invest With Us And I'll Kill You When You Want Your Money Back.'

Page knew it was game over. 'Yes, mine,' he said taking ownership of the doodle like a pair of handcuffs. 'I am pissed, depressed, can't give any money back … By that time I was on the floor, drinking daily, twenty-four-seven. I didn't know if I was coming or going.'

Then in a final flourish, he added: 'I'm here now.'

£ £ £

Fifty days of trial were over. All that remained were speeches from the prosecution and Page, and a summing up by the judge, then the jury could start its deliberations.

Page necked a can of Stella on his way into court for Day's closing speech. It was Friday, 7 July 2009 and Laura was still accompanying him on the walk from Fenchurch Street station along the Thames, past Traitors' Gate of the Tower of London. She hated the commute because of her husband's death breath from the previous night's drinking. Today he just smelt of stale booze and fear.

ULPD was an illusion designed to 'rescue' Page's family from a financial bind and 'feed' his gambling, Day told the jury. Investors bought into the illusion because of the lifestyle Page maintained from 'robbing Peter to pay Paul'.

There was no conspicuous consumption like you see in many single-handed frauds, but a nice house with an expensive car on the drive to maintain the illusion of success. 'All it needed was for one investor to ask some awkward questions and the whole edifice would have come tumbling down,' said Day. But his closing speech steered clear of explaining why no one ever piped up.

Page was dreading his closing speech to the jury on Monday. Plans to take the boys to the Essex coast for their last weekend together were abandoned for making rabbit traps in the fields behind Chafford Hundred.

Page's speech turned into a ninety-minute largely incoherent ramble with few periods of lucidity, some invention and patent lies.

'Was I the devious character, slimy money-grabbing, money-spending person I've been made out to be? No, I wasn't at any stage … I've admitted I've broken the rules,' he began.

> I want this over. I'm tired. … I've been accused of being a loser. I am a loser but how much has the police wasted … They had ample opportunity to stop it … There's a constant thing that happens in the Met. It's called shirking your responsibilities. Not one senior officer came here and took responsibility for their investigation. Not one … This mess was kept in house … The Met do what they do best: they cover up. I know, because I've done it … The culture [at SO14]: you cover stuff up. Do what you are told, keep your mouth shut and head down.

Page raised a laugh when he said those doing the covering up would no doubt be rewarded with an invitation to one of the Queen's garden parties at Buckingham Palace.

Next he turned his attention to his investors who'd turned on him.

> How many property companies give a cash return? What property company can produce these types of returns? The Sharmas £11,000 in a day for investment in the barns … Where did they think I was getting returns from – a set of barns that were [not completed] … The money has gone. They knew it and everyone knows it … I tried to do what I thought was best. It went wrong. I blew it. I burned out.

374

You can either close the door or open it. I will always say whatever happens that I've not been given a fair trial. That's all I've got to say, my Lord.

The three of us got into the lift and pressed the button for the ground floor. As the doors closed, the soothing automated voice said: 'Going down.' No one laughed.

At a bar by the train station we all drank our fill. Page said he had 'no regrets' about how he ran his defence. Laura joked that she had been secretly preparing his going-away bag.

'That's some cold shit, love!'

'It's good to be prepared,' Laura replied.

Rivlin took the next three days to sum up the 'somewhat unusual case' to the jury. Fraud trials are usually dry and document heavy, he told them, but 'this is more down to earth. It's about people and their experiences and whether they've been telling the truth.'

The judge made clear it was not a defence to claim some investors had stolen money or that the Met should have intervened earlier or to use as an excuse one's alcoholism and gambling addiction.

As for prosecution witnesses Rahul Sharma and Anjam Khan, 'it goes without saying that anyone who will threaten serious harm against another person is behaving in a thoroughly reprehensible way and that should never be condoned,' Rivlin told the jury. And yes, Beatrice Humby had 'feigned' a mental breakdown to get her money back and others had got loans on 'false premises'.

No, Bimal Lodhia was 'not an honest witness' and therefore shouldn't be relied on. Yes, some other witnesses blamed Steve Phillips, but they all blamed Page; however, it was for the jury to decide if the DPS had been fair.

Rivlin reminded them that a senior former SO14 boss had confirmed there was an officer with a steroids problem, officers were charged with drink driving and that large sums of cash had been transported by police escort. In addition, McGregor had admitted falling asleep on duty, sitting on the throne and being disciplined and fined seventeen years ago for 'falsehood and prevarication'.

But the crucial question, said Rivlin, was did investors put money into property or spread betting? It was for the jury to decide if Page's returns were too good to be true.

> You may think it is human nature for people to be attracted by a bargain or good deal. You may think that if someone was minded to make money out of others, they would know that. But also there are people who can talk the talk, especially if a police officer is at the helm of an impressive company at the time of a property boom.

Page, he said, had told so many lies that it was difficult to keep track of them. Some were not evidence of guilt but others, the prosecution claimed, were indicative of a guilty mind.

On Wednesday, 15 July, Rivlin sent the jury out and told them not to come back unless they were unanimous. Page was planning to shave his head in time for the verdict. 'I'm tired. Laura's off, I want closure. I was obsessed … The truth is they trusted me and I fucked up … I was running the show. It went tits up and it's my fault. I never … I was good Old Bill. I realize I was an obsessive compulsive,' he told me while we waited for a verdict.

The next day, on their way into court, Page had been drinking since 6 am and was being particularly nasty to Laura. On the commuter train, between sips of white wine from a plastic bottle, he threw insults at his wife. 'You're shit. You never supported me. You're shit in bed.'

Laura knew he didn't mean it. Her husband was afraid and weak and could never handle the pressure. She always picked up the pieces for him and everyone else in their family.

After lunch and a few beers, the usher announced that the jury had reached a verdict. 'You know what's going to happen,' Page told Laura from the dock, which was separated from the rest of the court by Perspex panels. Page had already warned his wife not to show any emotion in front of the assembled DPS officers.

After just over three hours, the jury found him guilty of fraudulent trading. Laura started crying as Page handed his cufflinks and tie to a security guard. He looked at his wife in a way that said 'Stop crying!' As Page was taken to the cells under the court he mouthed to Laura, 'This is the end'.

It wasn't. The following day he was returned from prison to hear the verdict on the second count: witness intimidation. Not guilty.

Rivlin had received a number of 'impact' statements from victims of the fraud. Former SO14 officer Lenny Thiel had lost over £200,000 and was now living with his mother. He wrote:

I hate my life now, it is a miserable existence and I can see no way out. I wasted £40,000 of other people's money. I struggle to come to terms with this. It is my fault. I really did give him my last penny. He took my money, any prospects that I might have and my self-respect. He must have a callous streak a mile wide and I missed it.

Constable Surinder Mudhar wrote how he lost the money set aside for his children's future and now had to work harder at

Buckingham Palace but found it difficult to focus on his job. Bristol publican David Williams said he lost his business and homes as a result of investing with Page. Meanwhile, Nicola Phillips told the judge how she and Steve came close to separating and how she became depressed and reclusive. 'I felt embarrassed and guilty due to other investors being friends of mine.'

On Page's behalf, the judge was told how much he had lost. 'In 1998 Paul Page was a man whose life was on the up. He'd made his way from being a lifeguard in a leisure centre to becoming a police officer. He had skills that allowed him to progress. Self-defence skills made him a man in demand.

Today everything is in ruins. He's lost his career. He's gone from being a provider to prisoner. He's hurt his family. They've lost their home. And the reason for this massive fall from grace he knows is his own failings. Page caught the bug of shares. As far as he was concerned he had a talent, a talent to make money. Spread betting was chasing the dream. It's plain that this is no more than a form of gambling to which he became completely ensnared and enamoured and certainly that which destroyed this man. The lure of money completely buried him. He was a true believer blind to reality, blind to risk. Now his family are in a small flat on state benefits. On the day of his conviction his father had a stroke and is still in hospital. Page knows he bears responsibility for the damage to those who invested and those he loves.'

Judge Rivlin sentenced Page on 30 July 2009 to six years. He told him the Ponzi fraud was

> breath-taking, relentless and callous and, by a process of countless lies and very cunning manipulation, you managed to create what amounted to a false world of property development, and using this to deceive a large number of

innocent victims, you tricked many of them into parting with what most people would regard as huge sums of money. Nearly all of them have been seriously affected, some have been so crippled financially that your fraud led to their virtual financial ruin. I've no doubt your personal gain was in excess of £2.5m all of which the prosecution are satisfied you have lost.

Rivlin was angered by Page's lack of remorse.

Underpinning your desire not to go down was the extremely vindictive attitude that if you did you would ensure that those who had the temerity to give evidence against you would suffer most. You accused investors of deceiving their wives, entering into sham agreements with you, making you sign false documents. You accused [the DPS] of dishonesty, gross impropriety and unfairness. All of this rebounded on you – as it must have become clear to the jury, each of these descriptions really applies to you.

While Page left the court for Her Majesty's Prison Wandsworth, Rivlin made a point of commending the Operation Aserio team.

However, outside the court, the jurors were overheard disagreeing with the judge's praise for the DPS. One juror recalled telling a senior DPS officer in the pub after they had given their verdict that the investigation was 'corrupt.'[8]

Afterword

At Her Majesty's pleasure

In his sentencing remarks, Judge Geoffrey Rivlin found four aggravating features to Paul Page's Ponzi scheme: it was a blatant fraud, it involved a lot of money, it took place over a long period of time and the human cost was significant.

'I regard this as being an extremely grave case,' the senior judge told Page before jailing him in July 2009. 'If ever there was a case which demonstrates that fraud can have dire consequences to the ordinary man, it's this one.'

Rivlin's remarks could as easily have been made to the bosses of any number of City banks, hedge funds, insurance companies and credit agencies for their global Ponzi-type deception and market manipulation. Only no senior suit looked remotely like gripping the rail at Southwark Crown Court, where the UK's major frauds are tried.

Six years later, that remains the position. No prosecutions in the UK and most other countries of those responsible for the biggest fraud in history. Or put another way:

£3 million	lost by Paul Page
$3 trillion	lost by international bankers
£300 billion	taxpayers' bank bailout
30 million	worldwide unemployed
1	prosecution of Page
0	prosecutions of UK and US bankers

In June 2014, one year before the general election, Tory Chancellor George Osborne announced that bankers caught rigging financial markets *will* go to prison under new changes to the law.

The announcement came two years after Barclays Bank was fined £290 million for interest-rate rigging to increase profits at the expense of those with mortgages, car loans and credit cards. You again.

The so-called Libor scandal unfolded very slowly after the 2008 crash because of the too cosy regulatory environment of the old chaps. More recently a similar banking fraud involving the fixing of foreign exchange rates – a Currency Club of bankers – has emerged and led to a £1 billion fine on UK banks by a regulator keen to show it had found its teeth.

All three scandals – subprime mortgages, Libor and ForEx – meet the Rivlin test. In other words, they are lengthy, blatant and massive frauds with dire consequences for the ordinary person. Yet not even the obscene bank bonus culture of incentivized high risk taking with other people's money has been radically changed, and nothing as humiliating as a Leveson-style inquiry into banking is on the horizon.

Asked why no government has carried out a more systematic investigation after the financial crash, Nouriel Roubini, an economics professor at New York University Business School, replied: 'Because they would find the culprits.'

These are not just the 'banksters' who fixed the game and rolled the dice with other people's money, but the politicians and regulators who encouraged, and then failed to control, the casino capitalism that gambled away the public's future.

The public trusted the banks when they mis-sold them toxic investments as low-risk, high-yield opportunities. Why wouldn't they? These were pukka financial institutions, not crooks operating from back-street offices. They also trusted politicians of all hues and the regulators when they too talked up what the banks were doing.

This is one reason for no prosecutions or public inquiry in the UK. Another is the mantra much loved of politicians here that such action against senior suits would stifle the risk-taking culture necessary for a successful capitalist economy, and make bankers flee the UK with their bulging pockets to less risk-averse shores. A third reason was encapsulated in the telling comments of Mervyn King, the former Governor of the Bank of England, as protestors from the Occupy movement blockaded the City with tents between October 2011 and June 2012 demanding economic justice. King said many like him in the financial sector wondered why it took the British people so long to demand their heads. In fact, it was just a small group of activists.

King's replacement as governor, Mark Carney, more recently remarked that reckless bank bosses had 'got away' with compensation packages and retained their membership to the world's 'best golf courses'. Fining errant banks and bankers was not enough of a deterrent, he admitted.

So the suits stayed, and laugh as they stick two fingers up at the society they impoverished. Some publicly murmur there might be a need for restraint while secretly paying lobbyists to ensure politicians pass no new overly restrictive financial laws.

Ironically, while the politicians protected the bankers, their own greed and fraud was being exposed at the same time as Paul Page's trial.

The MPs' and Lords' expenses scandal dominated the news agenda in 2009, with daily revelations of fraud at the taxpayer's expense over second home allowances. The high degree of public revulsion at greedy politicians soon translated into prosecutions.

Scotland Yard was brought in to investigate the abuse that had largely been exposed by journalists despite the best efforts of the political establishment to cover it up.

In 2011, Page found himself at Her Majesty's pleasure alongside disgraced Tory peers Lord Hanningfield of Essex and Lord Taylor of Warwick and the Labour MP Jim Devine.

My colleague Jonathan Calvert, the editor of the *Sunday Times* Insight team, has done more than most investigative journalists to expose politicians for hire and those who fiddled their expenses. It was an Insight investigation that first exposed Lord Taylor and also the Royal Protection scandal.

Page was released from prison in 2012. 'The most difficult thing has been being away from my wife and kids. Nothing is worth that, not even if I had £9 million hidden away. Which I don't,' he told me.

The wannabe City trader had served half of his six-year sentence and is currently working as a driver with hopes to be a private bodyguard. If he wrote a book he said it would be called 'How Not To Spread Bet'.

'I regret what I did and I deserve what I got,' Page told me just before publication of this book.

Laura remained intensely loyal and insanely jealous, even with her husband banged up. During one prison visit, a female warden told off Page for touching his wife's knee under the table.

'Inappropriate?' Laura exploded. 'We're married with five children! Either you fancy me or me fucking husband. Which is it?'

The couple now have a sixth child, a girl at last.

Meanwhile, Lord Loughborough, the head of Royalty Protection since 2003, has retired from the Met after thirty-four years in public service. He was immediately appointed Master of the Household at Clarence House in charge of Prince Charles's domestic arrangements.

Loughborough declined to be interviewed about Page and other security scandals. There was no internal inquiry into what happened under his watch. All the blame was hung on Page. As such, and despite what Judge Rivlin said, no SO14 officer was disciplined for any of the admissions that emerged during the trial. The DPS said they were 'historic.'

However, six months after Loughborough's departure, in October 2014 it was announced that his old department would be reformed to 'tackle one or two pockets where [it] found a culture had built up in an unacceptable way over a period of time,'

The shake-up of SO14 followed a spate of new protection squad scandals, from selling royal secrets to the tabloids and fitting up a former minister who had called one of their number a 'fucking pleb', to claims that protection officers at Buckingham Palace had planted ammunition in the lockers of colleagues and stole items confiscated from visitors.

The Met is merging SO14 (1) and (2). The senior officer in charge of the reform explained that 'rotation and churn stops pockets of culture building up in one place which then over a period of time can cause problems.'

There was no mention in all this reformist zeal about any lessons learned from the Paul Page scandal, where the fraud trial showed that a problematic culture inside SO14 had developed across the main London palaces.

Michael Orchard, the DPS officer in charge of the Page investigation, has since been promoted to a detective chief inspector. His next high-profile inquiry also caused embarrassment to the Queen. Orchard led the team that helped convict her official portrait artist, Rolf Harris, for child abuse.

The senior officer who in 2003 authorized the registration of ULPD as a business interest is now Commissioner of the Metropolitan Police and a knight of the realm.

Sir Bernard Hogan Howe was appointed commissioner in September 2011 and knighted by the Queen the following year. The phone-hacking scandal had claimed his predecessor and, at the time of writing, Hogan Howe is dealing with several other scandals that I was involved in exposing. Among them, the Met's cover-up of police corruption and the murders of Daniel Morgan and Stephen Lawrence.

Business as usual.

21-year-old Essex Police cadet Paul Page, 1992. © **Paul Page**

Making money rather than guarding the Queen was the priority for one royal policeman. Michael Gillard reports

FRAUD AT HEART OF THE PALACE

A
s Paul Page opened a can of Stella Artois, his wife Laura gave him a withering stare. The Belgian lager is not generally regarded as a breakfast beer.

The royal protection officer was not thinking clearly. His life was in freefall, his mind frazzled by the inescapable pressure of losing sum of other people's money.

Like a gambling addict, though, Page believed salvation was at hand with a few bets on the financial markets, or maybe Arsenal to win against Chelsea. He had hardly slept in a week, he later recalled.

Six days earlier, on November 16, 2006, detectives from the anti-corruption squad of the Metropolitan police had warned Page that they had "specific intelligence" that his family's lives were in danger. The written warning also said: "Threats have been made that you may be subjected to violence to recover debts you apparently owe."

Detectives informed him he was under investigation and should he offer his resignation, it would be happily accepted.

They were on the brink of unpicking his massive fraud, which had sucked in many of his colleagues. In doing so they would also expose a remarkable culture below stairs at Buckingham Palace.

Many of the men who were supposed to be focused on protecting the Queen and her family seemed as concerned with making money through financial investments and property schemes. Others, it has since emerged, were also moonlighting, running a series of other businesses alongside their day jobs.

Since receiving the police

warning, the Page family had been in a state of high alert. They confined themselves to their rear bedroom home in a cul-de-sac in Chafford Hundred, Essex, near the Lakeside shopping centre.

Laura and their five sons, aged from two to 16, slept barricaded in a bedroom upstairs, while Page kept watch downstairs by the front door, with a bulletproof vest and a selection of swords and replica guns.

He was more than capable of handling himself; as a teenager he had represented England in karate and he was used to carrying a gun on duty.

On the morning of November 22, Page spotted a car parked oddly in a side road across the way. The driver was constantly on the phone and kept looking towards the home. The police would not be so conspicuous if they had him under surveillance, reasoned Page, who suspected an attempt on his life was imminent.

He had hidden a small plastic case under the living room sofa, inside which was a silver imitation Beretta handgun. He discreetly retrieved it. Putting on his jacket and some wrap-around sunglasses, he picked up the keys to his car which was parked on the driveway. As Page got into the car, he saw the man across the road partially emerge and level a long metal object directly at him.

He was not sure if it was an assassin's rifle or a photographer's lens, but there was no gunshot and as the man sped off in his car, instinct took over and Page started in pursuit.

Soon drawing level with the other driver, he screamed: "Get out of the car — police!" The driver gestured in response, as if to say, "What?" So Page drilled and explained what was happening. He did not end the call, as the operator gave instructions for an army officer to be locked sufficient qualifications for an army officer cadetship, while his second choice, the London Fire Brigade, was not recruiting.

Page's karate skills brought him to the attention of a senior Metropolitan police officer, who suggested he join the force. After three years on a central London beat, in June 1996 Page moved to Buckingham Palace as one of SO14's main self-defence trainers.

SO14 is the responsibility of the only hereditary peer in the Met, Commander Peter Loughborough, the Earl of Rosslyn. Under him are 400 officers who protect all the royal residences in London, Windsor and Scotland. Most are uniformed officers armed with Glock 9mm handguns, who patrol the grounds and man security posts around and inside the palaces. A small number of SO14 officers work in plain clothes, guarding individual royals, who have antique call signs. The Queen, for instance, is Purple One.

Page's first job was to man the garden gate at Buckingham Palace, which leads to the Queen's personal quarters. He was expected to have the wooden gates open so Her Majesty could be driven through without stopping. "But I was dawdling in my post," Page told The Sunday Times. "She wasn't amused."

During his trial, SO14 emerged as a sleepy hollow with lax management control over the excessive financial interests of officers, some of whom seemed to have forgotten that their main job was protecting the royal family during a time of heightened security threats from terrorism.

It was an environment in which younger, entrepreneurial officers such as Page felt they could flourish. "The prevailing attitude was that it was a licence to print money. Thousands could be earned on overtime for doing very little," Page wrote in his defence statement.

With genuine returns of 6 per cent a year, it was not long before officers from St James's Palace and other police squads were wanting a piece of the action. More than 40 officers were involved, according to evidence given at the trial, and according to Page's defence statement it was common to have SO14 officers "using their time to make money from business interests outside the police".

The apparent toleration of such activities was remarkable. During his trial it emerged that in 2001 Page was allowed to disappear for three years on various forms of unpaid special leave. He would still appear at the palace in his black Range Rover, but only to hand out bonus envelopes of cash to his police investors.

In 2003 Page registered a company, United Land & Property Developments (ULPD), as a business interest with the Met. This became the vehicle for the sum fraud carried out under the force's nose.

He used money invested for a property renovation project to fund a worsening gambling addiction. As losses mounted

he lured new investors and used their money for further gambling, or to keep existing investors sweet with envelopes full of cash. What could have been a successful investment scheme had now become a Ponzi fraud like that operated by Bernard Madoff, the American fund manager.

Police intelligence documents disclosed during the trial reveal a remarkable series of failures and questionable decisions.

As early as January 2006, a financial investigator for the anti-corruption squad had identified a serious problem with Page and ULPD, which he felt made the royal protection officer susceptible to corrupt approaches from organised criminals. Page had amassed debts of £600,000.

The anti-corruption investigation discovered that Page was acting criminally or was breaching police discipline, but it did make some welfare recommendations to the chief superintendent at SO14.

A disclosed note by the SO14 boss said: "[Page] should not serve in a [command] which could bring embarrassment to the Met or leave the officer open to inappropriate approaches from outside influence of persons."

Remarkably, almost nothing was done until November 2006, by then Page was sum in debt, according to an internal estimate, and descending into paranoia.

DURING his trial Page, 38, made repeated requests for a public inquiry into the handling of his case and the culture at SO14.

Some of his claims — involving members of the royal family — were outlandish and unsubstantiated. But several prosecution witnesses who had lost money admitted under cross-examination that they had never taken it, and police cars to escort cash returns from Page's business, sleep while on duty and allowed friends and family to use the police car park.

The lax culture at the palace is still apparent. Neil Watson, 41, another royal protection officer, is being investigated after moonlighting with a string of businesses.

He has been removed from frontline duties after allegations that he made £20,000 from a business partner. He is also facing a misconduct inquiry after repeatedly using his police e-mail address to pursue private commercial activities.

He was a director or company secretary of six firms, including a shipping contractor set up with an Iranian woman and a business making picture frames.

There are further indications that Page's activities were merely the most serious at SO14. Another case involved a pyramid scheme known as the Hearts Club, which a royal protection officer ran until he was moved to Windsor Castle.

After the jury brought in its guilty verdict on Page for fraudulent trading, the Met ruled out any further investigation into the culture at the palace. "The Page case reiterates how perilously [easy] take the standards in [the Met] on perils of employees, and how robustly we will act when those standards are not met," it said in a statement.

Clearly there is still work to be done.

> **SOMEONE COVERED MY SHIFTS WHILE I SOLD SHARES**

The author's 2009 exposé of the scandal in The Sunday Times.

© The Sunday Times

Paul and Laura Page at home in March 2015. "I often wonder why didn't the Met stop me earlier when it was painfully obvious I was ruining people's lives and out of control in so many other ways. People were nearly killed but the Met was more interested in protecting itself and the palace."

Note on sources

For Queen and Currency is a human story: the tragic rise and fall of a young couple in the boom and bust years. It is based on extensive interviews with the key players, witnesses and documentary evidence that emerged in the Page trials and official documents I have seen or obtained.

There is a lot of dialogue in this book. Some of it is based on the recollection of one or all of the participants in that conversation. Alternatively, they are based on transcripts of secretly recorded phone calls by one of the participants, contemporary documents such as witness statements, police logs, letters, official reports and the direct evidence on oath given by witnesses during the trials.

On occasion, I have carefully re-created the conversation or given someone's state of mind. This is not invention for dramatic purposes but faithfully based on the primary sources cited above. Any conflict in recollections or positions has been harmonized to present an agreed essence and account of the conversation.

I was the only reporter to cover the entire fraud trial. I also extensively interviewed the Pages and members of their families. Only a few of the key investors were willing to talk to me. The opinions and actions of those who declined are represented in the book based on their witness statements and evidence at court.

Only one person, Anjam Khan, an investor who became a prosecution witness, offered to sell me his story and those of unidentified people he claimed to represent. The offer was rejected.

Metropolitan Police officers involved in the case also refused requests for interviews. Their views are based on the evidence they gave in court and internal police documents.

Notes

Chapter 1 Essex princess

1 Details of the couple's early relationship are taken from interviews with Paul and Laura Page between 2008 and 2011. Unless otherwise stated, all details of their personal life come from the same source.

Chapter 3 Road to royalty

1 Page claimed in his 2008 defence-case statement ('statement') that he was given a heads-up during his application to join SO14. The Met and prosecution never denied it.

2 Elliot Philipp's carer told me he was too old to be interviewed. Details of the Hills–Snowdon relationship and the inquest are taken from press coverage at the time.

Chapter 4 Gripper meets Purple One

1 Page detailed the lap-dance incident in his statement. The Palace and prosecution never denied it.

Chapter 5 Bubble bath

1 From *Memoirs of Extraordinary Popular Delusions and the Madness of Crowds* (1841).

Chapter 6 The Currency Club

1 Evidence on 20 May 2009 of SO14 officer Phil Williams at Page's fraud trial ('the trial').

2 McGregor's discipline finding was set out in a disclosure note prepared by the prosecution for the trial.

3 McGregor declined to be interviewed. The account of his early relationship with Page is taken from his police interview on 7 December 2007; his witness statements (11.12.07, 21.1.08, 18.2.08) and his evidence at the trial on 20–21 April.

4 The account of Mahaffy's early encounter with Page comes from the former's witness statements (1.2.06, 11.1.07, 17.10.07, 28.3.08) and his evidence at the trial on 28–30 April.

Chapter 7 Throne games

1 Page revealed his account of the Throne Room incidents in his statement. McGregor admitted having his photo taken on the throne when he was cross-examined during the trial.

2 Allegations of a drinking culture at SO14 were detailed in Page's statement. Peter Prentice, a senior SO14 officer, later corroborated some of these incidents at the trial.

3 McGregor's involvement with the Hearts Club is based on his trial evidence.

4   The Hearts scandal narrative is based on emails and corre-
spondence between civilian investors Jamie Ross and Terry
Belton, and from Christine O'Brien's complaint to CIB. I also
interviewed investors from Watford. McGregor's account
comes from his witness statements and trial evidence. The
prosecution was provided with a disclosure note from SO14,
which confirmed the plot to harm Ross and his transfer to
Windsor.

Chapter 8 ULPD: A firm within The Firm

1   Mahaffy's witness statement and trial evidence.
2   Details of Lisa's involvement in ULPD are taken from interviews with Paul and Laura Page, and from Lisa's witness
statement (18.12.07) and her trial evidence on 20 April.
3   The investment details in this section are taken from the witness statements and trial evidence of the McGregor brothers and Steve Tree.

Chapter 9 Jimmy's

1   Mortgage Guarantee had reduced the conversion loan from
£270,000 to £217,000. The money was mostly released
between May and August 2004 for Paul Ballard and his men
to start converting the three barns.
2   The Mahaffys' investments and attitude to Page are taken
from Jim Mahaffy's witness statement and his trial
evidence.
3   The Copleys' investment and dealings with the Pages are
taken from the witness statements of Mark (6.12.06) and
Sufia (20.9.07) Copley and their trial evidence on 27 April

and 19 May respectively.

4   This section is based on the witness statements of the Mudhars (6.2.08) and Suri (5.3.08) and their trial evidence on 27
and 30 April and 11 May respectively.

Chapter 10 Gripper Airways

1   Author's interview with Baree, 30 July 2008.

2   Author's interview with Baree and Khan, 30 July 2008.
Details of the investments by the three British Asians are
taken from their witness statements: Lodhia (26.6.07),
Solanki (6.6.07) and Hussain (5.4.07, 17.1.08); and their
trial evidence (2–3 June, 21 and 27 May respectively).

3   Mark Joyce declined to be interviewed.

4   Author's interview with Baree, 30 July 2008.

5   Craig Gunn witness statements (28.3.07, 7.8.07, 27.3.08).
McGregor's witness statement and trial evidence.

Chapter 12 Grand designs

1   Dave Newman's witness statement (1.11.07) and his trial
evidence on 19–20 May. Witness statements and trial evidence of the McGregor brothers.

2   The account of the Humbys' involvement is taken from the
witness statements of Richard (15.1.07, 11.10.07) and
Beatrice (11.10.07) Humby and their trial evidence on 5–7
May. Further details come from Richard Humby's police
interview (23.11.06).

3   The Mahaffys' witness statements and trial evidence.

4   McCallion's witness statement (8.3.07, 27.7.07) and his trial
evidence on 1 May.

5   Duane Williams's witness statement (23.3.07) and trial evidence on 7–8 May. Williams received some returns but lost half his investment.

6   Witness statements of Phil Williams and Linda Jolly (20.2.07, 30.1.08) and their trial evidence on 20 May.

7   Page wrote to SO14 management that his seventeen months of special leave was necessary 'to concentrate fully on my domestic, family, educational and similar commitments'. He added that if allowed back to SO14 he would 'repay at a premium' and save the Royal Protection Squad money from not having to train another officer. No decision had been made by the time his leave period finished at the end of July, leaving Page neither in nor out of SO14.

Chapter 13 Winter of discontent

1   When he gave his witness statement to the DPS in November 2007, Newman was a police community support officer. He made no mention of the £20,000 delivery to Mudhar at St James's Palace. Mudhar only gave the scantiest detail of it in his witness statement.

Chapter 14 The Bristol connection

1   Phillips paid his cousin in cash from Page. But after four months the loan repayments stopped. Paul Phillips said in his April 2007 witness statement: 'The last two years of my life have been hell. I am struggling financially and have constant money worries which will take me a few years to bounce back from.'

2   In his 20 April 2007 witness statement, Steve Phillips said: 'I never actually ever got any commission.' However, he admitted receiving wages and fees for money passing through his bank account and the CMC account in his wife's name. Nicola Phillips said in her witness statement of the same date that she believed her husband was on commission.

3   There was some truth in a connection between Premier League players and Page's syndicate. Financial adviser and ULPD investor Parish Solanki had arranged substantial mortgages of between half and one million pounds for two British Premier League players. He also had a business relationship with an African player. When cross-examined, Solanki said he couldn't recall the name of the African player. Phillips's mother Sheila never got her money back.

4   The witness statements of Steve Phillips (20.4.07, 3.9.08) and Nicola Phillips (20.4.07). She closed the CMC account in September 2006 because she was 'not happy'.

5   Three of the five were Andy Boucher, David Jones and Elaine Davey. On 7 February, Boucher called Page who said he was at his lawyers and couldn't talk but asked to borrow £40 to unclamp his car. Amazingly, Boucher transferred the money to the NatWest account of Terry Page. 'I don't know why but I agreed as I felt that I had to keep this man on my side if I was ever to receive any of my monies back,' Boucher explained in his witness statement.

6   According to prosecution figures, Gerry McCallion got back almost £20,000 of his £68,000 investment. His girlfriend lost all of hers.

7   Page's leave was coming to an end on 26 July 2005. In early June, SO14 human resources asked if he was coming back to work. Page replied positively on 15 June.

8   The others are Jason Molen, Rob Pearce and Lenny Thiel.

9   Mahaffy had a hearing listed for January 2006 at Basildon Crown Court.

10   Humby told the jury he was playing along to get Page talking and was not like he came across on the tape.

11   Lenny Thiel and Rob Pearce.

12   Molen emailed Page on 11 December 2005 asking for his money to pay a hospital bill and help pay off his son's student loan. The email mentioned the prospect of putting a charge on the barns. Page emailed back: 'I have to deal with a world of shit … I am making efforts to arrange payments for you all.' To which Molen responded: 'All anyone wanted was reassurance.'

13   Humby denied to the jury that he had recorded this conversation.

14   The owner of the premises leased by Wicked Wardrobe was owed £10,000 in rent. Laura, he discovered, was sub-letting a space in the back of the shop to a tailor who paid her in cash.

15   Mark Copley told the jury that he knew Mortgage Guarantee was the lender on the barns because someone from the finance firm would regularly visit the site. However, he denied that Page had told him about the mortgage.

16   Phillips maintained at trial that he believed he was promoting a property investment not a spread-betting scheme.

17   Page made sure Marsh got a £5000 cash return quickly. But no sooner had Phillips handed it over then Page was on the phone asking Marsh to hand it back so he could pay Anne Carter her return. Amazingly, Marsh agreed and gave Phillips the cash. However, later that afternoon the Bristol agent returned the £5000 to Marsh with the explanation that Carter had decided to reinvest.

18 McGregor ended up repaying most of Matthew Bainton's £10,000 investment.

19 Pennell transferred £10,000 to Phillips's bank account on 8 June 2006 and put 'loan' as a reference.

Chapter 15 Death threats, guns and gangsters

1 Matthew Smith knew Baree before BAT from another travel agency and had already met Page as a police officer. Smith approached Baree to invest and was shown the brochure. He said he didn't know Baree was the finance director of ULPD. In July 2005, Smith invested £20,000 by transfer to Baree who put it in his CMC account. Weeks later, Page gave Smith his money back plus a £11,000 cash return. Smith reinvested another £30,000 and his brother-in-law, Mike Beatty, put in £10,000 in September and October 2005. There were no contracts. The money went to Laura Page's ULPD account.

2 Baree, Solanki and Lodhia made these admissions and denials during the trial.

3 Baree's witness statements (29.3.07, 31.3.07, 4.4.07, 19.4.07, 22.5.07, 4.6.07).

4 Saeed Khan admitted during the trial that he understood his £10,000 payment was 'a drink' or 'back-hander' for an employee of the finance firm behind the barns. Saeed transferred the money to Steve Phillips's HSBC bank account, who transferred it to CMC. In his witness statement, Fahim Baree described the purpose of his £10,000 payment was to 'sweeten Mortgage Guarantee'. Khan and Baree were never investigated for this. The Mortgage Guarantee employee falsely accused of soliciting bribes complained about Page

to the Independent Police Complaints Commission.

5   Mick Hickman refused to answer any questions about his involvement with Page.

6   During the trial, Rahul Sharma gave details about the call to Laura and accepted it was a 'death threat'.

7   In her witness statement (11.06.07) Gina Plowman, CMC client relations manager, calculated losses of over £1.1 million on just six accounts that Page controlled. £397,000 was lost on his own CMC account, £337,000 on Baree's, £139,000 on the Phillips account and £200,000 on those opened by Page's father and mother-in-law.

8   Anne Carter, David and Marcus Williams, and their friends Esther Smith and Jeff Pennell. Marcus Williams had reported the matter to Essex Police who referred him to Avon and Somerset Police on 25 October 2006. Six days later a crime report named Page and Phillips as suspects. Carter, David Williams, Esther Smith and Adrian Marsh said in their witness statements to Operation Aserio that they believed Phillips was part of the deception.

9   Thiel told the jury that he didn't notice the date of May 2005 until much later. He signed another strange loan agreement, apparently to placate Laura's bank over a recent £80,000 deposit. Thiel wrote in this agreement: 'I have agreed to make a personal loan of £80,000 to my good friend Laura Page on 21 November ... to be repaid at my discretion.'

Chapter 16 Royal Protection: the Osmans

1   Before the killings, Potter, the teacher, had spread false rumours that Osman junior and his neighbour, a fellow student, were in a gay relationship. Consumed with jealousy, Potter changed

his name to Osman by deed poll, something he had done before when infatuated with another schoolboy at a different north London school. A psychiatrist had examined Potter and described his relationship with Osman as 'reprehensibly suspect' but said he should remain teaching at the school. Then the Osmans had their windows put in and tyres slashed. After a further psychiatric assessment the teacher was transferred to another school. Attacks on Osman's property continued. Potter was also suspected of deliberately ramming a car with Osman's neighbour and school friend inside. The teacher claimed his foot had slipped on the pedals. The police continued to deny receiving warnings from school authorities. Potter, it emerged, had told the education authorities he was going to do a 'sort of Hungerford', a reference to Michael Ryan's massacre months earlier in August 1987 of sixteen people before he turned his automatic weapon on himself.

2   In 2008, the Crown Prosecution Service wrote to Page's solicitors that: 'Paul Page's business interest was not reviewed after it was first approved (in November 2003) and the questionnaire that should be completed each year before the annual review is not on the file and does not appear to have been submitted.'

3   The judge ordered the prosecution to make inquiries with the DPS about who was behind the threat to Page. Anjam Khan was named in a prosecution note disclosed to the court. Page's solicitors were also trying to establish links between Khan and the Essex underworld figures who they claimed had invested £20,000 in the scheme. Khan, who denies any connection with the Essex underworld, was interviewed under caution on 31 March 2009. He denied any involvement in a plot to harm Page and his family. No further action was taken.

Chapter 17 Royal hunt of the Sun

1   Page had been trying to return to paid police work since late 2005, but his application for an armed officer's position at London City Airport was turned down on 14 February 2006. Two days later, the SO14 human resources manager wrote offering the option of a five-year career break. But Page ducked several meetings until 20 July. The official told him he could no longer remain on special leave, as this was only meant to be for a year and he was well over. It was agreed he would have to apply for a career break until 31 December. The official also demanded a report from Page about what he had been up to because there was nothing on file since 2004. Page never produced the report and no document was ever produced showing he was on a career break at the time of the Lakeside gun incident.

2   At Page's trial, Lodhia denied he had kept any investors' money.

3   The Met also paid for Page to have counselling. But he said it didn't help him much.

4   Nigel Gore didn't make a witness statement.

Chapter 18 Annus horribilis

1   Page said of the ledgers: 'The first one had names of all the people – civilians and police and military and [Royal] Household, chefs and cooks – names of all the people who put money in, how much they put in, what their deals were. The second one was the holidays – who's had what holidays.' The third ledger contained members who had use of a leased car, he said.

2   During the Osman Gold group meeting the Met discussed rehousing Page. Shortly after handing over documents to the DPS, Anjam Khan went to Page's house on 24 March to check it had been repossessed. He was considering buying it to recoup his losses. When the property was sold, Jim Mahaffy recovered £27,000 and Mike Tinsley recovered £40,000.

3   On 20 June 2006, Baree asked CMC for more time. They had been waiting for money since November 2005 and were now threatening solicitors. Baree wrote: 'I am on the verge of losing everything or gaining much from an investment made last year on property, however I have a third party involved who has complicated matters and I may need to take further action against him to retrieve my money.' On 31 July 2006 he emailed CMC that he could not clear the debt because the refinancing of a development property investment had fallen through. 'I am desperately trying to resolve this without having to go legal. It's a very awkward situation as he is a close friend and he has used my remortgaged money so I cannot even draw any more equity to cover my debts. This situation is causing immense stress and anguish in my family as I face the possibility of selling my flat. I have dependents and I will do what is necessary to recover my money and pay my debtors. At this stage I have no other means to submit even a token gesture as my credit cards cannot be extended and my wages are just covering my two mortgages.' By early 2007, Baree still hadn't named Page or provided CMC with the December 2005 letter indemnifying him for the gambling debt. He did say that the person responsible was awaiting trial on a 'sensitive' matter. Finally, in late March 2007, he wrote naming his former best friend as responsible for the gambling debt. 'Mr Page was

known to me as a trusted childhood friend and has used my personal details to spread bet with your selves [sic]. I have been advised not to protect him any longer and he has admitted the debt in the supporting letter. I apologise for the inconvenience that this may cause but Mr Page has caused me extreme financial hardship and I cannot cover the debt.'

4   The *News of the World* editor Rebekah Brooks admitted that the newspaper paid police officers for information when questioned by a committee of MPs in March 2003. The tabloid had gone to great lengths to mislead Operation Caryatid that the accessing of royal voicemails was the work of a rogue reporter. Meanwhile, Operation Aserio was building a rogue-officer narrative, which would protect its senior officers and the Palace from criticism.

5   A recently retired Beck told me by phone on 22 July 2011: 'It's history, at the end of the day I did something [invest] that I thought "OK, in for a penny in for a pound". It didn't come to much so I didn't worry about it. Paul phoned me and said "Do you know someone?" And I can't remember who it was. We used to come into contact with loads of people from the press, I have done through my career from Downing Street in 1985.' Beck admitted being a member of the Currency Club, but said the Page scandal 'didn't affect me'. Others had been 'done quite badly'. Beck said he had put in some capital, not that much, over a two-month period and the return was 'next to nothing' so he didn't get further involved. He knew that a lot of the witnesses against Page were from St James's Palace but said the DPS never approached him. He said he had never taken money from any journalist and only the PPOs had access to the Green Book and must have been 'desperate' if they sold it for just

405

£1000. He put the phone down when asked if he ever had access to other phone books in the control room at St James's. Beck has never been investigated in connection with any of these events.

In his 2014 trial for allegedly paying policemen for information, Clive Goodman denied that 'David Farish' and 'Ian Anderson' were Met officers. At the time of writing, Goodman is awaiting a retrial.

6   During the fraud trial, Khan denied any involvement in the kidnap plot.

7   Anjam Khan contacted me after seeing my *Sunday Times* Insight article on 6 July 2008 about the scandal. We met on 29 July. Khan wanted money for his story. He got nothing. Page said Khan had asked him for £250,000 to undermine the threats to kill prosecution. Khan told me he had offered to withdraw his evidence in return for his money back.

Chapter 19 God save the Prince

1   The Page story bore many of the trademarks of a similar chancer centuries earlier whose antics were described by Charles Mackay in *Memoirs of Extraordinary Popular Delusions and the Madness of Crowds.* John Law came from nowhere to beguile and rob the establishment with his bogus housing and gambling schemes. 'He soon became a regular frequenter of the gaming houses, and by pursuing a certain plan, based upon some abstruse calculation of chance, he contrived to gain considerable sums. All the gamblers envied his luck, and many made it a point to watch his play, and stake their money on the same chances ... The extraordinary present fortune dazzled his eyes, and prevented him

from seeing the evil day that would burst over his head, when once, from any cause or other, the alarm was sounded … After he had been for nine years exposed to the dangerous attractions of the gay life he was leading, he became an irrecoverable gambler. As his love of play increased in violence, it diminished in prudence. Great losses were only to be repaired by still greater ventures, and one unhappy day he lost more than he could repay without mortgaging his family estate. To that step he was driven at last.'

2   Erin Arvedlund, *Madoff: The Man Who Stole $65 Billion*, Penguin, 2009.

3   Madoff was arrested on 11 December 2008 for America's biggest financial fraud. On 12 March 2009 he pleaded guilty. Madoff was suspected of secreting funds in London and Switzerland.

4   Michael Gillard, 'CPS acts to strike out claims about royal protection squad made by former officer', *The Times*, 5 December 2008. A spokesman for Prince Andrew refused to comment on the matters contained in Page's statement.

Chapter 20 God save the Queen

1   A source close to Day told me that when the prosecutor took over the case he was 'surprised' at the decision not to charge McGregor and questioned whether the DPS had put the full facts before the CPS.

2   McGregor was never disciplined for any of these admissions.

Met Sergeant Steve Tree, who McGregor had brought in after a round of golf, told the jury, 'I blame Adam. I don't know how much he did and didn't know.' Tree accepted that his £60,000 investment for a 30 per cent return was down to greed. 'It's that old cliché: if it seems too good to be true, it is too good to be true.'

3   James Mahaffy, Gerry McCallion, Lenny Thiel, Surinder Mudhar and Adam McGregor all admitted involvement in the movement of cash returns. Phil Williams claimed there was a special system whereby friends and family members of Royal Protection officers would be allowed to park in the palace on weekends to go out on the town or shopping. He said it was an 'unwritten rule'.

4   Before the trial, Baree told me on 30 July 2008: 'I've got family members that really are out for him [Page] at the moment, and I said, "You can't do that because it's going hthrough the system. Let it go through the system."'

    Mubasher Hussain and Abishake Gill told the jury they had no involvement in threats against Page and his family. Gill said, crying: 'I've lost my marriage over this. I can't see my son. I don't care about the money.'

5   A relative of Lodhia, Mrs Madavani, told the jury she was waiting for the trial to end before making a criminal complaint against Lodhia for the alleged theft of £27,000.

6   DS Mark Beckett told the jury he hadn't gone to Bristol to keep the focus on Page, even though investors there had also implicated Phillips in deception. Beckett denied Phillips was treated with 'kid gloves' and said Orchard had made the decision not to treat him as a suspect.

7   The prosecution believed Mick Hickman had lost £100,000. He never made a witness statement. Page warned Day during the trial that if he continued to ask questions about his relationship with Hickman, he would start talking about Prince

Andrew. Rivlin warned Page that the Prince's antics were irrelevant to the case. Page spat back that the same applied to Hickman. Consequently, his involvement with Page was never fully explored in court. At the time of writing he was still employed by the Met and refused an interview request.

8   The jury were unanimous on their first vote that Page was guilty of fraudulent trading. However, they felt that some prosecution witnesses also should have been in the dock. They didn't believe that every witness had invested in property only. They were unimpressed by most DPS officers' evidence and did not believe the prosecution had made its case of money laundering against Laura Page. They felt that others should have been charged on the same evidence.

Index

411

Acknowledgements

My first thanks go to renaissance man, Alistair Fraser, for his support, insight and the inspired title; followed by journalists, Mark Olden, who also laid his fair eyes on the manuscript and *The Sunday Times* Insight editor Jonathan Calvert, with whom I wrote the original newspaper expose in 2008.

More recently, I have had the pleasure of working with scriptwriters and funny men Michael Holden and David Whitehouse who also saw the potential for a dramatised version of the Paul Page story and an aftershave called Folly for men.

A special thanks goes to Fleet Street legend, Alastair Brett, who gave the manuscript its first legal going over followed by barrister, Lucy Moorman.

A large raised glass to Leslie Gardner, my implacable agent, and Bloomsbury editor Miranda Vaughan Jones. Finally, thank you to NL, who had to go before the 'pinche libro' was published. Somewhere.

A NOTE ON THE AUTHOR

Michael Gillard writes for *The Sunday Times* on corruption and organized crime. In 2004, he co-authored *Untouchables: Dirty Cops, Bent Justice and Racism in Scotland Yard*. A two times winner of Investigation of The Year in the British press awards, in 2013 he was voted Journalist of the Year for his investigation of organized crime and the London 2012 Olympics, his next book.

If you would like to contact Michael, please use the
following email address:
forqueenandcurrency@hotmail.com

Printed in Poland
by Amazon Fulfillment
Poland Sp. z o.o., Wrocław